The Believers' Church

Library of Congress Cataloging in Publication Data

Durnbaugh, Donald F.
  The believers' church.

  Reprint. Originally published: New York:
Macmillan, 1968.
  Includes bibliographical references and index.
  1. Free churches.   2. Dissenters, Religious
3. Protestantism.   I. Title.
BX4817.D8   1985   280'.4   85-7599
ISBN 0-8361-1271-7 (alk. paper)

*Permission to quote from copyrighted material for this edition was granted by the following publisher, whose
courtesy is gratefully acknowledged:*

Macmillan Publishing Company. Excerpts from Henry Charles Lea, *A History of the Inquisition of
the Middle Ages,* Walter Rauschenbusch, *A Theology for the Social Gospel,* and Frederick B. Tolles,
Quakers and the Atlantic Culture.

90 89 88 87 86 85 10 9 8 7 6 5 4 3 2 1

Donald F. Durnbaugh

The Believers' Church

THE HISTORY
AND CHARACTER OF RADICAL
PROTESTANTISM

HERALD PRESS
Scottdale, Pennsylvania
Kitchener, Ontario

To M. R. Zigler, churchman and prophet

Permission to quote from copyrighted material for the first edition was granted by the following publishers, whose courtesy is gratefully acknowledged.

CHARLES SCRIBNER'S SONS AND CONSTABLE & CO., LTD. Excerpts from George Santayana, *The Last Puritan.*
COMMONWEAL PUBLISHING COMPANY. Excerpts from Daniel Callahan, "Church and Sect" (November 3, 1967).
DOUBLEDAY & COMPANY, INC. Excerpts from Franklin H. Littell, *The German Phoenix.* Copyright © 1969 by Franklin Hamlin Littell.
FORTRESS PRESS. Excerpt from *Liturgy and Hymns*, Vol. 53 of *Luther's Works* by U. S. Leupold.
HARPER & ROW PUBLISHERS. Excerpts from Angus Dun, *Prospecting for a United Church*, and Elizabeth O'Connor, *Call to Commitment.*
THE MENNONITE PUBLISHING HOUSE. Excerpt from *The Complete Writings of Menno Simons.*
MENNONITE HISTORICAL SOCIETY. Excerpts from the *Mennonite Quarterly Review:* John C. Wenger, "The Schleitheim Confession of Faith," XIX (1945), and Robert Friedmann, "The Oldest Church Discipline of the Anabaptists," XXIX (1955).
THE WESTMINSTER PRESS, WEIDENFELD & NICOLSON LTD., and GIULIO EINAUDI EDITORE S.P.A. Excerpts from *The Radical Reformation*, by George Huntston Williams. Copyright © 1962, W. L. Jenkins.
THE WESTMINSTER PRESS and SCM PRESS LTD. Excerpts from *Spiritual and Anabaptist Writers*, LCC, Vol. XXV, edited by George H. Williams and Angel M. Mergal.

CONTENTS

Preface to First Edition

The term "Believers' Church" offends some people. To them it smacks of partisanship and self-satisfaction. It seems to relegate all not of that persuasion to the camp of the unbelievers. Others sense an implication that the Church is held to belong to the individuals within it, as a kind of private club.

Several responses can be made to these charges. First, other commonly accepted ecclesiastical names are at least as presumptuous, e.g. "Orthodox," "Catholic," "Reformed." Then, members of the religious movements discussed under the rubric in this book sincerely held that they were believers in a sense which they had to deny others, either implicitly or more often quite explicitly. Therefore, the use of a delimiting concept is accurate historically. Most importantly, no better term commends itself. "Free Church" is the usual label applied to the strand of Christian history here discussed, but major difficulties attend its use. A large part of the introduction is devoted to a discussion of this problem.

It was Max Weber in his seminal work on the Protestant Ethic who coined the term "Believers' Church" in the course of a description of the Anabaptists and Quakers. In their rejection of the visible church as a kind of "trust foundation for supernatural ends, an institution necessarily including both the just and the unjust," these groups, held Weber, sought a "community of personal believers of the reborn, and only these."[1]

Two study conferences have used the phrase as a focus for their work. The first was the Study Conference on the Believers' Church held by the General Conference Mennonite Church (August 23–25, 1955).[2] The second was the Conference on the Concept of the

[1] Max Weber, *The Protestant Ethic and the Spirit of Capitalism*, trans. T. Parsons (New York: Charles Scribner's Sons, 1958), pp. 144–145.
[2] For a report of this conference, see *Proceedings of the Study Conference on the Believers' Church* (Newton, Kan.: Mennonite Press, 1955), 246 pp.

Believers' Church (June 26–30, 1967). At the latter, some one hundred and fifty participants—from seven different denominational families—affirmed in the final resolution that they had "discovered in history, and in our present fellowship, a common scripturally based heritage, which is relevant for contemporary life and which is developing in churches of other traditions." This heritage, it was agreed, included these acknowledgments: "the Lordship of Christ, the authority of the Word, church membership regenerated by the Spirit, the covenant of believers, a need for a perpetual restitution of the church, the necessity for separation from the world, proclamation and service to the world, and a special conception of Christian unity."[3]

This book has two major predecessors and has profited from both. The first is Franklin H. Littell's *The Free Church*,[4] an incisive and provocative demonstration of the ways in which the concerns of the Left Wing of the Reformation (held to be the source of the Free Church concept) are of significance to modern Protestantism. The second, by the Swedish scholar Gunnar Westin, *The Free Church Through the Ages*,[5] is a careful and dispassionate historical treatment which avoids thematic discussion almost entirely.

The attempt is here made to strike a course between Littell's book with its topical treatment and Westin's with its narrative coverage. This method should present adequate historical data while eschewing encyclopedic coverage, at the same time allowing the most important themes to be clearly stated.

Following an introduction which looks at ways in which the topic has been previously approached with a view to establishing the bounds of the study, selected Believers' Churches are described. Those chosen are considered typical of others here neglected, and will provide a fair picture of the varieties which have taken form in

[3] Baptist and Mennonite churchmen of the Netherlands originally suggested such a meeting for August 1964, but this plan was not carried out. The Southern Baptist Theological Seminary at Louisville, Kentucky, aided by an interdenominational planning committee, sponsored the conference. The first report appeared in the *Watchman-Examiner*, LV (August 10, 1967), 383–389. See also Maynard Shelly, "Deliberations on the 'Believers' Church,'" *Christian Century* (August 23, 1967), 1077–1080. Conference papers and the responses to them are to be published.

[4] Boston: Starr King Press, 1957.

[5] Virgil A. Olson, trans., (Nashville: Broadman Press, 1958), first edition, 1954; there is a German edition, 1956.

history. The chronological span is the later Middle Ages to the present. Dependency on the standard treatments will be obvious and little original scholarship is claimed in these chapters which emphasize the formative years in each case. Quotations from the sources will aid in the understanding of the genius of these movements. Then, the major emphases and common characteristics of the Believers' Churches are portrayed.

Acknowledgments

Two scholars have been especially helpful in the initiation and completion of this project. Franklin H. Littell suggested that the book be written. Moreover, by his publications and in personal conversations, he has shown the ramifications of the Free Church ideal. More than any other person, he has put the movement on the map of ecumenical discussions. John Howard Yoder has contributed most penetrating theological, as well as historical, analyses of many of these groups, particularly those within the Anabaptist tradition. He also gave this manuscript the benefit of a critical reading. While both men have contributed greatly to the position of this book it would be unfair to assume that they are in complete agreement with the conclusions reached in it.

Hedda Durnbaugh has efficiently executed her now-accustomed wifely collaboration in typing the several drafts of the manuscript under the pressures of deadlines, despite the demands of family and teaching responsibilities. In so doing she has manifested some of the winsome qualities of faithfulness described later in these pages. Appreciation is also extended to the publishers indicated elsewhere, for permission to use copyrighted material.

DONALD F. DURNBAUGH

Lombard, Illinois / December 31, 1967

Preface to Second Edition

This book, first published by the Macmillan Company in a hardbound version in 1968 and in paperbound in 1970, appears again at the request of a different publisher. As author I find this gratifying for two reasons. In the first place, it indicates continuing interest. In the second place, instructors in several institutions once again will have copies available for the use of their students. Some twenty-five colleges, universities, and seminaries, to my knowledge, have used *The Believers' Church* as assigned reading. About half of these have built courses around it.

Some friends of the book have encouraged me to undertake a thorough revision reflecting the large number of monographs and articles related to the topic that have been published since 1968. This would enable me to bring the story up to date by adding material on more recent manifestations of the recurrent impulse toward reform and restitution chronicled in the book. It could include, for example, the striking development of base communities in Latin America.

Such major revision was not possible in this edition. It is republished substantially as it first appeared. The only changes are corrections of a dozen small errors or infelicities which have come to my attention. The reader is thus cautioned to note the original date of publication, so as not to be disappointed by not finding a record of quite recent developments.

Reviewers were remarkably kind in their assessment of the contribution and literary quality of the original publication. It is, therefore, sent forth again in the hope that it can find a new set of readers and thus, in some measure, bear witness to the renewal of the church—so desired by the founders and members of the several religious movements described in these pages.

Donald F. Durnbaugh

PART ONE

The Concept of the Believers' Church

· I ·

The Believers' Church Defined

Introduction

AFTER successfully defying both pope and emperor with his revolutionary doctrines, Martin Luther was faced with the practical problems of organizing an evangelical church. One urgent need was a revised liturgy which would incorporate the new teachings into the traditional form. In 1526 he published his own vernacular mass. In his preface Luther noted that he would personally be happy with the Latin service of 1523. Still, he saw the need for a mass in the common tongue for the "simple unlearned lay folk," the greater part of whom "stand around and gape, hoping to see something new, just as if we were holding a service among the Turks or the heathen in a public square or out in a field."

What he thought really needful, however, was a "truly evangelical order." This would not be held in a public place for a mixed assembly as were the previously mentioned services, but should be held privately for those "who want to be Christians in earnest and who profess the gospel with hand and mouth." This was his suggestion as to how such a group should be formed:

> [They] should sign their names and meet alone in a house somewhere to pray, to read, to baptize, to receive the sacrament, and do other Christian works. According to this order, those who do not lead Christian lives could be known, reproved, corrected, cast out, or excommunicated, according to the rule of Christ, Matthew 18 [15–17]. Here one could also solicit benevolent gifts to be willingly given and distributed to the poor, according to St. Paul's example, II Corinthians 9. Here would be no need of much and elaborate singing. Here one could set out a brief and neat order for baptism and the sacrament and center everything on the Word, prayer, and love.[1]

[1] Ulrich S. Leupold, ed., *Liturgy and Hymns*, Vol. 53 of *Luther's Works*,

Luther never worked out the order sketched here, nor did he establish a group of "earnest Christians." His explanation was the sheer lack of personnel for it. What he could do, though, was to "train the young and to call and attract others to faith" until "Christians who earnestly love the Word find each other and join together."[2]

Later he concluded that this was an impractical dream, and that to be realistic, given the mixed multitude, he would have to turn to the prince in order to get on with the task of securing the Reformation. "Luther's dilemma was that he wanted both a confessional church based on personal faith and experience, and a territorial church including all in a given locality. If he were forced to choose, he would take his stand with the masses, and this was the direction in which he moved" (Bainton).[3] As it happens, Luther's sketch of those for whom the third order was intended is an excellent résumé of the character and concerns of members of the Believers' Churches. Earnestness, witness, covenant (signing their names), discipline, mutual aid, simple pattern of worship—these are hallmarks of the believing people. The tragedy of Protestantism is that when such groups did emerge in history, Luther and his colleagues could see nothing in them but enthusiasts, fanatics, and rebels. This prejudice has not been completely overcome to this day.

The Free Church Concept

Ordinarily, the term "Free Church" has been used both by those within the heritage and those outside it to describe this "third order," rather than "Believers' Church." Why should there be a change in nomenclature?

The truth is that "Free Church" is one of those concepts which mean virtually all things to all people. A British writer began a recent discussion on the future of the Free Churches in England by granting that the situation is confused and any decision on

ed. Helmut T. Lehman (Philadelphia: Fortress Press, 1965), p. 53ff. See George H. Williams, " 'Congregationalist' Luther and the Free Churches," *Lutheran Quarterly*, XIX (August 1967), 283–295, for a discussion of the passage.

[2] Leupold, *op. cit.*, p. 64.

[3] Roland H. Bainton, *Here I Stand: a Life of Martin Luther* (Nashville: Abingdon Press, 1950), p. 311.

terminology rather arbitrary. As a working convenience, he announced his usage: "By the 'Free Churches' of my title I normally mean those communions whose names strike a faint spark of recognition in most English people: Baptists, Congregationalists, Methodists, and Presbyterians." But he went on to say that much of his discussion might "embrace without difficulty" smaller bodies such as the Moravians and the Churches of Christ. "In some contexts the category might be extended to the Presbyterian Church of Scotland, which is not exactly free, and in other contexts to the Society of Friends and the Salvation Army, which are not exactly churches." Also in some cases he wished to include the Unitarians but usually would not.[4] This is a rather typical example of the confusion attending use of the term "Free Church." Winthrop S. Hudson observed in 1961:

> Sometimes "free church" is used to mean churches with a congregational polity; sometimes it is used to describe non-liturgical churches (whatever they may be); sometimes the term is used for non-credal bodies; and sometimes it is appropriated by the churches of a "liberal" spirit, such as the Unitarians and Universalists. . . . The term "free church," however, was first used in England as a designation for those major churches of dissent which were separate from the state. . . .[5]

Here, then, in brief compass, are five definitions, all current, each seemingly adequate and coherent. These need to be examined more closely.

First is the common use of "Free Church" as a definition of a religious body which prefers congregational polity to presbyterian (synodal) or episcopalian systems. A typical approach is found in an article in *Christianity Today*: "The term 'free church' is employed here to designate those Christian groups which are locally free to choose their own affiliations and are not obligated to accept commitments made for them by a collective or hierarchical action." During the recent discussion (1966) within the American Baptist Convention on the Consultation on Church Union, several "distinctives" were laid down as guidelines for such ecumenical negotiations. Two of them were "the freedom of each local church to order its own life without control by an episcopacy" and "the

---

[4] Christopher Driver, *A Future for the Free Churches?* (London: S.C.M., 1962), p. 13.

[5] "Define Your Terms," *Foundations*, IV (1961), 99.

advisory and cooperative nature of our associations and denominational organizations."[6]

Nonliturgical, as a synonym for "Free Church," has its problems, as hinted by Hudson. Liturgy, understood as the total life and work and worship of the church, will be found in any faithful congregation. Even in the common use of "nonliturgical," to denote the rejection of specified forms and orders of worship (low church), there remain questions. To be true, Free Churchmen agreed in rejecting the course of Lutheranism and Anglicanism in retaining but reforming the medieval mass. This, they maintained, inhibited the free flow of the Spirit. But distaste for programmed worship is not sufficient criterion for church typology.

That "Free Churches" are ordinarily noncreedal is an apt description. These have confessions of faith, not creeds, is the way it is sometimes expressed. However, this is not to be understood as disbelief in or rejection of the doctrinal formulations of the Nicene or Apostolic creeds. Most Free Churchmen were quite orthodox in this respect. The point was rather their conviction that formal adherence to creeds tended to make Christianity a sterile matter of intellectual assent. Moreover, they desired to keep themselves open to new apprehensions of God's Word. This is something different, however, than the point of view upheld by advocates of "liberal religion."

"The Free Church is free of dogmatic tests. It is open to all who will come in" is a recent Unitarian formulation.[7] A contemporary Unitarian tract thus defines the basis of their persuasion: "A Unitarian is one who believes that in religion, as in everything, each individual should be free to see the truth for himself, unhampered by official creeds. He regards creeds as negative: they say 'no' to new truth. . . . The basic principle is individual freedom of belief."[8]

The problem with these formulations is that many who have been classed as Free Churchmen would be as quick to reject them as the orthodox. The objectionable feature is their unrelieved indi-

[6] A. Dale Ihrie, "The Free Churches and Ecumenics," *Christianity Today*, (May 25, 1962), 12–14; Kyle Haselden, "Baptist Ambivalence," *Christian Century*, (June 1, 1966), 705–706.

[7] Joseph A. Schneiders, "How Free Is Our Free Church?" *Crane Review*, VI (Spring 1964), 117–122.

[8] A. Powell Davies, *Unitarianism: Some Questions Answered* ([n.p.]: Church of the Larger Fellowship, Unitarian Universalist, [n.d.]).

vidualism. In the phrase "Believers' Church," the placing of the apostrophe after the "s" in "believers" is done purposely to emphasize the communal and collective quality of belief, in opposition to the individual alone.

Individualism, for that matter, has its critics within the ranks of liberal religion, who themselves repeat such jibes as the one reported by H. L. Mencken that "Unitarianism is not a kind of Christianity at all, but simply a mattress for skeptical Christians to fall on."[9] This was evidently in the mind of Santayana as he described the feelings of his Last Puritan:

> It was a relief to be safe within the high enclosure of the family pew
> . . . out of sight of everyone. . . . The music was classical and
> soothing, the service High Church Unitarian, with nothing in it
> either to discourage a believer or to annoy an unbeliever. What did
> doctrines matter? The lessons were chosen for their magical archaic
> English and were mouthed in a tone of emotional mystery and
> unction. With the superior knowledge and finer feelings of today
> might we not find in such words far deeper meaning than the
> original speakers intended?[10]

Even discounting heavily for caricature, this portrays a far different world than that of others called Free Churches, for example Anabaptists or early Quakers.

To use separation of church and state as the key to a definition of the "Free Church" certainly has much in its favor. Yet, the historical realities are such as to make this much too inclusive a criterion. Given the triumph of the "wall of separation" in the United States since the Revolution, and the growing spread of the principle in other countries, east and west, communions as far apart as Roman Catholics and Pentecostalists would all be classed as "Free Churches." A category this broad is not particularly useful.

[9] Quoted in Ralph W. Burhoe, "Some Thoughts on the Future of Liberal Religion," *Crane Review*, V (Fall 1962), 15.
[10] George Santayana, *The Last Puritan* (New York: Charles Scribner's Sons, 1949), pp. 18–19. Also note pages 32–33: "The great error of our forefathers had been to make religion a subject of wrangling. Controversy might be inevitable in science, when points of fact were not clearly determined by the evidence available: but why dispute about faith, about hope, about love? Why shouldn't each man form his conception of God and of heaven— if he need such conceptions at all—according to the promptings of his own breast?"

From a different point of view, there are complications with this usage. In England, where the term was first popularized, all Presbyterians, most Congregationalists, and even a few Baptists and Quakers, during the Protectorate, were committed to an organic collaboration of church and state, not to strict separation. Yet these, as Hudson rightly notes, have the best historical claim to the title Free Churches.[11] The paradox is resolved, of course, by the fact that the Glorious Revolution of 1689 scotched for all time the hopes of the Puritans for establishment by reaffirming the status of the Church of England, and provided for toleration, within limits, for these dissenters. It would perhaps be well for the sake of greater clarity to consider the Puritan Nonconformists as the Historic Free Churches.

The German church historian Peter Meinhold, after a briefer but similar discussion, concluded:

> It is clear from this confusion, that the concept "Free Church" in its traditional sense is no longer useful. Inasmuch as the general tendency of the newest development leads to a separation of church and state, it would be well either to abolish completely the concept "Free Church," or to fill it with a new meaning and to use it for those churches which are based on the principle of voluntaryism.[12]

Another solution, followed in this book, is to use a new term for *some* of those usually called Free Churches, without attempting to deny the term to those who wish to claim it. That this is a necessary step is further indicated by a review of the theories of the *origins* of the Free Churches.

Theories of Free Church Origins

It is striking that no agreement has been reached as to when "Free Churches" can be first discerned as distinct bodies on the ecclesiastical horizon. The numerous writers on this problem can be classified into three schools of thought, the "sectarian," the "Puritan," and the "Anabaptist."

[11] A Free Church Congress was held in England in 1892. The name became official in 1896 with the formation of a National Free Church Council— Horton Davies, *The English Free Churches* (London: Oxford University Press, 1952), p. 1.

[12] *Ökumenische Kirchenkunde: Lebensformen der Christenheit heute* (Stuttgart: Kreuz Verlag, 1962), p. 90.

THE SECTARIAN SCHOOL

The "sectarian" view of Free Church origins can be quickly described as traditional church history seen from the other side of the barricades. In this view, there is an apostolic succession of suffering dissenters stretching from the early Christian church through the medieval movements labeled as heresies by orthodoxy in both East and West to the left wing of the Reformation times and thence to modern times. Some in this school have been at pains to document the transmission, and to this end veritable catalogues of heretics in contiguous geographical areas and eras have been compiled. More usually, proponents have simply asserted that God would not have left Himself without faithful witnesses in any age, even if their obscure lives have made no impact upon the historical record. A writer in a Dutch Mennonite martyrology of 1660 explained:

> The divine and heavenly church, which is a separate holy flock and people of God, originated upon earth at the beginning of the world; has existed through all the ages up to the present time; and will continue to the end of the world. [Just as] the moon . . . is not always seen in her full light, . . . even so it is with the substance and appearance of the church of God upon earth. The latter, though never perishing entirely, does not always show herself in her full form to us; at times she seems to have vanished altogether, yet not in all, but only in some places, whether through the slothfulness of some people who . . . neglect the external, manifest commandments of God, or on account of some misconceptions or errors that have arisen, so that its characteristics, light, and virtue could not be seen, much less known, by the common world.[13]

Nineteenth-century Baptist historians in Great Britain and the United States favored this interpretation. One reason they did was the intense denominational rivalry of the time which motivated writers to search for ancient foundations for their own beliefs. An influential history issued by the English Baptist minister G. H. Orchard gave his position in the title: *A Concise History of Foreign Baptists: Taken from the New Testament, the First Fathers, Early Writers, and Historians of all Ages; Chronologically Ar-*

[13] Quoted from *The Martyrs' Mirror* in Cornelius Krahn, "The Anabaptist-Mennonites and the Biblical Church," *Proceedings of the Study Conference on the Believers' Church* (Newton, Kan.: Mennonite Press, 1955), p. 84.

ranged; Exhibiting their distinct Communities, with their Orders in various Kingdoms, under several Discriminative Appellations, from the Establishment of Christianity to the Present Age.[14] He began the fifteen years of research entailed in his book when a Congregationalist minister patronizingly praised William Carey as the individual "who had raised the Baptists out of obscurity" remarking that "they had no existence before the days of the Commonwealth." In 1869 a West Virginia Baptist elder attacked the Church of the Brethren by noting their foundation in 1708. He triumphantly concluded that they were thus about "1675 years too late to be the church founded upon a rock, against which the gates of hell never were to prevail" and went on to establish Baptist rights to that honor.[15]

Some "mainline" Protestant groups also delighted in tracing their antecedents back to the early church. High-church Anglicans emphasized the Catholic character of their communion and played down the Reformation. Presbyterians and others in the Reformed tradition also looked beyond the sixteenth century for their antecedents. When Philip Schaff came to North America in 1844 he found the leaders of the German Reformed Church in America contending for an ancient genealogy. A synod president devoted a major address to "establishing a claim to apostolic order and succession" by way of Christian churches in southern France and the Waldensians. "This is not a fanciful chain, nor a rope of sand," he exhorted.[16]

A self-styled polemic in the same vein was published in 1966 by a conservative leader of the Disciples of Christ, James DeForest Murch, to demonstrate that "the Free Church has had an unbroken existence in Christendom from the first Christian Church in Jerusalem, A.D. 30, to the present day." The path is traced through the followers of Priscillian (350–385) of Spain and Vigilantius of Lyon (fl. 400), in which locale he places the origins of the Waldensians. Another strand is said to lead from the Milan area, which early "assumed a free church stance," under the lead-

[14] The twelfth edition was issued by J. R. Graves (Nashville: 1855).
[15] M. Ellison, *Dunkerism Examined* (Parkersburg, W. Va.: Gibben Bros., 1869), p. 14.
[16] Bard Thompson and George H. Bricker, eds., "Editor's Preface," in Philip Schaff, *The Principle of Protestantism* (Philadelphia and Boston: United Church Press, 1964), pp. 11–12. The clergyman was Joseph F. Berg of Philadelphia.

ership of bishops defying the papal prerogatives. When the episcopal defiance was finally crushed, the people in the Alpine valleys
continued their independent spirit, finally merging with the followers of Peter Waldo, thence to the Anabaptists, the left-wing Puritans, the revival in Scotland led by the Haldane brothers, culminating in the Restoration sparked by Thomas and Alexander
Campbell.[17]

Lest it be assumed that such a view of Free Church origins is
the prerogative of the denominational controversialist, let it be
said that it was defended by the church historian credited today
with having introduced the objective approach to ecclesiastical historiography. Gottfried Arnold (1666–1714) stood the scholarly
world of his day on its ear with his massive *Impartial History of
the Church and Heretics.* This was a meticulously documented
claim that true Christianity had been preserved over the centuries,
not by the proud and secure church or prelate, professor, and
priest, but by the despised dissenters. Arnold took the standpoint,
made popular by Luther and his followers, that a fall had occurred in the church, but pushed back the date of the fall to the
fourth century with Emperor Constantine's fateful embrace of
the church, and extended the duration of the fall *past* the Lutheran Reformation. Again, he took the idea of the Lutheran
polemicist Flacius that there had been "Witnesses of Truth" during the dark ages of medieval corruption to testify to God's saving
plan, and expanded it to the thesis that throughout all of church
history the persecuted "heretics" had been these witnesses.

How could this be demonstrated? According to Luther's own
paradoxical formulation, a sure sign that God is present is the
experience of suffering. God and the world are enemies. Those
who serve God will be called fools by the world. Truth must
suffer. To Arnold, it was quite clear as he contemplated the history of the church that it was the "heretics" who had suffered
under the Inquisition, at the stake, and from church-instigated
crusades. Just as Jesus experienced the persecution of the hierarchy before the Sanhedrin, so His simple followers had endured
suffering at the hands of the established church.[18]

The sectarian view of the origins of the Free Church received

[17] James DeForest Murch, *The Free Church* ([n.p.]: Restoration Press,
1966), pp. 36–48.
[18] Erich Seeberg, *Gottfried Arnold* (München: Albert Langen, 1934), pp.

most detailed treatment from the German archivist and scholar Ludwig Keller (1849–1915).[19] In *The Reformation and the Older Reformed Parties* (1885), he worked out the genealogical tree of "Old Evangelical Brotherhoods" in unbroken continuity backward from the Reformation period to early Christianity, and forward from the Reformation to his own time. Although sharply attacked by scholars for his "enthusiastic" claims, he embarked on a program to bring together the descendants of these Old Evangelical Brotherhoods into a living alliance. This concern even reached across the Atlantic. In 1887 he wrote in an optimistic vein to the foremost American Mennonite scholar of the time, John Horsch:

> Would your churches . . . be willing to send representatives to a general conference in 1890 in Berlin? [Thus] . . . the Mennonites of various branches could join with the Quakers, Schwenkfelders, Arminians, Remonstrants, Dunkers, several branches of the General Baptists, the Hutterian Brethren, several wings of the Presbyterians, etc., in brief, all the parties that grew out of Old Anabaptism, in an "Old Evangelical Alliance."[20]

Keller's thesis won new life when the great German theologian and historian Ernst Troeltsch (1865–1923) brought out his magisterial *Social Teaching of the Christian Churches* (1911), a book which to this day retains deep influence. According to Troeltsch, from the very beginning, and hence at the very essence of the Christian Church, a dualistic tendency can be identified. One line is drawn from Paul, through Augustine, Thomas Aquinas, and the major Reformation bodies to the present day; the other comes from the Gospels, through the monasteries and the medieval sectarians to the Reformation, and then on to modern times. The former line provides the basis of the inclusive,

20–22; Walter Nigg, *Die Kirchengeschichtsschreibung* (München: C. H. Beck, 1934), pp. 76–97.

[19] For a recent sketch of Keller's life, see the biography by a daughter, Amalie Keller, "Ludwig Keller—a Scholar With a Mission," *Mennonite Life*, VIII (October 1954), 159–160, 192. She characterized the mission in this way: "In all the writings he aimed to demonstrate that the reformatory movements were considerably older than was usually assumed; that the 'old evangelical' congregations had taken over ideas from the early Christian congregations. . . ."

[20] Elizabeth Horsch Bender, ed., "The Letters of Ludwig Keller to John Horsch," *Mennonite Quarterly Review*, XXI (1947), 202.

sacrament-dispensing institutionalized Church; the latter the basis for the disciplined, obedient sect which works as salt. Troeltsch explained the upsurge of sectarianism during the Middle Ages as a reaction to the organizational perfection of the church and its intellectual completion in Thomism. The stark contrast between the radical law of the Scriptures and the medieval marriage of natural law with canonical jurisprudence precipitated the formation of the sects. He went on to pinpoint the origin of the modern-day Free Church in Puritan England, but emphasized that they "approximate more and more to the sect-type, even when the idea of the Church is preserved. . . ." One effect of his work was the intellectual validation of the sects.[21]

No less a personage than Walter Rauschenbusch (1861–1918), the prophet of the Social Gospel in America, advocated and incorporated in his person the sectarian view. It was W. A. Visser 't Hooft, long-time World Council of Churches leader, who in 1928 first saw that at the base of the Social Gospel movement lay sectarian foundations. "The Social Gospel is a revival of this sectarian ideal (Troeltschian sense) but now applied to the whole of society and not only to a limited group." More recently, Reinhold Niebuhr singled out the "radicalism of sectarian Christianity" which Rauschenbusch had inherited from his father August Rauschenbusch, along with the secular idea of progress, as the starting points of Rauschenbusch's message.[22]

In his career as a seminary teacher Rauschenbusch emphasized the early church, the medieval sectarians, and the left wing of the Reformation to the virtual exclusion of other topics. His writings on social issues return again and again to the early movements as the source of creativity and prophetic utterance. Here is a typical statement:

Genuine prophecy springs up where fervent religious experience

[21] Troeltsch called Keller's research "very instructive and stimulating" but thought that the idea of the "old evangelical congregations" as he developed it "may be a fantastic picture." The section on the Free Churches is found in the *Social Teachings,* trans. Olive Wyon (London: George Allen & Unwin, 1931), II: 656–673; on Keller, II: 949.

[22] W. A. Visser 't Hooft, *The Background of the Social Gospel in America* (Haarlem: H. D. Tjeenk Willink and Zoon, 1928), p. 64; Reinhold Niebuhr, "Walter Rauschenbusch in Historical Perspective," *Religion in Life,* XXVII (1957–1958), 530. A full discussion of his sectarian stance is in Donovan E. Smucker, *The Origins of Walter Rauschenbusch's Social Ethics* (Chicago: Department of Photographic Reproductions, University of Chicago, 1956).

combines with a democratic spirit, strong social feeling, and free utterance. . . . We have the same combination in those manifold radical bodies which preceded and accompanied the Reformation. They all tended toward the same type, the type of primitive Christianity. Strong fraternal feelings, simplicity, and democracy of organization, more or less communist ideas about property, an attitude of passive obedience or conscientious objection toward the coercive and militaristic governments of the time, opposition to the selfish and oppressive Church, a genuine faith in the practicality of the ethics of Jesus, and as the secret power in it all, belief in an inner experience of regeneration and an inner light which interprets the outer word of God. . . . They have been the forerunners of the modern world.[23]

An interesting corroboration of this point of view, from quite a different perspective and scarcely sympathetic comes from the Austrian scholar, Friedrich Heer, writing on the intellectual history of Europe. He posits a recurring struggle between the "upper culture" of Christianity, educated humanism, and rationalism against a "lower culture" of the masses, a struggle which can take both religious and political form. Increasing social tolerance after the French Revolution meant abandonment of the suppression previously used by the elite to keep the undertide of dissent in its place:

> When the new popular movements came out into the open, the most remarkable and exciting fact of all European intellectual history was unconsciously brought to light: despite a persecution lasting 1,000 years not one "heretical" idea, philosophy, or conviction had been exterminated. . . . Persecution by the orthodox and the secular rulers had only succeeded in pushing heretical movements underground, forcing them to put on disguise. . . . The fate of Spain and Russia, where suppression from the fifteenth to the twentieth century was most thoroughly carried out, and the oppression of the free churches in Germany afford instructive examples.[24]

Another recent historical work which sounds the same theme is a study of the left wing of the Reformation by the Dutch Reformed pastor, Leonard Verduin. He pictures the radicals as opening a

[23] Walter Rauschenbusch, A Theology for the Social Gospel (New York: The Macmillan Co., 1918), pp. 195–196; see also his Christianizing the Social Order (New York: The Macmillan Co., 1912), p. 83.
[24] Friedrich Heer, The Intellectual History of Europe, trans. J. Steinberg (Cleveland: World Publishing Co., 1966), pp. 1–2.

"Second Front" against classical Protestantism by their insistence on a full reformation. This was designed to work out the logical consequences of the Reformers' dicta on the sole authority of the Scriptures and the priesthood of all believers. But more importantly, he contends these "stepchildren" in fact represented a resurgence of "those tendencies and opinions that had already existed over against the medieval order." As a text, as it were, for which his book is the exegesis, Verduin calls attention to the statement by Luther: "In our times the doctrine of the Gospel, reestablished and cleansed, has drawn to it and gained many who in earlier times had been suppressed by the tyranny of Antichrist, the Pope: however [these elements] have forthwith gone out from us . . . for they were not of us even though for a while they walked with us."[25]

The author of the most complete history of the Free Churches, the Swedish professor Gunnar Westin (1890–1967) accepts a cautious version of the theory of continuation. His account begins with the early Christian church, and proceeds with a chapter on the medieval period entitled "Free Church Movements as Heresies." The method is to treat the major heretical movements—Marcionism, Montanism, Novationists, Donatists, Paulicians and Bogomiles, Cathari, Waldensians, Lollards, and Hussites (including the *Unitas Fratrum*)—without claiming direct connections in every case. An example is the discussion of the relationship between the heretical movements of east and west:

> When the Cathari appeared . . . they revealed that their way of thinking and customs were in principal agreement with the opinion and order of the Paulicians and the Bogomiles. It is natural then to affirm that there is a direct historical connection, even though it is impossible to point out all the links in the chain. This portion of history is obscured by the same problem as the study of movements already mentioned. . . . The historical material documenting these groups was often destroyed because these groups were heretics.

Nevertheless, by calling these movements Free Churches, Westin creates a kind of chain by association.[26]

Arnold, Keller, Troeltsch, Rauschenbusch, Heer, Verduin,

[25] Leonard Verduin, *The Reformers and Their Stepchildren* (Grand Rapids: W. B. Eerdmans, 1964), pp. 11–20; the quotation from Luther is on page 18.
[26] Gunnar Westin, *The Free Church Through the Ages*, trans. V. A. Olson,

Westin—all these share to considerable degree the belief that the origin of the Free Church is found in early Christianity. This is the sectarian view.

THE PURITAN SCHOOL

In contrast to the preceding interpretation of Free Church origins is that which locates its beginnings within English Puritanism. It is a briefer, more direct link, stretching directly from seventeenth-century Anglo-Saxon Christianity to the present.

Here one finds impatience with suggestions that radical Continental developments influenced Puritanism, and scorn for the idea of the *Heimliche Kirche* of suppressed believers throughout the ages. The Free Church is seen as the peculiar contribution of the Puritan dissenting wing, which slowly took its unique shape under the aegis of the Lord Protector, Oliver Cromwell, in the revolution of 1640–1660.

This position is put neatly and concisely in the *Oxford Dictionary of the Christian Church*. The entry under "Free Churches" reads: "See Nonconformity." The editors define "Nonconformity" as:

> Refusal to conform to the doctrines, polity, or discipline of any Established Church. Originally in the 17th cent[ury] used of those who agreed with the doctrines of the C of E but refused to conform to its disciplines and practices, particularly in matters of ceremony, the term has come to be applied to all dissenters, esp[ecially] those of Protestant sympathies.

Individual denominations listed in the rest of the article are English Presbyterians, Congregationalists, Methodists, Quakers, and Baptists.[27]

More recently, American church historians have adopted this viewpoint, attacking earlier views which attempted to show the dependency of the English dissenters upon left-wing movements of the Continent. They insist that the Free Churches are native products of England. Winthrop S. Hudson, for example, states flatly that the Baptists were not Anabaptist, but rather were Puritan; the

---

(Nashville: Broadman Press, 1958), pp. 9–38; the quotation is on pages 24–25.

[27] F. L. Cross, ed., *The Oxford Dictionary of the Christian Church* (London: Oxford University Press, 1957), pp. 527, 963.

recent study by Hugh Barbour discounts the claims of Rufus Jones and others that Quakers were influenced by the "spiritual reformers" of the continent, and sees them as understandable only within the Puritan matrix; Sidney Mead discounts the view propounded by William Warren Sweet that the rise of religious liberty in the United States was primarily owing to the contributions of the left-wing sects, and locates the shift in a combination of practical necessity and Puritan theology.[28]

The most articulate proponents of the Puritan-origins school are Hudson, James F. Maclear, and Horton Davies. Hudson maintains in his important book on the "Great Tradition" of the American churches that the voluntary principle in religion is their one great contribution. He quotes approvingly from the visiting James Bryce, who asserted: "Of all the differences between the Old World and the New, this is perhaps the most salient. All religious bodies are absolutely equal before the law and unrecognized by law, except as voluntary associations of private citizens."[29] Because of this, according to Hudson, "church life became strong and vigorous, being based upon personal conviction rather than nominal adherence, and a new surge of spiritual vitality produced a missionary outreach that brought the gospel to every new settlement established in the westward march of the American people, sent missionaries into every corner of the earth, and created colleges and hospitals and charitable foundations." However, the basic point is that Hudson sees all of these accomplishments as rooted in Puritanism—left-wing Puritanism to be sure, but still Puritanism. The "distinctive contribution" was made by radical Puritans during the turbulent seventeenth century in carrying the basic beliefs of the Protestant Reformation to their logical conclusions.[30]

A corollary theme of Hudson's is the identification of denominationalism as a new church form within Puritanism. For him, the idea of "denominations" emerged as a kind of *modus vivendi* from

[28] Winthrop S. Hudson, "Baptists Were Not Anabaptists," *Chronicle*, XVI (1953), 171–178; Hugh Barbour, *The Quakers in Puritan England* (New Haven: Yale University Press, 1964); Sidney Mead, *The Lively Experiment* (New York: Harper & Row, 1963), pp. 33–37.

[29] Winthrop S. Hudson, *The Great Tradition of the American Churches* (New York: Harper & Brothers, 1953), pp. 27–41; the quotation is on page 28.

[30] *Ibid.*, pp. 19–20.

the practical necessities and theological tendencies of the several vying Puritan bodies. It is a "theory which had been hammered out by a group of Puritan divines . . . and which had won sufficiently widespread acceptance so that its theological justification could largely be taken for granted."[31] (Left unexplained is the reason why Puritan bodies in New England clung so desperately to establishment.)

Very closely related to Hudson's position is that put forth by James Fulton Maclear who set himself the problem of pinpointing "The Birth of the Free Church Tradition." Like Hudson, Maclear sees the free church form as dominating much of both English and American church life; this stems "primarily from the shaping of Non-conformity in seventeenth century England." However, Maclear makes the additional point that this free church development is unlike that which occurred later on the Continent because of its close and enduring connection between church and state. "The free churches of Non-conformity developed within the fabric of Christian state and society and not out of any fundamental conflict with secularized authority." This puts him squarely athwart the interpretations of those who would define the Free Church as that ecclesiastical organization separate from the state. Maclear joins Hudson in grounding the denominational concept in Puritanism. "In England and America the free church form was moulded in the unique environment of religious multiplicity which Puritan divisions produced."[32]

Horton Davies, a noted scholar of English non-conformity, is another leading exponent of this school of thought. In his brief summary of the history and beliefs of the non-Anglican churches, he places the origin of the movement squarely within Puritanism, but notes: "Into the ancestry of Puritanism this is not the place to enter." Theologically, however, for Davies the source of Puritanism is traced to Calvin's Geneva.[33]

THE ANABAPTIST SCHOOL

The third and last school of thought is that which we are calling "Anabaptist." In this view the Free Church rose within the evangelical wing of the Radical Reformation. This wing, the Anabap-

---

[31] Winthrop S. Hudson, "Denominationalism as a Basis for Ecumenicity: a Seventeenth Century Conception," *Church History*, XXIV (1955), 32–50.
[32] James F. Maclear, "The Birth of the Free Church Tradition," *Church*

tist, took as norms for authority the scriptures and practices of the early Christians. Because of fierce persecution by Protestants and Catholics alike, Anabaptists were not free to develop and articulate their basic beliefs, and were forced underground, withdrew into isolation, or, indeed, were exterminated. Yet, scholars conclude that the theological ideas and claims enunciated by the Anabaptists were transferred to England where the political developments of the Commonwealth period allowed their flowering within the left wing of Puritanism.

It can be seen that this view combines something of the sectarian school and of the Puritan school. It recognizes the normative appeal of primitive Christianity for the Anabaptists of the Radical Reformation, and can even accept parallels in medieval sectarianism, but does not accept the theory of some unbroken line of apostolic succession of dissent. It agrees that many Free Churches as we know them today emerged from Puritanism, but believes that left-wing Puritanism is not fully explained by sole reference to Calvinism.

Among twentieth-century scholars who would largely subscribe to the "Anabaptist School" can be named Franklin H. Littell, George H. Williams, Roland Bainton, all of the United States, and Ernest A. Payne and Peter Taylor Forsyth of Great Britain. The Methodist Littell, especially, has been vigorously promoting the Anabaptist cause, itinerating across the country with a gospel of the contemporary relevance of Anabaptist beliefs like a latter-day circuit rider. His books *The Anabaptist View of the Church* (recently reissued in paperback with the significant title: *Origins of Sectarian Protestantism*) and *The Free Church* have been responsible for creating much of the current interest in this tradition. Restoring church discipline to nominally converted congregations, furthering religious liberty upon religious grounds, fostering the ministry of the laity, improving race relations—these are but a few of the ways in which he is applying Free-Church principles to modern problems.[34]

History, XXVI (1957), 99–131. See also his "'The True American Union' of Church and State: the Reconstruction of the Theocratic Tradition," *Church History*, XXVIII (1959), 41–62.

[33] Davies, *op. cit.*, pp. 1–3.

[34] Franklin H. Littell, *The Anabaptist View of the Church*, second rev. ed. (Boston: Starr King Press, 1958); the paperback edition was published in 1964. *The Free Church* (Boston: Starr King Press, 1957). See also his "The

In his massive synthesis of scholarship on the left wing of the sixteenth century, *The Radical Reformation,* George H. Williams has documented many of Littell's contentions. The title itself reflects the conviction that alongside the "magisterial state-church reformations" of Lutheranism, Calvinism, and Anglicanism, there arose an equally important and coherent position. This was composed of those who wished to cut to the root of the church if need be in order to be faithful and obedient disciples. A veritable cascade of scholarly attention to the Radicals bears out this idea. Equally opposed to the long-standing, if unhallowed, tradition of interpreting the radicals as "fanatics" [*Schwärmer*] and divisive enthusiasts is Williams' description of what he calls "Sectarian Ecumenicity." He means by this the universal, missionary, and zealous concerns of the Radical Reformers for all men, which flowed from their basic disagreement with the territorial principle of church organization accepted by most early Protestants. Williams concluded his introduction by noting:

> Again in our own times, when, in a new context at once secular and ecumenical, the European state churches are being disestablished, the large churchlike American denominations are being reorganized, and the younger churches of Asia and Africa are being challenged by renascent ethnic religions and the international religion of the proletariat, when, in short, the mission of the churches everywhere is being reconceived in a basically hostile or alienated environment, Christians of many denominations are finding themselves constitutionally and in certain other ways closer to the descendants of the despised sectaries of the Reformation Era than to the classical defenders of a reformed *corpus christianum.*[35]

Of modern American church historians Roland H. Bainton has been the most influential in focusing attention on the "Left Wing of the Reformation" (a phrase which he popularized). In numerous works he demonstrated their role in enlarging the area of freedom in that long struggle or "Travail of Religious Liberty." For Bainton, it was the Anabaptists who "anticipated all other religious bodies in the proclamation and exemplification of three principles which are on the North American continent among

Historical Free Church Defined," *Brethren Life and Thought,* IX (Autumn 1964), 78–90.
    [35] George H. Williams, *The Radical Reformation* (Philadelphia: Westminster Press, 1962), p. 31.

those truths which we hold to be self-evident: the voluntary church, the separation of Church and state, and religious liberty." But he also cautions that this initiative did not itself directly inform later centuries, but had to be transmitted through the Puritan revolution.[36]

The English Baptist Ernest A. Payne, an ecumenical executive and scholar, is sharply critical of those who would dissociate the Radical Reformation of the Continent from religious reform in England. He marshals detailed evidence to show interchange of people and ideas, highlighted by personal contacts of English dissenters (including the Pilgrim fathers) with Dutch Anabaptists in the Netherlands. John Smyth, the leader of the first Baptists, for example, wished himself baptized by Dutch Mennonites and his followers, in large part, received the rite.[37]

One of the leading English Congregational theologians of the first part of the twentieth century was Peter Taylor Forsyth (1848–1921), whose works are coming again into prominent theological position. He maintained vigorously that it was Anabaptism—in his eyes the exponent of the Spirit rather than the Word—which fructified Puritanism and made it powerful. "The Christian gospel escaped from Calvinism, from the systematic creed of the Puritans by the aid of ardent Anabaptism only to return for protection from its Anabaptism to the cardinal Calvinism in which it first rose." For the Free Church, he uses the image of the motherhood of Anabaptism, and the fatherhood of Calvinism; perhaps we could add that he saw England as the cradle. In this way the "true church principle was carried into modern affairs." From the father, Calvinism, came the positive and theological Gospel of the Word; from Anabaptism came the personal and subjective religion of the Spirit, and from England "its free constitution of the Church, non-dynastic, non-territorial and democratic." If Forsyth had known the Radical Reformers better, he would have found other elements in their thought besides mere emphasis upon the Spirit.[38]

Some of the disagreement between these scholars about the

6 Roland H. Bainton, "The Left Wing of the Reformation," *Journal of Religion*, XXI (1941), 125–134. The quotation is from his "The Anabaptist Contribution to History," in G. Hershberger, ed., *The Recovery of the Anabaptist Vision* (Scottdale, Pa.: Herald Press, 1957), p. 317.

37 Ernest S. Payne, *The Anabaptists of the 16th Century* (London: The

origins of the Free Church goes back to the lack of consensus on definition. Another way to focus on the problem is to look at ways in which the various traditions of Christianity, including the Free Churches, have been categorized.

The Categorical Imperative

Given the multiplicity of expressions of Christendom, there has been a persistent quest for categories or typologies which would enable ready identification and labeling. To be true, for Eastern Orthodoxy and Roman Catholicism until quite recently, this question has not occasioned overconcern, confident as each has been in its identity with the one, holy, catholic, and apostolic church. Professor Georges Florovsky, speaking for Orthodoxy, explained that "there is more than just an unbroken *historic continuity* [with the early church], which is indeed quite obvious. There is above all an ultimate *spiritual and ontological identity*, the same faith, the same spirit, the same ethos."[39] And it has only been since Vatican II that Protestant churches have been granted ecclesiastical significance in themselves by Rome. Therefore their standard books of "symbolics" have traditionally had something of the character of a religious insect collection as they impaled curious specimens of Protestant heresy.

It is no accident that the first attempts at classification upon a different principle than orthodoxy and heresy come from the ranks of religious individualists (often called Spiritualists since the sixteenth century), skeptical as they were of all institutions. For them the only true church was an invisible church, and organization itself was a sign of the fall. Foremost in this endeavor was the brilliant Sebastian Franck (1499–1543), who coolly classified his contemporaries into four main groupings—Catholic, Lutheran, Zwinglian, and Anabaptist. His standpoint was pointedly expressed in his hymn entitled "On the Divisive Churches, Each of Which Hates and Damns the Others." The first verse begins: "I

Carey Kingsgate Press, 1949), p. 5ff. See also his article, "Contacts Between Mennonites and Baptists," *Foundations*, IV (1961), 39–55.

[38] Peter Taylor Forsyth, *Faith, Freedom, and the Future* (London: Independent Press, 1912), pp. 5, 97–98.

[39] Georges Florovsky, "The Ethos of the Orthodox Church," *The Ecumenical Review*, XII (1960), 186.

will not and do not wish to become Papist," and continues in succeeding verses in the same manner, by substituting Lutheran, Zwinglian, and Anabaptist. Elsewhere he wrote that a member of any of the four, "indeed a Turk, is my good brother."[40]

A host of other listings have been made since then, but by far the most persuasive and pervasive typology was that of Ernst Troeltsch already mentioned. More than one hundred books and major articles have been devoted to his tri-partite—Church, Sect, and Spiritualist—scheme itself, to say nothing of the innumerable studies it has influenced. Ironically, although Troeltsch himself indicated that he believed that modern western society was tending more and more to his third position, religious individualism, it has been the Church-Sect distinction which has attracted most attention.

Troeltsch summarized his extensive description of the three categories in this way:

> The Church is an institution which has been endowed with grace and salvation as the result of the work of Redemption; it is able to receive the masses, and to adjust itself to the world, because, to a certain extent, it can afford to ignore the need for subjective holiness for the sake of the objective treasures of grace and of redemption.
>
> The sect is a voluntary society, composed of strict and definite Christian believers bound to each other by the fact that all have experienced "the new birth." These "believers" live apart from the world, are limited to small groups, emphasize the law instead of grace, and in varying degrees within their own circle set up the Christian order based on love; all this is done in preparation for and expectation of the coming Kingdom of God.
>
> Mysticism means that the world of ideas which had hardened into formal worship and doctrine is transformed into a purely personal and inward experience; this leads to the formation of groups on a purely personal basis, with no permanent form, which also tends to weaken the significance of forms of worship, doctrine, and the historical element.[41]

Despite the widely accepted usefulness of this analysis, it has been under constant attack. One criticism, mounted independently

[40] Christian Neff, "Franck, Sebastian," *Mennonitisches Lexikon* (Frankfurt/Main: 1913ff.), I: 668–674; Hans Hillerbrand, *Fellowship of Discontent* (New York: Harper & Row, 1967), pp. 31–64, is the latest appraisal.
[41] Troeltsch, *op. cit.*, II: 993.

by both H. Richard Niebuhr and Ellsworth Faris in 1928/1929 was that the typology did not allow for the dynamics of change, especially for the second and later generations of the sects. Inasmuch as the zeal of the parents could hardly be experienced by their children in the same intensity, the sect would find itself faced with the same problems of nurture, organization, and continuity as had the church. Furthermore, as the growth of tolerance removed the conditions which made the original protest of the sect necessary, the acculturation of the sectarians in a more relaxed society would proceed apace.[42]

The very strictness of the sectarian ethic, moreover, with its rigid prohibition of amusements, cultural diversions, and socially approved luxuries, when paired with religious sanctions against idleness, would result in the accumulation of wealth. The rise in class standing brought on by prosperity and increased educational opportunity would lead to discomfort with the old practices, and a leveling-up process would ensue. In sum, "the sect will mellow its protest nature and slowly begin to adopt the theology, organization, and practice of the established religious structures in its environment."[43]

Theologians and church historians discounted Troeltsch's theory because of its sociological methodology and because it did not provide for "denominationalism," seen as the distinctive form of Christianity in the United States. Furthermore, sociologists of religion, such as Johnson, Wilson, and Berger, have come to criticize the typology as not especially helpful in concrete situations. It must be said that many of the critics have not grasped Troeltsch's use of "ideal types," which he borrowed from Max Weber. The types are meant to *clarify*, not to *classify* specific religious movements. Peter Berger suggests that a more generic difference could be established by focusing on the "inner meaning" of the religious activity. Thus the sect would be defined as a "religious grouping based on the belief that the spirit is immediately present." The church is a grouping which holds that the "spirit is remote." This

---

[42] H. Richard Niebuhr, *The Social Sources of Denominationalism* (New York: Henry Holt and Co., 1929); Ellsworth Faris, "The Sect and the Sectarian," *American Journal of Sociology*, LX (May 1955), 75–90, originally published in 1928.

[43] Calvin Redekop, "The Sect Cycle in Perspective," *Mennonite Quarterly Review*, XXXVI (1962), 155–161.

then affects the attitude toward the world, education, ministry, and other issues.[44]

Another approach to the question of categories is that proposed by theologians Angus Dun and Lesslie Newbigin. Although the two developed their ideas separately, they are closely enough related to be treated together. For them, the three basic divisions of Christian viewpoints may be called the "catholic," the "classical protestant," and the "fellowship of the spirit." In Dun's words:

> The first of these is the view that the Church is the great society with its essential institutions, established on the earth by God to bring men into right relation with himself and with one another under him. It is the ark of salvation, city of God, earthly aspect and embodiment of his kingly rule, which is in heaven and is to come. . . . God's approach to man, and man's answering approach to God, are through the Church in its visible, institutional, official character. . . . The second major way . . . is that which thinks of it as the community of those who, having received by faith the Word of God, embodied in the Bible or communicated through the Bible, live and shape their common life in obedience to that Word. God and man meet in the Word. The Church stands forever under the Bible. . . .
>
> The third view . . . is that which identifies it as the fellowship of the Spirit or the community of the Perfect Way. The emphasis here is on personal experience, on the converted heart, on moral purity and the spontaneity of the Spirit-moved or Spirit-guided life, and on the immediately realized fellowship of believers in face-to-face meeting. The tendency . . . is to view all outward forms with suspicion— formulas of faith, forms of worship, forms of ministry and of organization. . . . God and men meet in the Spirit.[45]

[44] Benton Johnson, "A Critical Appraisal of the Church-Sect Typology," *American Sociological Review*, XXII (1957), 88–92, and "On Church and Sect," *ibid.*, XXVIII (1963), 539–549; Bryan Wilson, "An Analysis of Sect Development," *ibid.*, XXIV (1959), 3–15; Peter Berger, "The Sociological Study of Sectarianism," *Social Research*, XXI (1954), 467–485, and "Sectarianism and Religious Sociation," *American Journal of Sociology*, LXIV (1958), 41–44. The quotations from Berger are from the former article.

[45] Angus Dun, *Prospecting for a United Church* (New York: Harper & Brothers, 1948), pp. 46–58; Lesslie Newbigin, *The Household of God* (New York: Friendship Press, 1954). Newbigin's summary characterizations of the three are posed in terms of the "manner of ingrafting into Christ": (1) by incorporation through "sacramental participation in the life of the historically continuous Church"; (2) by incorporation through "hearing and believing the Gospel"; and (3) by incorporation through "receiving and abiding in the

It will be seen that Dun-Newbigin's third category—the fellow-ship of the spirit—has affinities with the sect type as defined by Troeltsch. By fusing these two categories, one comes close to an adequate description of the Believers' Churches. It will be helpful, though, to take yet another tack in arriving at a viable delineation of the movement in question by way of political comparisons.

Political Analogies

One device to attain clarity about variations among Christian bodies is by comparing them with political models. This is not as arbitrary as it may seem, for it has long been observed that churches tend to take on, either consciously or unconsciously, the organizational form of the state system under which they exist. It is a truism that the early papacy modeled its polity after that of the Roman Empire. Today, in the United States, even those denominations of episcopalian polity stress in their promotional literature how democratically organized their churches are, and do so with considerable justification. A quick review of the history of the church will demonstrate the essential truth of this contention, of course oversimplifying greatly in the process.

Scholars generally agree that the early Christian churches demonstrated great variety in their organization and procedures, which only slowly became regularized and standardized as the Catholic church took form by way of bishop, creed, and canon. Thus Benz summarizes: "Before Constantine the major Christian communities in East and West had their individual creeds, their individual systems of doctrine, their treasure of special traditions in all realms of life."[46]

These congregations were hit hard by the effective persecutions of the Emperor Diocletian (ruled A.D. 284–304), who made a vigorous effort to revitalize the empire and change its course from decline to improvement. Besides striking at the growing body of Christians who he felt threatened the peace, he created what would later be called an absolute monarchy. He degraded or abolished the erstwhile republican agencies of Rome, and set up

Holy Spirit." His designations are: the Body of Christ, the Congregation of the Faithful, and the Community of the Holy Spirit.

[46] Ernst Benz, *The Eastern Orthodox Church*, trans. R. and C. Winston (Chicago: Aldine Publishing Co., 1963), p. 75.

an elaborately graded hierarchy of officials dependent on his person alone. Every phase of life was controlled from the central government.

In order to rule more effectively, and also to provide a more orderly succession to power, he divided the empire into east and west, each part further subdivided into two prefects. The church followed suit. "The genius of the early Christians has decided that the Church, to achieve the widest possible influence, must model itself upon the organization of the secular state; and since the days of the Apostles the central sees of Christendom had been placed in the three capitals of the Mediterranean world, Rome, Alexandria, and Antioch, other cities and towns having their bishop and hierarchs according to their civil importance" (Baynes).

The pattern is seen most clearly when Constantine (ruled 312–337) succeeded in wresting sole power from his colleagues. One of his important acts was to move the center of government eastward to Byzantium, which was then renamed after him. The foundation of the new capital by Constantine revolutionized the ecclesiastical as well as the secular administration. The Second Ecumenical Council of 381 awarded the Byzantine patriarch a position second only to that of Rome, because "Constantinople is the New Rome." The swift ascension did not come easily, given the jealousy of the other hierarchs, but it came, and has persisted. To this day the patriarch enjoys ecclesiastical preference over all of the Eastern Orthodox church.

With the fall of the western empire, the vacuum was filled, as is well known, by the rising papacy. This was made possible by the competence of the church's leadership and the tolerant policy of the already Christianized "barbarians" who seized military control. Augustine, in his *City of God*, provided the theological and philosophical justification for this shift in power. "To Augustine, the great counterpart of the doomed pagan empire was not Christian Byzantium, but the Catholic Church. This had been created by Christ and was itself the visible sign, the embodiment and representation upon earth of the kingdom of God."[47] In his classic study of the Holy Roman Empire, Bryce drew the same conclusions: "Just as with the extension of the Empire all the independent rights of districts, towns, or tribes had disappeared, so

[47] Benz, *op. cit.*, p. 168.

now the primitive freedom of diversity of individual Christians and local churches, already circumscribed by the frequent struggles against heresy, was finally overborne by the idea of a visible, Catholic Church, uniform in faith and ritual."[48]

In the continuing eastern (Byzantine) empire the merging of church and state into the *symphonia* or concord as it was called by Greek theologians resulted to considerable degree in the church's subservience to the state, known technically as caesaropapism. Although individual patriarchs followed the injunctions of their ordination charges to remain independent and to speak the truth even to the emperor who placed them into office, the verdict of history demonstrates that the emperor usually was able to have the last word.

In the west, however, the imperially styled papacy increasingly challenged the authority of the secular rulers. When in A.D. 800 Pope Leo III seized the crown of Charlemagne in his own hands during the coronation service, this clearly symbolized the superior rights of the church. Light on the developed theory of papal monarchy is shed by the forged "Donation of Constantine," created sometime around the ninth century, which purported to document the grant to Pope Sylvester and his successors of extensive secular rule in the west. "The notion which prevails throughout, that the chief of the religious society must be in every point conformed to his prototype the chief of the civil, is the key to all the thoughts and acts of the Roman clergy; not less plainly seen in the details of papal ceremonial than it is in the gigantic scheme of papal legislation."[49]

Of course this was not completely accepted by the secular rulers. In principle there was to be cooperation, with the church caring for religious concerns, and the empire responsible for civil affairs. Ambitious rulers moved in on church business, and reform-minded and ambitious prelates expanded the church's realm, leading to endless strife and tension.

It is obvious that in this sweeping scheme, there was no place for religious expression which differed in points of faith (heresy) or on church organization and obedience to the pope (schism). These were literally outside the pale, and had to be annihilated.

[48] James Bryce, *The Holy Roman Empire* (New York: Hurst & Co., 1886), p. 29.
[49] *Ibid.*, p. 97.

The Inquisition of the late Middle Ages was the perfected device to perform this office.

The situation in east and west might be diagrammed in this fashion:

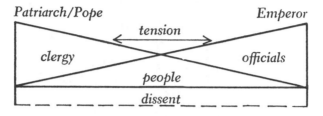

With the coming of the Reformation the brilliant conception of the unity of church and state in the *corpus christianum* was shattered in fact, although it lingered in theory for centuries. The terms of the Peace of Augsburg (1555) reiterated once again at Westphalia (1648) enthroned the particularist claims as over against the universal. National states had come to stay, and with them national churches. The right of each prince to determine the religion of his principality (*cuius regio, eius religio*), from among the four now-established faiths—Anglican, Lutheran, Reformed, and Roman Catholic—preserved the conviction that there could be only one acceptable faith in the now numerous territories. In but few isolated areas were dissenters tolerated on the condition that they would confine their beliefs to their immediate families.

Parallel then to the multiform state system was the co-existence (despite the horrified denunciations of the popes) of the several territorial churches. This could be portrayed in graph form (see next page).

In modern times, in the west at least, has come the growth of parliamentary government and democracy. The analogy on the British scene would be the two-party system, the government and the loyal opposition, or the Church of England as the established church, and the dissenters. A better model would be the French legislature, with its great fractionalization of parties, from monarchist to communist ranged from right to left in the assembly hall. Ecclesiologically, the range would be from the Roman Catholic and Eastern Orthodox, to the Spiritualists on the left. (It is not accidental that historically the "rightist" parties in the church spectrum have been most comfortable with monarchial govern-

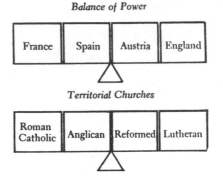

Balance of Power

| France | Spain | Austria | England |

Territorial Churches

| Roman Catholic | Anglican | Reformed | Lutheran |

ments, and that communistic experiments have emerged from the left.)

With this background, and using the typologies of Troeltsch and Dun-Newbigin, it is possible to construct a diagram which will both explain the classic positions of the major Christian traditions as they emerged and indicate which section may appropriately be called the Believers' Church. The three corners of the triangle represent the source of authority, respectively Tradition, the Word, and the Spirit. The middle ground is occupied by movements which are inherently unstable. The monastic orders, for example, have been largely preserved within the Catholic rubric, but have sometimes broken loose toward the sectarian side, e.g. Spiritual Franciscans. Pietism has used sectarian principles to renew the church (as seen clearly by Troeltsch), but has often led to separation. Methodism, for example, began as a renewal movement within Anglicanism, separated as a voluntary church, and now is moving back into the Anglican orbit. The Calvinist bodies have historically been torn by their ambivalence between church and sectarian motivations. The ecumenical movement can be explained from one point of view, as the drive to recover full churchly status, with the tendency to move to the right. Sectarian movements also shift to the right as they become denominations.

The Believers' Churches, as indicated on this diagram, lie in that sector ranging from center to left center, which balance the Word and the Spirit and largely ignore tradition. Historically, they have found themselves in opposition to the Spiritualist or Mystic, with their emphasis upon the Spirit to the practical (and occasion-

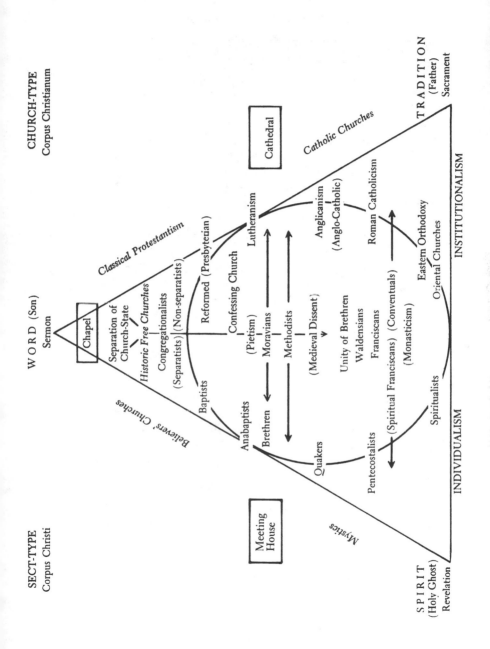

ally theoretical) exclusion of the scriptures, on the one side, and in separation from the church type on the other.

The Believers' Church Defined

How then should the Believers' Church be defined? Let us return to the likeness sketched by Luther, which was quoted earlier.

First, they are those who "want to be Christians in earnest and who profess the gospel with hand and mouth." The church consists of the voluntary membership of those confessing Jesus Christ as Lord. To them an uncoerced faith is the mark of true religion. For this reason, infant baptism as the rite of entrance into the church, or membership by virtue of citizenship in a certain territory, must be rejected.

Second, they "sign their names and meet alone in a house." The covenant is made between God and themselves and with each other to live faithfully as disciples of Christ. They reject a mixed assembly. Separation from the world means living according to the high ethic of the New Testament. There is no union of church and civil community, although they wish to be good citizens in everything that does not conflict with their belief.

Third, they "perform Christian works." Unlike the Spiritualists, who could proclaim a moratorium on outward actions because of the inherent imperfection of mankind, they are confident that even their halting and stumbling efforts will be blessed by God who had first extended his grace to them. As regenerate Christians, they will be expected to maintain a higher level of life than the common man.

Fourth, they accept the necessity of being "reproved, corrected, cast out, or excommunicated," according to the principle of Matthew 18:15–20. True Christian love, they contend, consists not in an easy tolerance, but in faithful admonition and edification. Being a disciple means being under a discipline, which is not legalism at its best, but rather like the loving chastisement of concerned family members.

Fifth, they urge "benevolent gifts to be willingly given and distributed to the poor." Mutual aid is a striking reality for the Believers' Churches, taking expression in the attitude that they are only stewards of their possessions, to be held ready for sharing with a brother in need. In cases of unusual emergency, communal possession might emerge, but this was exceptional.

Sixth, a "brief and neat order for baptism" and other church practices is developed by the group. There was to be neither complete formalism nor complete spontaneity; forms evolve from the group, and can be changed if need be.

Seventh, they "center everything on the Word, prayer, and love." The Word given in the scriptures and apprehended through the Holy Spirit provides the sole authority. Tradition must bow if the clear statement of the Word as understood in the covenant community so demands. On the other hand, the voice of revelation must always be tested by the Word, for there could be no clash between the two expressions. The inner and the outer word are one in essence, if not in form.

George H. Williams, in describing the impact of "sectarian" ideas on American Protestantism, has provided a felicitous summary statement in speaking of the ideal of "the gathered church of committed believers living in the fellowship of mutual correction, support, and abiding hope."[50] The Believers' Church, therefore, is the covenanted and disciplined community of those walking in the way of Jesus Christ. Where two or three such are gathered, willing also to be scattered in the work of their Lord, there is the believing people.

---

[50] George H. Williams, *Wilderness and Paradise in Christian Thought* (New York: Harper & Brothers, 1962), p. 214.

PART TWO

The History of the Believers' Churches

If the "sectarian" interpretation of the origins of the Believers' Church is accepted, then, quite clearly, the historical study of the movement must begin with the New Testament Church and continue to the present by way of medieval dissent and the left wings of the Reformation and of Puritanism. "We Baptists began at the Jordan River, and have had a continuous existence ever since!" is the current position of the Landmark Baptists. Problems of historical continuity can be disposed of by pointing to similarities in doctrine and deed. As a Landmarker spokesman put it: "If I see a white horse in a pasture, and he disappears for a time in the woods, then I see a white horse coming out from the woods on the other side, I can be fairly sure it is the same white horse, even though I could not see him while he was in the forest!"[1]

It has already been indicated that this approach will not be followed here. The question then becomes: where should the historical narrative start? For some time Protestant historians have been accustomed to beginning with what they have called the "Forerunners of the Reformation"—the Waldenses, Lollards, Hussites—before proceeding with the sixteenth century itself.[2] To see these "Proto-Protestants" from the later perspective, however, does violence to their own genius as reformers within the context of the medieval church. There is the further complication that several of the movements had sectarian qualities, in the sense in which Troeltsch used the term, which were rejected by "mainline" Protestantism. The Swiss Reformers did unite with the Waldenses,

[1] Quoted in O. K. and M. M. Armstrong, *The Indomitable Baptists* (Garden City, N.Y.: Doubleday & Co., 1967), p. 17.
[2] A recent example is the series *Klassiker des Protestantismus*, ed. C. M. Schröder; volume one is G. A. Benrath, ed., *Wegbereiter der Reformation* (Bremen: Carl Schünemann, 1967).

to be true, but the post-Reformation Waldensians were a different entity than their medieval forebears. A sizable number of them, indeed, opposed the merger as being foreign to their own faith.[3]

For the purposes of this discussion of the Believers' Church, it will be helpful to initiate the historical description with two medieval movements, the Waldenses and the Unity of Brethren, because they conform in major ways with the profile developed in the introduction. However, it is with the appearance of the evangelical Anabaptists that the Believers' Church movement as such actually began. In the cases of both the Waldenses and the Unity, the matrix within the medieval church did not permit the full development of what is here considered normative for the Believers' Churches. A question which has by no means been clarified by scholars is to what extent the Waldenses and the Unity of Brethren (known to have had intimate connection) themselves influenced the rise of Anabaptism.[4]

Later chapters will be devoted to representative examples of the Believers' Churches. Two have been selected for each century from the sixteenth on, so chosen as to illustrate the varieties within the classification under study.

[3] See Enrico Molnar, "Two Ecclesiological Betrayals of Pre-Reformation Movements," *Anglican Theological Review*, XLVII (1965), 418–426.
[4] For a recent discussion, see Robert Friedmann, "Old Evangelical Brotherhoods: Theory and Fact," *Mennonite Quarterly Review*, XXXVI (1962), 349–354. A negative relationship was established by Jarold K. Zeman in his study *The Anabaptists and the Czech Brethren in Moravia: 1526–1628* (The Hague: Mouton & Co., forthcoming).

· II ·

Medieval Sectarians

THAT dissent from the doctrines of the church was too great a danger to continue unchecked was an early conclusion of the medieval church. Augustine of Hippo failed in the fourth century to convince the Donatists by persuasion and appeal to the scriptures that their insistence upon the worthiness of priestly life was mistaken. He thereupon decided that force was necessary: "Originally my opinion was that no one should be coerced into the unity of Christ, that we must act only by words, fight only by arguments, and prevail only by force of reason."[1] But, faced with the threat of the schism, he concluded that violence was the lesser evil. He found a biblical text to support his view—the parable of the banquet (Luke 14:15-24). When the host described in this story discovered that his invitations were being ignored, he commanded the servant to "go out to the highways and hedges, and compel people to come in." This became the standard justification throughout the Middle Ages for the use of force in religious disputes.

Dissidents pointed in reply to the parable of the wheat and the tares (Matt. 13:24-30). Here the servants were prevented from their desire to root up the weeds in the field when the householder directed: "Let both grow together until the harvest" when the sorting would take place. Since the field was compared in the parable to the kingdom of heaven, the meaning must be that coercion is illicit. Augustine's counter-interpretation accepted the presence of the unfaithful. He said to the heretics: ". . . if you were just, you would groan as grain among the chaff. For since there are grains of wheat in the Catholic Church, and they are true grains, they endure the chaff, until the floor be threshed. . . . The

[1] Erich Przywara, ed., *An Augustine Synthesis* (New York: Harper and Brothers, 1958), p. 275 (Ep. XCIII, v. 16-17).

wicked may be with us on the threshing floor, in the barn they cannot be."[2] Therefore they should be compelled to enter the church, and if they were intransigent, they should be dealt with accordingly.

Of the many movements during the medieval period which could not accept Augustine's virtual identification of the city of God with the church of Rome, there are two of primary interest in a discussion of the Believers' Church. They are the Waldenses and the Unity of Brethren (*Unitas Fratrum*). Both have succeeded under often desperate circumstances in perpetuating themselves to the present. Some claim that the Believers' Church begins with the Waldensians; others prefer the Unity. In fact, both incorporated many of the emphases enumerated as marks of this pattern, but retained other practices and beliefs of medieval Catholicism. Nevertheless, attention to the life and teachings of these movements is an appropriate beginning to the historical study of the Believers' Churches.

The Waldenses

"Foxes in the vineyards" (from the Song of Solomon) was the favorite epithet pinned on medieval dissenters by the institutional church. In the Age of Faith, when the church reached a pinnacle of power never since equaled, the thought alone of heresy brought shudders to the faithful. "Heretics," defined Bernard of Fontcaude in his polemic against the Waldenses, "are those . . . who declare that we owe no obedience either to the Church of Rome or to her priests—*quod dictu horrible est!*—but solely to God."[3]

Yet, the presence of these "limbs of Satan" is not hard to understand in the high Middle Ages, when many from within the church were leveling indictments against her. Henry Charles Lea drew upon these philippics to good advantage in compiling his massive history of the inquisition, a work which retains its basic validity despite its Protestant bias. The subtitles of his introductory remarks on the causes of the antagonism of the laity toward the clergy sum up the shortcomings which agitated medieval

---

[2] *Ibid.*, p. 259 (Ps. CXIX, 9).
[3] Quoted in Zoé Oldenbourg, *Massacre at Montségur: A History of the Albigensian Crusade*, trans. Peter Green (London: Weidenfeld & Nicolson, 1961), p. 77.

churchmen: "election of bishops, simony and favoritism, martial character of prelates, difficulty of punishing offenders, prostitution of the episcopal office, abuse of papal jurisdiction, oppression from the building of cathedrals, neglect of preaching, abuses of patronage, pluralities, tithes, sale of the sacraments, extortion of pious legacies, quarrels over burials, sexual disorders, clerical immunity, [corrupt] monastic orders."[4]

In contrast to this disorderly array, the lives of the dissenters as attested by even their clerical enemies shone brightly. Bernard of Clairvaux (1090–1153), one of the sharpest opponents of heresy, admitted that "if you inquire into [such a man's] faith, nothing is more Christian; if into his conversation, nothing is more blameless." Moreover, "he proves by his deeds what he speaks with his mouth. . . . What can be more faithful? As regards life and morals, he cozens no man, overreaches none, does violence to none. . . . He works with his hands for his livelihood."[5]

Bernard asked: "Where, then, is the fox?" Not surprisingly, he was able to answer his own question to his satisfaction, and to that of most of his contemporaries. This was not an age of tolerance. The very concept of tolerance, indeed, was unthinkable, for if one had the truth (and who doubted this?) then it was criminal not to bring others to that truth, even if force were needed. Far better that a few stubborn dissenters be tormented briefly, always with the possibility that they might repent and be saved, than to run the risk of infecting the whole body of Christendom with their bacillus. Louis of France (1226–1270), canonized by the church for his efforts on her behalf, had a typical answer for the unbeliever; rather than arguing with such a person, he maintained that the layman should "thrust his sword into the man's belly as far as it will go."[6]

THE MOVEMENT BEGINS

From this milieu emerged in late twelfth-century France what is now known as the Chiesa Evangelica Valdese or Waldensian Church, which thinks of itself as the oldest Protestant church.

---

[4] Henry Charles Lea, *A History of the Inquisition of the Middle Ages* (New York: The Macmillan Co., 1906), 3 vols.; the listing is in I: [vii].

[5] Quoted in G. G. Coulton, *Inquisition and Liberty* (London: William Heinemann, 1938; republished Boston: Beacon Press, 1959), pp. 51–52.

[6] Coulton, *op. cit.*, p. 81.

Historians of an earlier era, as we have seen, linked the Waldenses with earlier medieval dissent or directly with primitive Christianity. Recent scholarship finds a satisfactory explanation in the immediate response of a dissatisfied laity to a powerful medieval church establishment.[7]

The founder, Valdes or Waldo (1140?–1218?), was a rich merchant of Lyon. One day he heard a wandering minstrel relate the legend of Alexis, which honored the monastic life. According to the popular tale, young Alexis was pressed into marriage by his patrician Roman parents. However, the reluctant groom was dedicated to the ideal of chastity. He made a pact of virgin purity with his bride on their wedding night, and then fled to the Holy Land. The parents sought him, but in vain. Many years later he returned to his parents' house as a beggar. He was so emaciated and wasted from his austerities that he remained unrecognized. Permitted to live under the stairs of an outbuilding in their courtyard, he existed on food scraps from their table, continually tormented and scorned by the servants. Only as he lay dying did he reveal his true identity, too late for the grieving family to claim him. The moral: a true Christian must be willing to sacrifice everything in this life for the sake of the next.

Struck to the heart by the story, Valdes (who had been troubled by the practice of usury in achieving his wealth) went to a cleric to learn how to live like Christ.[8] He was directed to the answer of Jesus to the rich young ruler: "If you would be perfect, go, sell what you possess and give to the poor, and you will have treasure in heaven; and come, follow me" (Matt. 19:21). Valdes set out

[7] The extensive article written by Heinrich Boehmer and Alberto Clot in *The New Schaff-Herzog Religious Encyclopedia*, XII: 241–255, is one of the fullest and most convenient summaries. The latest review treatment is Herbert Grundmann, *Ketzergeschichte des Mittelalters* (Göttingen: Vandenhoeck & Ruprecht, 1963), pp. 28ff., in Kurt Dietrich Schmidt and Ernst Wolf, *Die Kirche in ihrer Geschichte*, Bd. 2, Lfg. G (1. Teil).

[8] Another version tells of the sudden death of one of Valdes' friends as the catalyst for the conversion; H. Daniel-Rops, *Cathedral and Crusade: Studies of the Medieval Church, 1050–1350*, trans. John Warrington (London: J. M. Dent, 1957), p. 525. Yet another version simply states: "A certain rich man of the city of Lyons, called Waldo, was curious when he heard the gospel read, since he was not much lettered, to know what was said. Whereupon he made a pact with certain priests, the one, that he should translate to him the Bible: the other, that he should write as the other dictated. Which they did." Quoted in Margaret Deanesly, *A History of the Medieval Church, 590–1500*, 8th ed. (London: Methuen & Co., 1959), p. 227.

to do just that. He determined to "follow nakedly a naked Christ," to be "forever a pilgrim, calling no place on earth his home."

Valdes provided his wife with an adequate income, placed his two daughters in a cloister, and then proceeded to give the rest of his estate to the poor. Some coins he threw into the street, saying: "Friends, fellow townsmen, I am not out of my mind, as you may think. Rather, I am avenging myself upon these enemies of my life who have enslaved me, so that I cared more for gold pieces than for God and served the creature more than the Creator."[9]

He employed two priests to translate into the vernacular the New Testament, parts of the Old Testament, and some of the patristic writings. Using these he began to teach others the truths he gleaned from them. He taught in the streets or wherever he could find someone to listen, living by begging. A contemporary described the result of Valdes' efforts: "Hence there flowed unto him a very great multitude of poor folk, whom he taught to practice voluntary poverty and to become imitators of Christ and His Apostles. . . . He taught them the text of the New Testament in the vulgar tongue, and being rebuked for his temerity, he contemned the rebuke and began to insist on his own doctrine."[10] The innovation of Valdes was in applying the counsels of poverty and discipleship as the guidelines for all true Christians, not just for monastics.

His followers went out two by two, after the apostolic pattern, into villages and market places, to teach and explain the scriptures. If the opportunity came they spoke in churches. Soon they adopted a distinctive form of dress, including the wearing of sandals. This brought them the nickname of the "Shooed" or *Insabbatati*. They referred to themselves merely as the Poor Ones, or the Poor in Spirit (*Pauperes Spiritu*).

THE CHURCH CONDEMNS

The idea of unordained laymen preaching without permission struck the local archbishop as an unwanted and dangerous novelty, and he officially banned their activity. Valdes and his followers desired to remain loyal members of the Church, but they

---

[9] Quoted in Walter Nigg, *The Heretics*, trans. Richard and Clara Winston, (New York: Alfred A. Knopf, 1962), p. 194.

[10] Riniero Sacconi, inquisitor in the Passau area, quoted in Coulton, *op. cit.*, p. 173.

also felt an apostolic call to preach. Their answer was to appeal the ruling to Rome. In 1179 two of their representatives appeared during the course of the Third Lateran Council, asking for papal permission to be itinerant preachers. They presented samples of their scriptural translation as evidence of their work.

A theological commission of curial divines was set up to investigate their doctrinal orthodoxy. It proved no difficulty to entangle the simple Waldenses in the snare of scholastic theology. An English member of the commission sneered: "Shall the Church give pearls to the swine, leave the Word to idiots whom we know to be incapable of receiving it? . . . Water ought to be drawn from the well, and not from puddles in the street." Moreover, there was the danger of the priestly caste being displaced: "They now begin with extraordinary humility because they have not yet found a firm footing. But if we let them in, they will throw us out."[11]

Pope Alexander III (1159–1181) praised the Waldensian dedication to poverty, but ruled that they could only preach with diocesan approval. This, unfortunately, they could not secure. Faced with an agonizing dilemma, the Poor Men of Lyon chose to follow Acts 5:29 and "obey God rather than men." They persisted in their preaching, at the same time regarding themselves as basically loyal to the church. In 1180 Valdes himself appeared in Lyon before the Cardinal Henry von Albano, and presented a perfectly orthodox confession of faith, along the lines of the Apostles' Creed. He specifically condemned the Manichean errors of the contemporary sect, the Cathari or Albigenses, with whom the Waldenses were often linked in the popular mind. All church sacraments were accepted by Valdes. The confession concluded:

And because faith, according to the apostle James, "is dead without works," we have renounced the world and all that we have, according to the Lord's own counsel. We have bestowed all on the poor and have decided to become poor, taking no thought for the morrow. We accept no silver or gold or the like except for daily food and clothing from those who give to us.[12]

The church could not countenance the outright rejection of its will, even though it recognized the sincerity of the Waldenses. In

[11] Quoted in Nigg, *op. cit.*, p. 197.
[12] Ray Petry, ed., *A History of Christianity: Readings in the History of the Early and Medieval Church* (Englewood Cliffs, N.J.: Prentice-Hall, 1962), pp. 350–351 and Grundmann, *op. cit.*, p. 29.

1184 they were formally condemned as heretics by Pope Lucius III and placed under eternal anathema. Many scholars have pointed out that a generation later, Francis of Assisi (1182–1226) and his followers, with almost precisely the same motivation and mission, were accepted within the framework of the church and proved to be a vital leaven. Catholic authors say that the crucial difference was that Francis was willing to submit to the papacy but that at bottom, Valdes was not. Probably more important was the insight of the able Pope Innocent III (1198–1216) in seeing how the reform impulse could be channeled in ways which would strengthen the church, instead of forcing sincere dissenters into outright defiance.[13]

The condemnation by the church and the persecution which set in some time after the formal anathema rather naturally led to a greater radicalism in the Waldensian beliefs. They may have been influenced in the organization which they developed by the Cathari, despite the major doctrinal differences which divided them. Also influential were dissident groups in Italy, with whom the French Waldenses came in contact and joined forces. These groups are often referred to as the *Humiliati,* and centered in Lombardy. One of their teachings, not formerly part of Waldensian belief, was the Donatist-like attack by the Italians on the validity of sacraments offered by unworthy priests.

Eventually a complete underground structure rivaling the institutional church formed along sectarian lines. Laymen were now permitted to hear confessions, absolve sins, give communion, and eventually to ordain church leaders. The link with the Lombardians was maintained for some time, despite the inability of a synod in 1218 to bring unity on all points. The Italian branch had spread to Cremona, Bergamo, Strasbourg, Mainz, and Bavaria by that time, while the French group had extended its influence through the Rhineland as far as Flanders.

[13] Albert Hauck, *Kirchengeschichte Deutschlands* (Leipzig: J. C. Hinrichs, 1920ff.), IV: 862, said that it was purely a matter of chance that Valdes became a heretic rather than a saint. According to Daniel-Rops: "The Church might have used this movement for her own ends, and Innocent III came to regret that he had not done so. But personal questions and blunders on both sides made this impossible. . . . The heretic [Valdes] proudly declined, in the first place, to recognize any authority superior to what he believed to be 'his' truth; and what had perhaps been mere misunderstanding developed into open revolt. . . . In many respects the Waldenses foreshadowed Protestantism," *op. cit.,* (p. 525).

NATURE OF THE WALDENSES

It is possible to glean a fairly adequate picture of the life and conduct of the early Waldenses from the writings of their opponents, even though there is little extant literature emerging from the movement itself. With the rise of the Inquisition in the thirteenth century, it became necessary to draw up manuals and guidebooks for identification of the heretics to be suppressed. One of the inquisitors, Peter von Pilichdorf, who wrote about 1300 in Germany, left this portrait:

> [Waldenses] are recognizable by their customs and speech, for they are modest and well regulated. They take no pride in their garments which are neither costly nor vile. They do not engage in trade, to avoid lies and oaths and frauds, but live by their labor as artisans; their teachers are cobblers. They do not accumulate wealth, but are content with the necessaries. They are chaste, . . . and temperate in meat and drink. They do not frequent taverns or dances or other vanities. They restrain themselves from anger; they are always at work; they teach and learn and consequently pray but little. Again, they go feignedly to church and confess and commune, attend sermons, but this is in order that they may catch the preacher in his speech. They are to be known also by their modesty and precision of speech, avoiding scurrility and detraction and light speech and lies and oaths.[14]

A second inquisitor drew up a long list of reasons for the success of the dissenters. He noted that the heretics, both men and women, old and young, never ceased to teach and to learn. The workman, busy by day, applied himself to learning in the evening. A convert with as little as ten days of membership went out to teach others. One swam an Austrian river in the dead of winter to reach a man he wished to convert. "Wherein we may blame the negligence of the Catholic teachers, who are not so zealous for the truth of their faith as these faithless heretics are for their false misbelief."[15]

An important reason for their progress was their translations of the scriptures into the vernacular. "In Waldensian circles laymen for the first time in the Middle Ages were face to face with the greatest religious instrument the Church possessed: the Bible." The

---

[14] Lea, *op. cit.*, I: 85.
[15] Coulton, *op. cit.*, p. 174ff.

scriptures were memorized by Waldenses, and it was not unusual for their ministers to memorize the entire New Testament and large sections of the Old Testament. They especially emphasized the Gospels and the Sermon on the Mount. A critic testified: "They know the Apostles' Creed excellently in the vulgar tongue. They learn by heart the Gospels of the New Testament . . . and repeat them aloud to each other. I have also seen laymen who were so steeped in their doctrine that they could even repeat by heart a great part of the Evangelists, as Matthew or Luke, and especially all that is said therein of our Lord's teachings and sayings, so that they could repeat them continuously with scarce one wrong word here or there."[16]

The scandal of the loose living of many in the priesthood aided Waldensian efforts. Their own conduct compared so favorably with many an incumbent's that this was a powerful inducement for the local people to flock to them. At a time when it was seriously debated whether any bishop could ever be admitted to heaven, it is easy to understand how a rigorous ethical standard would impress lay folk.

Another reason contemporaries gave for Waldensian success was the "insufficiency of the teaching of some [Catholics] who preach sometimes frivolities and sometimes falsehoods," in addition to the irreverence some priests exhibited in handling the sacraments. Waldensian criticism of lax priests was particularly infuriating for the clergy, for it struck at the heart of the sacerdotal system. Peter von Pilichdorf attacked this Donatist position, incidentally admitting the justice of the critique:

> Thou barkest also against the priests of the Church, saying: "They are fornicators, tavern-haunters, dicers, forgers"; and thou castest in their teeth many other vices. What then? Are they on that account not priests? God forbid! For even as a man's goodness does not confer priesthood, so also doth his wickedness not take it away. . . . Therefore, the worst man, if he be a priest, is more worthy than the holiest layman. Where is the layman so holy that he would dare to handle with his hands the venerable body of Christ?[17]

By the end of the fourteenth century, a list of practices or beliefs of the Roman church the Waldenses had come to reject

---

[16] Hauck, *op. cit.*, IV: 89; Coulton, *op. cit.*, p. 184.
[17] *Ibid.*, p. 177.

included: privileges of rank, clerical prerogatives, the title of "pope," churchly incomes and endowments, councils, synods, ecclesiastical courts, clerical celibacy, monasticism, catechetical instruction, the mystical interpretation of scripture, church feasts and feast days with few exceptions, candles, pilgrimages, processions, organs, bells, spires, canonical hours, the Latin liturgy, the cult of images, relics, purgatory, prayers for the dead, and all acts of worship not specifically directed by the Bible. This was a puritan movement with a vengeance![18]

Organizationally they developed a threefold ministry of "major minister," presbyter, and deacons. Periodic general meetings or assemblies were held in places of safety, usually once each year. Typically a senior minister would travel with a younger man from place to place, meeting in secret with the faithful who were identified by passwords. The visitors gave absolution, performed baptisms, and led worship meetings. At times it was possible to set up special schools to which others would come for training. Several years of training were required for leaders, in more protected areas.

There were two levels of membership—the "society" and the "friends" or "believers." The former involved a probationary period of several years and entailed breaking all civil ties, sometimes including marriage, in order to renounce world, property, and family. The less-demanding membership permitted more contacts with the secular world, and provided funds for support of the leadership.

Waldenses taught the priority and sole authority of the scriptures in the vernacular. They practiced nonresistance to violence and opposed the shedding of blood and capital punishment. They took no oaths. This latter stand was often used by accusers to identify them. "The Sermon on the Mount was the basis of their strict rule of living."[19] The two sacraments of baptism and communion came to be standard; some rejected infant baptism, some used it. Ordinarily communion was celebrated once a year on the evening of Maundy Thursday, with a special meal of fish, bread, and wine.

[18] See Boehmer and Clot, loc. cit., pp. 242ff.
[19] Gunnar Westin, *The Free Church Through the Ages*, trans. Virgil Olson (Nashville, Tenn.: Broadman Press, 1958), p. 29.

PERSECUTION

The first edict against the Waldenses came out in Spain a decade after the papal ban of 1184. King Alfonso ruled that anyone daring to give shelter, offer food or drink, or even listen to the dissenters would be punished by confiscation of property and prosecuted for *lèse majesté*. The heretics themselves could be punished in any form except by death or mutilation. Three years later the edict was renewed, demanding death by burning of Waldensian believers wherever taken.[20]

The papal inquisition, called into being by Innocent III, took special care to root out the Waldenses, while making a distinction between them and the Cathari, rightly considered to be more truly heretical. Eighty Waldenses were burned in Strasbourg as early as 1211. As was the case with the early Christians the laws against the heretics were not implemented with equal severity in all areas and all periods. But from the thirteenth century on, the specter of persecution was always hovering over them. Much depended on the energy and intelligence of their enemies in the established church. The stubborn Waldensian resistance excited the admiration of the chronicler of the Inquisition, Henry Charles Lea, who made more of their individualism than is apparent from the records:

> There are few pages of history of humanity more touching, few records of self-sacrifice more inspiring, few examples more instructive of the height to which the soul can rise above the weaknesses of the flesh, than those which we may glean from the fragmentary documents of the Inquisition and the scanty references of the chroniclers to the abhorred heretics so industriously tracked and so pitilessly despatched.[21]

Despite the persecutions the Waldenses won adherents throughout much of Europe. The Italian branch was especially vigorous. By the mid-thirteenth century there were flourishing congregations in Austria, and even more in Bohemia and Moravia. In 1245 Pope Innocent IV described the sect as widely and firmly established, embracing not only simple folk but also princes and magnates. The fourteenth century saw expansion throughout

[20] See Lea, *op. cit.*, I: 81.
[21] *Ibid.*, III: 645.

Germany, Hungary, and Poland; groups from these areas kept up contacts with the Latin homelands by visits and delegates. Collections were taken up to aid needy congregations across national lines.

THE MODERN PERIOD

In the sixteenth century the great majority of Waldenses made common cause with the Protestant Reformation. After sending emissaries to the Swiss reformers, the Waldensian leaders arranged for a synod in 1532 (Chanforan). This resulted in agreement with the Calvinists and increasing alignment doctrinally and organizationally with the Reformed tradition.[22] One result was a stiffening in the persecution, as the Waldenses emerged into daylight from their hiding places.

Some of the worst persecution came in the sixteenth and seventeenth centuries. In eleven days in June 1569, for example, the Waldensian population of the Calabrian area of Italy was eradicated by Spanish troops. Some two thousand were executed, sixteen hundred imprisoned, and many others condemned to the galleys. More and more of them fled for protection to the remote areas of the Alpine mountains, where their descendants are found today. During this period, the Waldenses gave up their non-resistant position, and sometimes were successful in fighting off Catholic troops. One particularly gruesome pogrom by Savoyard troops in the seventeenth century inspired the sonnet by Milton which begins "Avenge O Lord, thy slaughter'd saints, whose bones lie scatter'd in the Alpine mountains cold."[23] Oliver Cromwell intervened in 1655 with both diplomatic pressure and financial aid. Help came from other Protestant countries to the beleaguered Waldenses, considered to be the only survivors of the "primitive Christians." For a time many took shelter in Switzerland, but came back in 1689, a date still observed by their successors as the "glorious return."

It was not until 1848 that religious freedom was granted to the much-battered remnants who still clung to their tiny homes in the Cottian Alps. The first synod (August 1848) held after the coming of freedom turned its attention to the evangelization of all

---

[22] See Boehmer and Clot, *loc. cit.*, pp. 248ff.
[23] In James Montgomery, ed., *The Poetical Work of John Milton* (New York: Leavitt & Allen Bros., [n.d.]), I: 233.

Italy. To facilitate this, the synod members officially changed to Italian the church language which had remained French through the years. They established a theological seminary first located in Florence and later in Rome. The first Protestant church (with the exception of chapels for foreigners) was organized in the capital city by a Waldensian pastor in 1870, upon the unification of Italy.

Today about thirty thousand Waldenses live in Italy, with settlements elsewhere primarily in North and South America (Uruguay). The church is active in the ecumenical movement,[24] symbolized by the famous youth center Agape, near Prali, Italy. This was built in 1947–1951 by the voluntary labor of hundreds of youths of many countries in work camps. The key to the mountain retreat was given to officials of the World Council of Churches as a token of its ownership by all churches. Today, a staff living as a community keeps the center going year-round with conferences, institutes, and discussions; in 1966 youth and speakers from forty-one different countries participated.[25]

An offshoot of Agape is village rehabilitation and migrant work in Riesi, Sicily, and Kriftel, Germany (near Frankfurt/Main). Tullio Vinay, founder of Agape and leader of the Riesi project, articulates the current Waldensian theme: "The Church's task is not to save itself—Christ has already done that. It is rather to give itself in love and service—in fact to die for the world."[26]

Unity of Brethren

Exactly five hundred years ago (1467) a small band of Hussite religious reformers sought and secured confirmation of their newly elected ministry from a Waldensian elder. Some authorities accept this date as the beginning of the Believers' Church idea.[27]

[24] Ermanno Rostan, *The Waldensian Church of Italy and the Ecumenical Movement* (Genoa: Papini, 1962).

[25] A good description of Agape is found in Donald G. Bloesch, *Centers of Christian Renewal* (Philadelphia and Boston: United Church Press, 1964), pp. 69–82.

[26] Quoted in Ray Davey, "The Two Faces of Sicily," *Frontier*, I, vol. 8 (Spring, 1965), pp. 45–48.

[27] Franklin H. Littell, "The Concerns of the Believers' Church," Chicago Theological Seminary *Register*, LVIII (December 1967), p. 12: ". . . the Unity of the Brethren was the community within which a number of the testimonies most dear to modern Free Churches first took determined shape."

The Czech patriot John Hus (1373?–1415) welded the reform ideas of John Wyclif and the Lollards of England to the earlier-voiced Czech criticism of the Roman Church by his own scorching prophetic zeal to fashion the most dangerous weapon threatening the papacy in the early fifteenth century. When the fathers at the Council of Constance (1414–1418) bound him to the stake (while wearing a dunce's cap with demons on it) and applied the torch, they ignited a fuse which set off repeated explosions throughout Central Europe. The combination of repressed religious feeling and outraged nationalistic pride was so powerful that the united efforts of papacy and empire could not suppress the revolt. The rugged Hussites took the cup as the symbol of their determination to partake of both communion elements and to force other reforms, and then marched against their foes. They were not defeated.[28]

A compromise arrangement worked out at the Council of Basel, the *Compactata*, based on the earlier Four Articles of Prague, led eventually to a schism within the rebel ranks. In a decisive battle in 1434 the moderate nationalist and pro-Catholic party, the Calixtines or Utraquists, left twelve thousand bodies of the radical party, the Taborites, on the field of battle. The extremists were crushed.

Emerging as the spokesman for the victorious moderate party was the eloquent John of Rokycana (1390?–1471). He hoped to receive papal confirmation as archbishop of Prague as reward for his pro-Roman policies. This was doomed, however, because the compromise which permitted the Bohemians to enjoy the communion in both kinds was as repulsive to the papacy as was the conciliar effort to reform the church in head and members. Rokycana even turned to the Greek church for ecclesiastical sponsorship, but these negotiations failed with the fall of Constantinople (1453) before the invading Turks.

The Calixtine leader lost interest in conciliating Rome and mounted a series of blistering sermons against papal corruption. His hostility increased when Pope Nicholas V sent two of the western church's most able spokesmen in the attempt to bring the Bohemians and Moravians back under the papal sway, without so

[28] See the many writings of Matthew Spinka on the subject, especially *John Hus' Concept of the Church* (Princeton: Princeton University Press, 1966).

much as a nod to the Compactata, bought so dearly a few years earlier.

Despite the increasing radicality of Rokycana's speech, he held back from an outright rupture with the church. His favorite motto was "the middle way." His followers, to the contrary, caught up in the vision of a church restored in the pattern of primitive Christianity, purified of the involvement with wealth and the arrogance of hierarchy, and constituted by sincere believers, were not content with the message without the form. These "hearers," as they were called, pressed him to make concrete his reform talk.

A group of "students and scholars" from Prague, with some commoners as well, coalesced around the purpose of putting Rokycana's ideas into practice. Their leader was Gregory of Řehoř (d. 1474), Rokycana's nephew, an impoverished member of the gentry. Though evidently without extensive formal education, he knew Latin and, more importantly, was gifted with skills in leadership and inspiration.[29]

PETER CHELČICKÝ

Rokycana himself directed Gregory's group to the man who was to become their spiritual guide. This was Peter Chelčický (1390?–1460?), whom Tolstoy was to memorialize as having been to Christianity what Christianity itself was to the whole human community. Though so little famed in his own time that even birth and death dates are uncertain, and virtually unknown to later generations until recently, he has been called by an expert on Czech history "from certain points of view . . . more important, certainly more original than the great Czech Reformer" John Hus. Increasingly, following the rediscovery by Palacky and other scholars in the nineteenth century, Chelčický has been recognized as an innovator in both religious and political thought.[30]

Peter was born about 1390 in the village of Chelčice, from which his name was derived, and came probably of the yeoman

[29] Peter Brock, *The Political and Social Doctrines of the Unity of Czech Brethren* (The Hague: Mouton & Co., 1957), pp. 72ff.

[30] Matthew Spinka, "Peter Chelčický, the Spiritual Father of the *Unitas Fratrum*," *Church History*, XII (1943), 271–291, from which the quotation is taken; Harold S. Bender, review article of C. Vogl, *Peter Cheltschizki* (1926) in *Mennonite Quarterly Review*, IV (1930), 220–227; Brock, *op. cit.*, pp. 25–69.

class. He identified himself as a man of the people, and his writings demonstrate a lack of formal education. Yet, he acquired a remarkably good grasp of the theological issues of the day, and by 1420 is found debating the leading theologian of the Utraquist party. Though not proficient in Latin and therefore unable to enroll in the university, Chelčický secured translations of patristic and other religious literature from university men, and gathered a good background by discussing his views with scholars. He is known to have had conferred personally with Hus.

The issue he debated in 1420 was whether the cause of true religion could be defended with military force. The pope and the emperor were on the verge of launching a massive attack against the Bohemians to put down the outcry raised against the execution of John Hus. Despite the urgency of the situation. Chelčický upheld an absolute pacifist position, even though the moderates argued that the justness of the cause permitted an exception to biblical mandate.

Chelčický left Prague and spent the rest of the time in Chelčice, not far from the fortified city of Tabor which harbored for a time the extremist Hussite party. In the village he elaborated his ideas in his own unique way, unswayed by the welter of competing views raging about him. The leading influences in his thought came from Hus, Wyclif, and the Waldenses. There are explicit references to the first two in his writings. The Waldenses are not clearly referred to, but the congruence in belief is striking.

As Brock, the recent historian of the Unity points out, the question of Chelčický's debt to the Waldenses is linked to the broader topic of Waldensian influence upon the left wing of the Hussites. Before the phase of belligerent military resistance by the Taborites, there was great similarity in religious program to the earlier movement. There were actual Waldensian settlements in Bohemia at an early date, and strong centers in nearby Austria. The historical consensus today sees Waldensian influences among the common folk reinforcing the ideas of Wyclif and Hus among the theologians.[31]

Many of the themes which occur repeatedly in the history of the Believers' Churches are sounded forcefully in the writings of Peter Chelčický. These include the law of love (his predominant

---

[31] Brock, op. cit., pp. 28–30; Spinka, loc. cit., p. 274.

concern), separation of church and state, nonresistant pacifism, dissolution of class distinction, and the authority of the New Testament. The fierce independence which he displayed in contending for beliefs so radical in his day has impressed even his critics. His writings are marked by sharp and pithy prose, and a simplicity akin to those of John Woolman. "While Hus and other theologians of all [Hussite] parties wrote as scholastics, filling out their works with copious quotations from past and present church authorities, Chelčický relies mainly on the Bible and the weight of his own thought and argument, using a few church fathers and several of his most revered predecessors, such as Hus himself or Wyclif, to illustrate some of his points."[32]

For Chelčický the fall of the church came with the "poisoned embrace" of Constantine the Great. In the most important of his writings, *The Net of Faith*, he uses the image of the net—the church—being rent and ruined by two whales—the pope and the emperor. They tore such gaping holes in the integral fabric of the net of Peter the Fisherman that soon there was no difference between being inside and outside. Chelčický's solution to the problem was a radical separation of church from state. In contrast, John Hus was eloquent in his attacks on the worldliness of the church, but he did not believe that a state could or should be totally separated from the religious sphere. The right and duty of the state to intervene in church affairs, indeed, was one of the cardinal points in his church reform. A venal papacy which refused to reform from top to bottom should be called to task by a reforming council convened by the emperor, said Hus.

Even though Chelčický found that "all the heathen customs of the pagan world have found acceptance among outwardly Christian nations," he would not hear of the state stepping in to set things straight. Coercion has no place in religion: "Whoever is not sincerely brought to the Christian faith through preaching of the gospel will never be brought by force. . . ." "Faith supported solely by spiritual power stands firm without the power of authority, which only brings and which can only attain what it wishes under the threat of compulsion." This is not to say that Chelčický taught anarchy. Because of man's fallen condition the state was needed. Force was necessary to control man in his wicked state,

---

[32] Brock, *op. cit.*, p. 36.

but Christians should not involve themselves in the state, as "no one may stray from the way of Christ and follow the emperor with his sword, for this way is not changed just because Caesar has become a Christian."[33]

His pacifism has already been noted. Historians have remarked that nothing "excites the indignation and horror of Chelčický so much as war."[34] For him a soldier is the same as a murderer. The only possible behavior for a Christian is strict nonresistance. This is extended to a denial of the validity of capital punishment as well. To imitate the example of Christ is the "most exalted rule of life: to love God above all and one's neighbor as oneself, the supreme law." The law of love has become the basis of all Christian life since its explanation and example by Jesus Christ. One could say that Chelčický's entire literary production was devoted to elaborating this conviction.

Here the reformer is seen in sharp opposition to other Hussite leaders. The Taborites, under the one-eyed General Žižka, wrote a new chapter in military history with their deadly tactics and bloody zeal. Chelčický argued that wars waged by those claiming to be Christians were in fact more vicious than those waged by Turks and pagans, precisely because the ethic of Christianity was higher. The new law of love forbids all killing.. In like manner secular justice was not to be called upon. "Among Christians secular courts are a disgrace and a sin." They had been taught a better way to resolve disputes, namely arbitration and restitution to the wronged party. If this does not effect a settlement, then the Christian humbly suffers and allows injustice to be done. Within the covenant community, an evildoer will be reprimanded and corrected. If he perseveres in the wrong way, he is then to be expelled.[35]

Kautsky, the German Marxist, praised Chelčický for his critique of the accepted three-class system. His small treatise titled *The Three Estates* attacks Wyclif for accepting the medieval assumption that distinction between nobles, priests, and commoners was in the will of God. Christly love sweeps away all differences.

[33] *Ibid.*, pp. 45–50.
[34] Edmund de Schweinitz, *The History of the Church Known as the Unitas Fratrum* (Bethlehem, Pa.: Moravian Publication Office, 1885), p. 97.
[35] Brock, *op. cit.*, p. 52.

Therefore secular laws based upon class distinction have no place within the church. The one-class society would not be achieved by war or by revolution, but "behind the state's back" under Chelčický's teaching.[36]

Chelčický worked out a clear, coherent, and radical program. At any other time, these views—taken as whole or any part of them—would have been the occasion for a speedy trial for heresy, attacking as they did the most cherished pillars of church and state. But in Taborite and Utraquist-controlled Bohemia there was room for this voice.

THE UNITY FORMS

A body of eager listeners gathered around the charismatic leader, but it was not they who crystallized into the Unity of Brethren. It was Rokycana's hearers led by Gregory who organized with Chelčický's teaching as their basis. Certain theological controversies kept Gregory's group from joining directly with "Brother Peter's" immediate circle. Chelčický himself was reluctant to make a decisive break by setting up an organized body. Sometime during the winter of 1457/1458 they formed a new religious community in the isolated village of Kunwald on the estate of Lititz (Litice) which belonged to the ruler of Bohemia, George of Poděbrad. Permission to settle there was facilitated by the benevolent sponsorship of John of Rokycana.[37]

They chose the name Brethren of the Laws of Christ (*Fratres Legis Christi*) for themselves, drew up a table of principles by which they would live, and began to make actual their goal of incarnating the kind of Christianity prophetically envisioned by Rokycana and detailed by Peter Chelčický. Gregory and a pious priest named Michael were chosen as leaders of the brotherhood. Because some people thought them to be a new order, they soon changed their name to Unity of Brethren or *Unitas Fratrum*

---

[36] Karl Kautsky, *Vorläufer des neueren Sozialismus* (Stuttgart: J. H. Dietz, 1920), pp. 368–369.

[37] The Moravian historian Heinz Renkewitz indicates in a recent encyclopedia article that the date of settling was likely 1458, rather than the 1457 which has usually been given: "Brüderunität," *Die Religion in Geschichte und Gegenwart*, I: 1435–1439. The year 1957 saw numerous observances celebrating the quincentennial. See also Rudolf Rican, *Das Reich Gottes in den böhmischen Ländern* (Stuttgart: Evang. Verlagswerk, 1957).

(*Jednota Bratrska*) which has persisted through the centuries. This appellation made clear that they did not at this time intend to establish a new church.

In 1461 the peaceful brethren were hit by persecution, the first of many waves of oppression until they were drowned in the Counter-Reformation. The reason for this outbreak was that the ruler Poděbrad had designs upon the imperial dignity. At pains to demonstrate his orthodoxy, he found himself embarrassed by the charge that he tolerated heresy on his own property. Gregory was in Prague when the monarch's drive began, and decided to remain with the brethren in the city although he was warned of the plans. The magistrate who appeared at the meeting to take them into custody announced: "All that will live godly shall suffer persecution. You, therefore, who here are gathered, follow me to prison." At the same time the brothers were driven from Kunwald.

The patriarch was placed on the rack and tortured to make him divulge information, but without success. Rokycana received letters from the brethren begging him as the ranking ecclesiastic to use his influence to save his own former followers who were forced to flee to mountain caves. "Have we deserved the persecutions which you have brought upon us? Have we not been your disciples? Have we not followed your own words in refusing to remain in connection with the corrupt Church? Is it right to invoke the civil power against us? Civil power is intended for the punishment of those who have broken the laws of society and must be coerced within proper bounds. It arose in the heathen world. It is absolutely wrong to use it in matters of religion."[38] The death of the king in 1471 finally brought relief to the beleaguered brethren.

Although they had originally been conscientious in seeking the ministrations of a priest of the national (Utraquist) church to take the sacraments, this persecution by the state church and the inner logic of their position led the Unity to set up more structure. A synod at Reichenau (1464) effected a complete organization. Their chief problem was that of ministerial leadership. Delegates sought to obtain a legitimate ordination from successors of the primitive church by traveling to India, Greece, and Armenia, but did not achieve their goal. In 1465 a synod resolved that it was

[38] De Schweinitz, *op. cit.*, pp. 115–119.

God's will to institute a ministerial order of their own. This was carried out two years later at Lhotka.

This date, 1467, can be taken as marking the real beginning of the Unity as a separate body. The ordination of ministers, followed by the rebaptism of the members, effectively broke their relationship not only with Rome but also with the Utraquist church. Before this they could be considered an informal brotherhood or society. Although they continued the seven church sacraments, and allowed infant baptism for children of members, this act set a new course.[39]

The first three ministers were chosen by lot from a panel of nine men nominated for their virtue and character. Gregory announced that the three had been present in a vision he experienced following the torture in 1461; this was taken as divine corroboration of the rightness of the choice. As the Brethren later related in a letter to the king: "Many of us recognized and felt that God had visited us and effected great things in our spirits to strengthen us. Therefore, we received them with firm faith, thanked God in the joy of our spirits, that He performed great acts at the end of the age and that His work is fruitful in these lands of the earth, in our nation."[40] A hymn of thanksgiving closed the memorable synod.

Following the ordination, it was thought well that the selection should be confirmed by a bishop. A deputation visited a Waldensian bishop, whose name was not recorded. (It was then believed that the Waldenses traced their origins to the early church; in this way the Unity could receive apostolic blessing.) The Waldensian leader performed the desired service. This led to close

[39] George H. Williams, *The Radical Reformation* (Philadelphia: Westminster, 1962), p. 211: "By 1467 the brotherhood of Kunvald Brethren, under Gregory's leadership, took their decisive step in their radical reconception of the Christian life, and at a synod at Lhotka (near Ruchnov) organized as a church separate from the Utraquists . . . and the Romanists. . . ." Brock wavers between 1457 and 1467 as the key date in the history of the Unity: "It is very improbable that he [Chelčický] lived to see the foundation in 1467 of their new church to be known in history as the Unity of the Brethren" (p. 41); "Founded during the winter of 1457–1458, the Unity finally broke both with Rome and the official Utraquist church a decade later, in 1467, by instituting its own separate priesthood" (p. 70); "The settlement of the Brethren at Kunvald marks the virtual foundation of the Unity as an independent group, though it was nearly ten years before a formal separation from the Utraquist church took place" (p. 75). The ecumenical news service of the Czech churches announced the five hundredth anniversary for 1967: *Ecumenical Information from Czechoslovakia*, XIV (June 1967), 3ff.

[40] De Schweinitz, *op. cit.*, p. 136 (translated here from the German).

relationships between the two similar groups, but because of several reservations the Unity had about the older party, full union did not result. Later, a certain number of Waldenses actually joined the Brethren.

NATURE OF THE UNITY

The polity of the Unity incorporated bishops, elders, and priests, aided by deacons and acolytes made up of youths preparing for church service. For much of the history of the Unity the word "Senior" was used in preference to bishop. Membership was divided into the "Beginners," the "Proficients," and the "Perfect." Advancement through these levels came by progress in knowledge of the will of God and in practical observance of church teachings. A parsonage or household (Zbor) was established in each town where a priest lived; it served also as a hostel for traveling churchmen and as an asylum for the poor and elderly.

A very strict discipline marked the Unity, patterned after Matthew 18. Gross transgressions or refusal to accept admonition were met with exclusion by church officials, to which action the people gave their seal by saying, "Amen." The *Ratio Disciplinae* or *Church Order* contains the regulations for this; it was applicable to all "from the child to the old man, the serf to the lord, from the acolyte to the bishop." It was carried out "neither in a hypocritical nor in a violent and tyrannical manner, but as the Apostles advised in the spirit of meekness, with deep compassion, in the name of and by the authority of Christ, to edification, and not to destruction."[41]

Unity literature reflected the same fraternal character. Books were only issued with the consent of the brotherhood and without the author's name. This was done to avoid vanity and also to testify to their united witness. They were quick to use the medium of the printed page, having three of their own presses which published several notable Bible translations in the vernacular.

Insight into the life of the Unity of Brethren in the sixteenth century is gained from a letter of Erasmus of Rotterdam. A Bohemian humanist, who was evidently critical of the practices of the Unity in his report to Erasmus, received a reply which contained this passage:

[41] *Ibid.*, p. 222.

That the Brethren elect their own teachers is not contrary to the custom of the Ancient Church, for in this manner St. Nicholas and St. Ambrose were elected. That they choose men who have not received a thorough education and who are unlearned, is excusable, because the piety of their lives may well be considered as a substitute for learning. That they call themselves brethren and sisters, I cannot recognize as wrong, but wish to God that this mode of address might become common among all Christians. That they have less faith in the teachers of the Church than in the Holy Scriptures is right. That Christ and His Apostles, when they consecrated the elements, wore their ordinary dress, is extremely probable, although I deem it improper to despise what the Fathers, for good reasons, have introduced. If, as you say, they take such great delight in the Lord's Prayer, we must not forget that this prayer constitutes a part of our own mass; and in regard to ecclesiastical feasts, their view seems to me to be not very different from that of Jerome's age, whereas in our day such feasts have enormously multiplied and, more than anything else, afford the common people occasions for vice of every kind, forcing them to be idle and preventing them from earning the daily bread which they and their families need.[42]

Before the end of the century a severe internal crisis wracked the Unity and resulted in the formation of two factions. The issue was raised by the desire of nobles and businessmen to join. The more rigorous early position—faithful to the teachings of Chelčický—demanded that all titles, honors, and government responsibilities be abjured upon becoming a member. Some university-trained leaders, of whom the most prominent was Luke of Prague (d. 1528), had been attracted to the Unity by its reputation for piety. They developed an articulate apology for allowing upper-class members to retain some of their prerogatives. A series of synods from 1490 to 1494 wrestled with the problem. Finally, the advocates of the compromise, the "Major Party," won out with an agreement that would allow military service, membership in guilds, oath-taking, and government service "if absolutely necessary." This, of course, opened the door to further adjustment with society.

The defeated minority party, the Old Brethren, lost out despite

---

[42] *Ibid.*, p. 230. For the relationship of Erasmus to the Unity, see F. M. Bartos, "Erasmus und die böhmische Reformation," *Communio Viatorium,* I (1958), 116–123, 246–256. There is a reference to the Unity in the preface of the second edition of Erasmus' Greek New Testament.

several surges of renewed vitality. It dwindled in numbers and died out completely during the sixteenth century. There was thus a somewhat acculturated church on the scene when the Protestant Revolt exploded. Even so, when the Brethren sought personal contact, first with Luther and then with Calvin, their chief criticism of Classical Protestantism was the insufficient emphasis upon church discipline. In repeated delegations to Wittenberg this point was continually raised. Luther for his part accepted the Unity members as brothers in the faith, but excused laxity in discipline because of the natural roughness of his Saxons. He took exception to the Bohemians' insistence upon their own national language and their practice of adult baptism (abandoned in 1534). Interestingly, Luther commonly refers to them as "Waldensians."[43]

A GOLDEN PERIOD

In the sixteenth century the Unity of Brethren experienced its golden period, even though it suffered years of sharp suppression and failed to achieve recognition as an accepted communion until the imperial charter (*Majestätsbrief*) of 1609. The Brethren upheld the Protestant side during the first war of Schmalkalden, which led to forced exile. Many found refuge in Poland, others in Prussia. In Poland, they were instrumental in bringing about the Consensus of Sendomir (1570) which awarded religious liberty to Lutherans, Reformed, and the Brethren alike and marked a high point of religious unity.

The latter part of the 1500s was easier for the Unity of Brethren in their homelands, but this was abruptly altered with the defeat of the Protestant forces at the battle of White Mountain in 1620 during the outset of the Thirty Years' War. Many Brethren leaders were executed by the victorious imperial forces for their part in the national uprising (Defenestration of Prague). Those who had means migrated to Poland and Hungary. Others remained to endure forcible Catholicization, preserving their faith within their own families as best they could.

John Amos Comenius (1592–1670) was the great figure who

---

[43] A recent discussion on the interaction between Prague and Wittenberg (as well as with the Reformed) is found in John T. McNeill, "The Ecumenical Idea and Efforts to Realize It, 1517–1618," in R. Rouse and S. Neill, eds., *A History of the Ecumenical Movement* (London: S.P.C.K. 1954), p. 42ff.

became the symbol of the Unity in these dark decades.[44] Educator, churchman, universal scholar, Comenius perpetuated in his person both the spirit and the official entity of the Brethren as the last regularly ordained bishop. Through his prolific publications on the history and genius of the Unity he strove to keep the spark alive. He transferred the bishopric to his son-in-law, Peter Jablonsky (d. 1670), from whom it passed to the son, Daniel Ernst Jablonsky (1660–1741). It was the latter, the court preacher of the court of Brandenburg, who ordained Count Zinzendorf, thus extending the chain of leadership into modern times, according to the Moravians. At any rate, the Renewed Moravian Church was recognized by the British Parliament in 1749 as an "ancient Protestant Episcopal church."[45]

A small handful of peasants and craftsmen in Bohemia, the "Hidden Seed," preserved the memory of the faith of the fathers under the harsh regimen of the Counter-Reformation. Inspired by the reports of a traveling carpenter, Christian David (1691–1751), a small group in 1722 crossed the nearby German border to seek refuge and religious liberty on the Upper Lusatian estate of Count Zinzendorf. From the community of settlers there emerged in 1727 the Renewed Moravian Church, a fusion of the older strain of the Unity with the dynamic revival spirit of Pietism.

The movement as such died out in its ancestral lands by the end of the eighteenth century, but was replanted a century later by Moravian missionaries. Most contemporary Czech Christian bodies feel themselves today to be the spiritual heirs of the Unity of Brethren.

[44] Comenius was offered the presidency of Harvard by John Winthrop in 1641: De Schweinitz, *op. cit.*, p. 580.
[45] William George Addison, *The Renewed Church of the United Brethren* (London: S.P.C.K., 1932), pp. 96–103.

· III ·

Radical Reformers

A STRIKING shift has taken place in the assessment of the events which shook Christendom in the sixteenth century. Roman Catholics, who previously summed up Martin Luther as a rebellious monk who wanted a woman, now give him credit for a sincere religious quest which, however painful in its outcome, was essentially salutary for the church. Lutherans, who for centuries were content to parrot the Saxon Reformer's condemnations of all those further left than himself, now accept the significance of evangelical Anabaptism as a historical identity in its own right. No aspect of church history has been pursued more avidly by researchers or has provided more excitement than the story of the once-despised dissenters.[1]

George H. Williams has brought together into one extensive synthesis the fruits of several decades of source publications and monograph investigations in *The Radical Reformation*. The book has been criticized for drawing within the rubric of the Radical Reformation too many heterogeneous personalities and movements, by the use of a negative criterion of including all those *not* encompassed by Classical Protestantism or Roman Catholicism in Western Europe.[2] Nevertheless, there is no question of the staggering diversity of opinion and belief which spewed forth once the rigid grasp of religious orthodoxy was successfully broken by the courageous acts of Luther and Zwingli. Stirred up by the preach-

[1] John P. Dolan, *History of the Reformation: a Conciliatory Assessment of Opposing Views* (New York: Desclee Co., 1965), is a good summary of current Catholic thinking; chapter five ("The Changing Reputation of the Anabaptists") in Franklin H. Littell, *The Anabaptist View of the Church*, second rev. ed. (Boston: Starr King Press, 1958) is a concise summary of the shift in historiography.

[2] See the review by John H. Yoder in *Theology Today*, XX (October 1963), 432–433.

ing of evangelical freedom, excited by apocalyptic currents, frightened by the threat of Turkish invasion, caught between an ambitious, rising middle class and an increasingly desperate peasantry, Europeans found themselves in a veritable caldron. The cool categories of scholars writing after the fact fail to capture the dynamic quality of the era. A pertinent image would be iridescent crystals of belief forming in a supersaturated solution.

There is substantial consensus, all the same, that it is to a small band of "Swiss Brethren" that one must turn to find the beginnings of the Believers' Church. They were the first to articulate these principles and witness to them with their lives. When in defiance of the authorities they began to baptize in January 1525, something qualitatively new took place in the history of Christianity. The Swiss Reformed expert on Zwingli, Fritz Blanke (1900–1967), expressed it in terms of the first Anabaptist congregation near Zürich: "In Zollikon, a new type of church had begun to differentiate itself, the Free Church type. Zollikon is the cradle for this idea, which from here entered upon its triumphal march through four centuries and through the whole world."[3]

Others would place the turning point among the same group, but somewhat earlier. For them the watershed was the emergence among Zwingli's closest circle of these who rejected his policy of delaying needed church reforms until the city council approved. "The decision of Conrad Grebel to refuse to accept the jurisdiction of the Zürich council over the Zürich church is one of the high moments of history, for however obscure it was, it marked the beginning of the modern 'free church' movement" (Bender).[4]

It is therefore appropriate to choose the Swiss Brethren (or evangelical Anabaptists) as the foremost representatives of Believers' Churches in the sixteenth century. The Mennonites, conscious of their direct line of inheritance from the Brethren, have been in the forefront of the scholarly reappraisal. Linked with their concern for historical accuracy and correction of misconceptions

[3] This is discussed in the introduction under the "Anabaptist School" of Free Church origins.

[4] Harold S. Bender, *Conrad Grebel* (Goshen, Ind.: Mennonite Historical Society, 1950), pp. 99–100; John H. Yoder, "The Turning Point in the Zwinglian Reformation," *Mennonite Quarterly Review*, XXXII (1958), 128–140, and *Täufertum und Reformation in der Schweiz: I. Die Gespräche der Reformatoren 1523–1538* (Karlsruhe: Mennonitischer Geschichtsverein, 1962), pp. 20–33.

has been the quest for the "recovery of the Anabaptist vision" in the life of their faith-community. This has issued in a worldwide program of such scope and vigor as to earn them the praise of providing (with the Lutherans) "the most remarkable energy to enter the Protestant scene in recent years" in the United States.[5]

To demonstrate the variety within Anabaptism itself, the Hutterites are also portrayed. They are the branch which developed a form of Christian communism able to perpetuate itself, despite many hardships, to the present. They share common rootage with the Mennonites in the Swiss Brethren.

The Swiss Brethren

In March 1558 a journeyman printer and Anabaptist leader in Cologne named Thomas von Imbroich was beheaded. He was twenty-five years old. Earlier two priests had come to convert him as he lay imprisoned in a tower. When they insisted on the necessity of infant baptism, he replied: "The scriptures teach no infant baptism, and those that are to be baptized according to the Word of God, must first be believers." They accused him of despising the Roman Catholic Church. He answered: "That I condemn your church and do not come under your communion, is for the reason that you do not keep your church pure: for perjurers, whoremongers, and the like are pious brethren among you." During the months in prison he wrote letters of encouragement to his young wife and an able confession of faith, later published in Europe and America.[6]

This episode reveals several important facts about the people called by their judges "Anabaptists," i.e. rebaptizers. They were ready to suffer and die for their faith. They were concerned for the purity and integrity of their church fellowship. They were able to give an account of the faith that was in them. (The record states that Imbroich's accusers were not able to prove that he was a heretic.) Further, they were convinced that baptism was meaningless before a person had been taught, converted, and become a

[5] Franklin H. Littell, *From State Church to Pluralism* (Garden City: Doubleday & Co., 1962), pp. 139, 141–144.
[6] Thieleman J. van Braght, comp., *The Bloody Theater or Martyrs' Mirror*, trans. J. Sohm (Scottdale, Pa.: Mennonite Publishing House, 1950), p. 578.

convinced believer. Finally, their witness has been preserved for posterity despite the cruel circumstances.

THE MOVEMENT BEGINS

It was long thought that the source of Anabaptism was to be sought in the mining town of Zwickau in Central Germany. Here several volatile religious enthusiasts including Thomas Müntzer (1488–1525) were active in the early sixteenth century. Some of the "Zwickau Prophets" visited Wittenberg, where their claims to direct revelations from God impressed even Philip Melanchthon, Luther's chief colleague, until the doughty reformer himself hurried from his refuge in the Wartburg to set things straight. Thwarted in Saxony, the "infection" then is said to have spread to South Germany and to Switzerland.

This version, still found in some current literature, is no longer tenable. It is now clear that the Zwickau radicals led by Müntzer were a separate phenomenon. No personal contacts between Müntzer and the Swiss Brethren have been demonstrated. Two letters (or one letter and its postscript) from the Swiss directed to the German radical are extant, but they were never delivered. Their contents reveal support for certain parts of Müntzer's teachings, in so far as they had heard of them, but indicate also great unclarity about his total position. Sharp admonitions directed to Müntzer on such vital points as nonresistance, liturgy, believers' baptism, and the gathered church make obvious that the two movements can only be placed in the same camp by ignorance or prejudice. Scholars now know that the story of the origin of Anabaptism in Germany was intentionally put into circulation by Zwingli's followers to try to remove the onus of the radical movement from Zürich in the eyes of the world.[7]

The story of the Swiss Anabaptists begins with the reform efforts of Ulrich Zwingli (1484–1531) himself. The eloquent Catholic preacher and humanist friend of Erasmus was called in 1519 to become the people's priest at the Great Minster (cathedral) of Zürich. Zwingli immediately began to preach straight through the New Testament, rejecting the prescribed texts of the church year. As his excited auditors listened to his careful exposi-

[7] Heinold Fast, *Heinrich Bullinger und die Täufer* (Karlsruhe: Mennonitischer Geschichtsverein, 1959). The letters are cited in footnote 9.

tions from the original languages of the Bible, they began to accept his urging for reform of church life and practice along scriptural lines. This reform was independent from Luther, although Zwingli was encouraged by what Luther had done. As the confrontation of the two leaders in Marburg in 1529 demonstrated, they were of different spirits. Luther, the former monk, had been in an agony of spiritual travail about his personal salvation. His was a doctrinal question. Zwingli, the humanist, was concerned to go to the scriptural sources and reform church practices upon their authority. His was an ethical question.

Zwingli began his reforms in 1522 (by encouraging his followers to break the Lenten fast, for example) but his ecclesiastical superior, the bishop of Constance, attempted to curb the changes. The city fathers of Zürich, however, who disliked the bishop's jurisdiction for political reasons, soon came to feel themselves competent to direct church affairs. Their common-sense method of handling theological differences was to call for a public discussion or disputation. Whoever made the best case before the council was judged correct. Zwingli won a notable victory for his views of scriptural authority in January 1523, when the Catholic opponents refused to admit the validity of this sort of secular decision on church matters. The way was free for him to proceed.

With the burghers on his side, Zwingli attracted young scholar-humanists to himself, chief of whom were Conrad Grebel (1495–1526) and Felix Mantz (1498?–1527). They studied the Bible with Zwingli and became his most ardent followers. He was grooming them for important positions. However, the promising development hit a snag. Although the city council was willing to take responsibility for church affairs from the disliked Catholic bishop, they were very reluctant to countenance more changes in the customary pattern of church life than necessary. Zwingli was convinced that through a process of cultivation the canton could be brought to a more progressive position. It was of first importance to bring all the people along. Education was needed, not revolution.

A crucial case came in October 1523. Zwingli had become increasingly restive about performing the mass, as he could find no scriptural warrant for it. In a disputation in that month, he presented his arguments. Despite this, the city council refused for political considerations to permit a change, although they granted that the theology of the Lord's Supper presented by Zwingli was correct. In December, Zwingli announced that he would proceed to celebrate a reformed eucharist anyway. When the council refused to accept a *fait accompli*, Zwingli backed down, indicating that the pace of the reform was in the hands of the state. He rationalized his position by asserting the right of the authorities to control all "outward" actions. The claim of the Bible is for "inward" matters. It became clear that despite Zwingli's biblicism, he could not conceive of any other arrangement than the union of church and state—*corpus christianum*. And indeed, hardly anyone else at that time could either.

Disappointment spread among his followers. They insisted that it was wrong to allow the final authority for purely religious matters, such as the liturgical form, to rest in secular hands. One interchange in 1523 reveals the sharp difference:

Zwingli: My Lords [the council] will decide how to proceed henceforth with the Mass.
Simon Stumpf: Master Ulrich, you have no authority to place the decision in the hands of My Lords, for the decision is already made: the Spirit of God decides.[8]

The chasm widened between Zwingli and his erstwhile adherents during 1524. He had become for them a "halfway" man, afraid to face the consequences of his own teachings. They seemed to him to be misguided, to be pressing too fast and hence risking the reformation. Grebel, Mantz, and others began meeting to discuss and study the Bible in order to find the right answers. They wrote to the major Protestant leaders in Germany—Luther, Karlstadt, and Müntzer—seeking communication. The letters to Müntzer show that they were passing from a negative position of rejecting those church practices foreign to the scriptures to a consideration of how a true church should be rightly ordered. In admonishing him to "go forward with the word and establish a Christian church with the help of Christ and his rule," they asserted their own conviction. They believed that obedience to biblical teaching demanded not only the rejection of infant baptism, but also the adoption of believers' baptism following personal conversion. Baptism "signifies that a man is dead and ought to be dead

[8] Quoted in Cornelius J. Dyck, ed., *An Introduction to Mennonite History* (Scottdale, Pa.: Herald Press, 1967), p. 29.

to sin and walks in newness of life and spirit, and that he shall
certainly be saved, if according to this meaning by inner baptism
he lives his faith."[9]

Two Zürich priests associated with the group, William Reublin
(d. 1560?) and John Brotli (d. 1528), refused to baptize the children of their parishioners. This called forth disciplinary action and
a government investigation. A perfunctory disputation was called
to hear the views of the new group, but the verdict was obvious
before it began. On January 18, 1525, the city council laid down
the ruling that anyone refusing infant baptism for his children
must be expelled from the canton. Three days later they decreed
that independent Bible study groups were banned; several individuals were banished.

Although baptism had not been the initial issue, it had now
become the symbol of the opposing church views. Zwingli and the
city fathers were determined to retain a state church; the others
sought to develop a fellowship along apostolic lines. In the face of
the ultimatum from the authorities, a dozen men gathered on the
evening of January 21 at the home of Felix Mantz to decide what
should be done. With them was a newer member named George of
the House of Jacob (Cajacob), nicknamed Blaurock, a priest
from Chur. An old Hutterite account describes the meeting:

> They came to one mind in these things, and in the pure fear of God
> they recognized that a person must learn from the divine Word and
> preaching a true faith which manifests itself in love, and receive the
> true Christian baptism on the basis of the recognized and confessed
> faith, in the union with God of a true conscience, [prepared]
> henceforth to serve God in a holy Christian life with all godliness,
> also to be steadfast to the end in tribulation. And it came to pass
> that they were together until dread [Angst] began to come over
> them, yea, they were pressed in their hearts. Thereupon, they began
> to bow their knees to the Most High God in heaven and called upon
> him as the Knower of hearts, implored him to enable them to do his
> divine will and to manifest his mercy toward them. . . . After the
> prayer, George Cajacob arose and asked Conrad [Grebel] to bap-
> tize him, for the sake of God, with the true Christian baptism upon
> his faith and knowledge. And when he knelt down with that request
> and desire, Conrad baptized him, since at that time there was no

[9] George H. Williams, ed., *Spiritual and Anabaptist Writers* (Philadelphia: Westminster Press, 1957), pp. 71–85, vol. xxv of *The Library of Christian Classics*.

ordained deacon to perform such work. After that was done the others similarly desired George to baptize them, which he also did upon their request. . . . Each confirmed the other in the service of the gospel, and they began to teach and keep the faith.[10]

THE MOVEMENT EXPANDS AND CONSOLIDATES

This was no frivolous act. The participants realized perfectly that this baptism flaunted the decision of the Zürich council: "They well knew what they would have to bear and suffer on account of it," in the words of the Hutterite chronicler. It was also clear to them that what they had been led to was not something to be enjoyed quietly and for themselves. Rather, they were given a mandate to teach their conviction to family, acquaintances—anyone they could reach. "The first church meeting was a missionary meeting."[11] The brethren dispersed to their homes in the countryside or surrounding cantons and taught what they had learned. The response was impressive. Persecution scattered them ever more widely, but they continued their witness.

William Reublin traveled to the Swiss German border near Waldshut, the town where the learned theologian Dr. Balthasar Hubmaier (1481?–1528) was priest. In much the same manner as his friend Zwingli, Hubmaier had accepted the reform doctrines. Also like the earlier Zwingli he had come to question infant baptism on Biblical grounds. Unlike Zwingli, he was ready to go one step further. When Reublin came in April 1525, preaching the necessity of believers' baptism, Hubmaier was ready. He was baptized by Reublin along with sixty of his parishioners. On Easter Sunday he himself baptized three hundred more. This was the first case of an entire congregation joining the Swiss Brethren.

The dramatic events in Waldshut brought quick retaliation from the Catholic powers, who had already marked Hubmaier as a heretic. He had to flee to Zürich, where he was twice imprisoned. Earlier, when Zwingli attacked the Anabaptists in print, Hubmaier had answered him with a tract, in turn calling forth an immediate published rebuttal. Upon Hubmaier's release from prison in Switzerland he traveled to Nikolsburg in Moravia, known as the "America of the sixteenth century" because of the tolerant policy of some of its noble-landowners. At Nikolsburg the refugee busied

[10] *Ibid.*, pp. 43–44.
[11] Dyck, *op. cit.*, p. 36.

himself with his pen, and became the most prolific literary protag-
onist of the Anabaptist cause. His name and writings were later to
lie cheek by jowl with Luther, Calvin, and Zwingli as the main
heresiarchs in the Catholic Index of prohibited books. He was
seized by imperial forces in 1528 and taken to Vienna where he
was burned at the stake. His wife was sentenced three days later to
drowning in the Danube. Hubmaier was killed but his message
lived on. "Truth is immortal" was his favorite saying.

In Zürich itself, the authorities had begun imprisoning the
brethren as early as February 1525. According to the chronicler:

> Finally, it reached the point that over twenty men, widows, preg-
> nant wives, and maidens were cast miserably into dark towers,
> sentenced never to see either sun or moon as long as they lived, to
> end their days on bread and water, and thus in the dark towers to
> remain together, the living and the dead, until none remained alive
> —there to die, to stink, and to rot. Some among them did not eat a
> mouthful of bread in three days, just so that others might have to
> eat.[12]

Seeing that imprisonment was no deterrent the Swiss proceeded to
capital punishment, a fit measure they felt for stubborn sedition-
ists. Felix Mantz was the first to die at the hands of a Protestant
government, although others had been killed by Catholic authorities before his death. He was sentenced to die by drowning in the
Limmat River, a mordant play on the practice of adult baptism.

One by one the leaders were tracked down and destroyed. Because they persisted in their public teaching and preaching, it was
not particularly hard to catch them. Within a few months of one
meeting in Augsburg in 1527, the so-called "Martyrs' Synod,"
almost all participants had met their death. Grebel was one of the
few early leaders who did not die a violent death at the hands of
the state. After evangelizing in several cantons in Switzerland and
winning many converts, he was mortally stricken with the plague,
less than two years after the first baptism. He was twenty-eight.

Suppression from above was not the only problem for the rapidly spreading movement. Equally important was the determination of their own principles and basis to prevent division within
their ranks. There were reports of antinomian activity by some

[12] Williams, *op. cit.*, pp. 45-46.

who had broken with the state church. With the loss of leadership by execution, there was more danger of excesses which could disrupt and lead astray. The answer was to call meetings of members from different areas to decide disputed issues and to establish limits. The most important of these early meetings was held at Schleitheim near Schaffhausen in February 1527. Michael Sattler seems to have been the one who put in writing the consensus of the gathering.

The account which was surreptitiously printed and circulated makes clear that there was much difference of opinion when they met at Schleitheim. But following the meeting they testified that "they had been brought into unity . . . without any brother's contradiction, fully satisfied." It is worth excerpting from this confession, because it largely fixed the direction of the movement from that time on. There are seven points:

(1) Baptism: "Baptism shall be given to all who have learned repentance and amendment of life . . . and to all those who walk in the resurrection of Jesus Christ. . . ."

(2) Ban: "The ban shall be employed with all those who have given themselves to the Lord, to walk in his commandments . . . and yet who slip sometimes and fall into error and sin, being inadvertently overtaken. . . ."

(3) Lord's Supper: "All those who wish to drink of one drink as a remembrance of the shed blood of Christ, shall be united beforehand by baptism in one body of Christ which is the Church of God and whose head is Christ. . . ."

(4) Separation: "A separation shall be made from the evil and from the wickedness which the devil planted in the world. . . . To us then the command of the Lord is clear when he calls upon us to be separate from the evil. . . ."

(5) Pastors: "The pastor in the Church of God shall, as Paul has described, be one who out-and-out has a good report of those who are outside the faith. This office shall be to read, to admonish and teach, to warn, to discipline, to ban in the Church, to lead out in prayer for the advancement of all the brethren and sisters, to lift up the bread when it is broken, and in all things to see to the care of the body of Christ. . . ."

(6) Sword: "The sword is ordained of God outside the perfection of Christ. It punishes and puts to death the wicked, and

guards and protects the good. In the Law the sword was ordained for the punishment of the wicked . . . and the same is ordained to be used by the worldly magistrates."

(7) Oath: "Christ, who teaches the perfection of the Law, prohibits all swearing to his [followers], whether true or false. . . ."

"Dear brethren and sisters in the Lord: These are the articles of certain brethren who had heretofore been in error and who had failed to agree in the understanding, so that many weaker consciences were perplexed, causing the name of God to be greatly slandered. Therefore there has been a great need for us to become of one mind in the Lord, which has come to pass. To God be praise and glory! . . ."[13] Their opponents rightly saw the importance of the confession, and both Zwingli and, later, Calvin directed polemics against it.

EXPANSION: SOUTH GERMANY AND STRASBOURG[14]

One of the most important consequences of the basic Anabaptist decision that the state is not the arbiter of faith was their disregard of governmental boundaries. Although classical Protestantism also expanded greatly beyond its places of origin, it held basically to the medieval conception of the union of church and state. For this reason, more emphasis was placed by them on the strategy of converting the influential and the powerful to Protestant belief. These were then to introduce the new teachings from the top down. The Anabaptist approach was precisely the opposite. This was essentially a lay movement, even though most of the early leaders were trained clerics. Their method—which was not consciously adopted but represented the spontaneous urge of the newly converted to share the good news with their fellows—was spreading the word person to person, aided by traveling missioners who spoke wherever they found hearers. The success was such as to create fear in the minds of the state and church that the movement would sweep Europe before it. It was this fear which explains the campaign of suppression which was mounted against

[13] John C. Wenger, "The Schleitheim Confession of Faith," *Mennonite Quarterly Review*, XIX (1945), 247–252.

[14] One school of thought believes that the South German movement was an independent movement, somewhat differently oriented in theology—see Jan J. Kiwiet, *Pilgram Marbeck* (Kassel: J. G. Oncken Verlag, 1957), pp. 40–46.

the defenseless brethren. In Swabia, four hundred special police (*Täuferjäger*) were appointed to apprehend Anabaptists and kill them on the spot. But soon one thousand police were needed. In 1529 the imperial diet of Speyer placed the dissenters under the ancient law against heretics: "Every Anabaptist and rebaptized person of either sex should be put to death by fire, sword, or some other way."[15]

Sebastian Franck, one of the best informed of the contemporaries, described what took place:

> The Anabaptists spread so rapidly that their teaching soon covered, as it were, the land. They soon gained a large following, and baptized many thousands, drawing to themselves many sincere souls who had a zeal for God. For they taught nothing but love, faith, and the cross. They showed themselves humble, patient under much suffering; they broke bread with one another, as evidence of unity of love. They helped each other faithfully, called each other brother, etc. They increased so rapidly that the world feared an uprising by them, though I have learned that this fear had no justification whatsoever. They were persecuted with great tyranny, being imprisoned, branded, tortured, and executed by fire, water, and sword. In a few years very many were put to death. Some have estimated the number of these who were killed to be at above two thousand. They died as martyrs, patiently, and humbly endured all persecutions.[16]

When Balthasar Hubmaier was on his way to Moravia, he passed through southern Germany. In Augsburg he baptized the noted Latin scholar and humanist John (Hans) Denck (1495–1527), one of the most irenic of the Anabaptist leaders. Denck had earlier lost his position as director of a Nuremberg school because of the sympathy he showed for reformation radicals. As an Anabaptist he was doomed to a pitiable life of wandering, but on his unwilling travels he was influential in spreading his faith from Augsburg to Strasbourg. He ended his days in Basel, wearied and harried by the defenders of the new orthodoxy.

One of those Denck baptized was John (Hans) Hut (d. 1527),

[15] Harold S. Bender, "The Anabaptist Vision," *Church History*, XIII (1944), 5–6.
[16] Quoted in John C. Wenger, *Even Unto Death* (Richmond, Va.: John Knox Press, 1961), p. 103. The statement was written in 1531. A recent article discounts the numbers involved; Hans J. Hillerbrand, "Luther's 'Deserting Disciples'," *McCormick Quarterly*, XXI (1967), 105–113.

a former follower of Thomas Müntzer. Hut escaped execution when the peasants' rebellion was put down in 1525, and renounced violence when he joined the Brethren. Impelled by eschatological fervor, Hut became one of the most vigorous of the Anabaptist missioners, covering Franconia, Bavaria, Austria, and Moravia. During the two years between his baptism and his death by suffocation in a prison, the fiery preacher is said to have won more converts singlehandedly than all of the other Anabaptists together. His corpse was solemnly tried, sentenced, and burned at the stake.

Strasbourg, one of the places visited by Denck, became an important center for the Anabaptists. As a border town between Germany and France and a juncture of trade routes, the Rhine River port had a tradition of independence. This explains why it was one of the few places to afford a relative sanctuary for hounded Anabaptists. Here, also, they were able to hold a series of conferences from 1554 to 1609. Here a congregation was able to exist, though its leaders were expelled. Anabaptist popularity in Strasbourg led the local reformers—Zell, Capito, and Bucer—to accept some of their convictions on church discipline in order to take the wind from their sails. When John Calvin spent some years there, he was introduced to the innovations, and in this way Anabaptism helped to influence Calvinism.

The strongest leader in Strasbourg was Pilgram Marpeck (d. 1556), who was employed by the city as a civil engineer. This gave him a privileged position, although he was finally driven out as a heretic in 1532. He had already lost his original home in the Tyrol along with his considerable wealth. Marpeck had many discussions with the Strasbourg church leaders, but his chief antagonist was Caspar von Schwenckfeld (1489–1561) of Silesia. He was a one-time associate of Luther who had come to the conclusion that there was so much wrong with current religious practices that it was best to declare a moratorium (*Stillstand*). Marpeck replied that Schwenckfeld would not have been content with Jesus Christ's own fellowship.

The only true church for Schwenckfeld was the invisible church; any attempt to organize a church was futile. Since truth was an inward quality, outward things must be de-emphasized. The most that could be allowed were small cells of like-minded souls who would seek to mutually edify. A high personal ethic was expected, but overt mission efforts such as Anabaptists undertook were unnecessary. Even as mild a position as this got Schwenck-feld into trouble, but he found influential support among some of the nobility. Paradoxically, a small movement did grow up around him in Silesia, Switzerland, and Italy, which has persisted in a quiet way, and now numbers some two thousand primarily in Pennsylvania.

Despite the attraction of Schwenckfeld's teachings, Marpeck was able to counteract them among Anabaptists, and in this way played a major role in furthering the movement. He was especially concerned for the unity of all Anabaptist groups, but met with indifferent success. Following his exile from Strasbourg, Marpeck traveled about in southern Germany and Moravia, finally finding a home in Augsburg. Here again his skills and technical knowledge compensated for his heterodox belief, and he died a natural death in 1556.

EXPANSION IN NORTH GERMANY AND HOLLAND

Another visitor to Strasbourg, but of quite a different tempera-ment was Melchior Hofmann (1493–1543). He is first heard of as a self-taught Lutheran preacher in Scandinavia and northern Germany. On his erratic travels he shifted to a Zwinglian position, and then came into contact with Anabaptist teaching. He was converted and baptized, but retained some of his peculiar views. To be the most fateful were, first, his apocalyptic conviction that the Second Coming was at hand, and second, a curious Christol-ogy which minimized the human nature of Jesus. Forced to leave Strasbourg, he converted large numbers in Emden, North Ger-many, and in the Netherlands and also wrote popular tracts. Some of his extremist followers convinced him that the New Jerusalem would be established by heavenly powers in Strasbourg and that he was a "second Elijah" called to prophesy and announce the great event. First, however, he would have to be imprisoned for six months to bring this about. Hofmann rushed to Strasbourg where he had no difficulty in persuading the city officials to fulfill the jailing requirement. He languished in prison for ten years, his meager food lowered through a hole in the ceiling, before he died still convinced that the millennium was imminent.

Misguided though he was, there was nothing belligerent about his eschatological quirks. For that matter, he was by no means alone in his expectations. In 1521 Luther announced that the end would come in 1524, and rushed the publication of the book of Daniel before the rest of his Old Testament translation, so that everyone could understand the prophecy before the violent end of the world.[17] It was among the "Melchiorites," Hofmann's followers, that the apocalypticism became dangerous. They took the fatal step from passively awaiting the divine establishment of the millennium to bringing it about themselves by force.

John Matthys (d. 1534), a baker in Haarlem in the Netherlands, took up the Melchiorite mantle, and sent out apostles two by two to convert the populace and prepare them for the end of the world. The harsh rule of the Spanish king in the Netherlands, accompanied by floods and plagues, conditioned the Dutch for radical teachings. Isolated episodes of fanaticism resulted. In Germany, the apostles found a field ripe for harvest in Münster, a fortified city in Westphalia. Bernhard Rothmann (1495–1535?), a protégé of Luther, had preached the evangelical message, and the townspeople were ready recipients of the heady news that not Strasbourg but Münster was to be the site of the New Jerusalem. Moderate elements in the city were driven out without mercy when the radical party seized power. John Matthys arrived to take charge himself in early 1534. Religious communism was introduced, and the Bible was declared the book of law for the city. The publicity of the heralds of the millennium sent off to all corners of Europe soon brought about the siege of the town by the forces of the outraged bishop in whose lands the city lay, aided by Protestant armies as well.

Matthys died in a foolhardy sortie outside the walls following one of his revelations, and a more reckless personality, John of Leyden, took over. Showing a bizarre mixture of military skill, ruthless hunger for power, and demagogical genius, the self-styled "King David" introduced a theocracy, based in equal part on Old Testament texts and his inspired revelations. Polygamy was introduced, and a reign of terror alternating with religious ceremonial kept the beleaguered populace in check. The news of the multiple wives both shocked and titillated Europeans, few of whom knew of the bigamy of Prince Philip of Hesse of about the same time, or of Luther's advice to the prince to lie heartily about it.

[17] See the documentation in John S. Oyer, *Lutheran Reformers Against Anabaptists* (The Hague: Martinus Nijhoff, 1964), p. 238.

When the "Davidic Realm" of Münster fell by treachery in June 1535, the half-starved survivors, reduced to making soup from wall scrapings, were slaughtered mercilessly. Three of the ring leaders were tortured to death with red-hot pincers, and their bodies hoisted in cages to the steeple of St. Lambert's church. The bones hung there for centuries, until men of a more sedate age removed the contents but left the cages hanging for the warning and edification of passers-by.

The aberration of Münster very nearly dealt a deathblow to the Anabaptist movement. This was more than enough to convince the authorities that their war against the Brethren was justified. No matter how many testimonies of their inoffensive conduct might be given, it was now evident to all that this was but a ruse to lull the state and church into carelessness, at which time an uprising could be staged and power wrested from the state. The name Anabaptist would ring through the centuries with an opprobium hardly less than "Bolshevik" for the good bourgeoisie of the 1920s. Indeed, the Anabaptists were called the "Bolsheviks of the Reformation" (P. Smith). Bainton comments: "The whole ugly episode discredited Anabaptism. Despite the fact that for the first ten years under frightful provocation they had been without offense, yet when a handful of the fanatics ran amuck the entire party was besmirched with the excesses of the lunatic fringe, and well into the nineteenth century historians of the Reformation did little more than recount the aberrations of the saints rampant."[18]

A Dutch priest named Menno Simons (1496–1561) heard with dismay the news about Münster. He had made a name for himself preaching against the errors of the wild spirits, but he was far from self-satisfaction. His pastoral concern was with the deluded but well-meaning remnant who were now like sheep without a shepherd. A group of them were killed when they took refuge in an old cloister near his parish. An autobiographical statement reveals the path of his own pilgrimage. Some years before, he had come to question the mass and the practice of infant baptism, and even preached his views, but continued his soft religious assignment:

After this had transpired the blood of these people, although misled,

---

[18] Roland H. Bainton, *The Reformation of the Sixteenth Century* (Boston: Beacon Press, 1952), p. 106.

fell so hot on my heart that I could not stand it, nor find rest in my soul. . . . I saw that these zealous children, although in error, willingly gave their lives and their estates for their doctrine and faith. And I was one of those who had disclosed to some of them the abominations of the papal system. But I myself continued in my comfortable life and acknowledged abomination simply in order that I might enjoy physical comfort and escape the cross of Christ.

. . .

I began in the name of the Lord to preach publicly from the pulpit the word of true repentance, to point the people to the narrow path, and in the power of the scripture openly to reprove all sin and wickedness, all idolatry and false worship, and to present the true worship; also the true baptism and the Lord's Supper, according to the doctrine of Christ. . . .[19]

Following a year of preparation in 1536, he was ordained an Anabaptist elder and thenceforth spent the rest of his life traveling through the Low Countries and northern Germany. There were other prominent leaders, for example Dirk Philips (1504–1568) and Leonard Bouwens (1515–1582), who baptized more than ten thousand persons in thirty-one years. But such were Menno's accomplishments that a grateful people accepted his name as a designation for their fellowship. Menno wrote and debated against the critics of Anabaptism, and exercised a far-flung ministry to shepherd a severely tried brotherhood. Something of the agony he and they endured can be felt in this moving summary found in one of Menno's writings:

For how many pious children of God have we not seen during the space of a few years deprived of their homes and possessions for the testimony of God and their conscience; their property and sustenance written off to the emperor's insatiable coffers. How many have they betrayed, driven out of city and country, put to the stocks and torture? Some they have hanged, some have they punished with inhuman tyranny and afterward garroted them with cords, tied to a post. Some they have roasted and burned alive. Some, holding their own entrails in their hands, have powerfully confessed the Word of God still. Some they beheaded and gave as food to the fowls of the air. Some have they consigned to the fish. They have torn down the houses of some. Some have they thrust into muddy bogs. They have cut off the feet of some, one of whom I have seen and spoken to.

[19] *The Complete Writings of Menno Simons*, trans. L. Verduin (Scottdale, Pa.: Herald Press, 1956), pp. 670–671.

Others wander aimlessly hither and yon in want, misery, and discomfort, in the mountains, in deserts, holes, and clefts of the earth, as Paul says. They must take to their heels and flee away with their wives and little children, from one country to another, from one city to another—hated by all men, abused, slandered, mocked, defamed, trampled upon, styled "heretics."[20]

LATER DEVELOPMENTS

Despite these concerted Protestant and Catholic pogroms against the Anabaptists, remnants did survive until the seventeenth century when Europeans, sickened by wars of religion, stopped killing those who believed differently. Nevertheless, survival was purchased at a price—either by accepting a tenuous toleration as the "quiet ones in the land" [*Die Stillen im Lande*] in isolated mountain valleys and rural areas, or by leaving the homeland to migrate to the thinly settled border regions or overseas. The first course was followed by some in Switzerland (although still liable to repeated waves of persecution through the eighteenth century) and Germany; the second by those who went from the Low Countries and northern Germany eastward to Prussia and Poland where freedom from military service and their own religious exercise were promised them. The first migrants to North America arrived in the seventeenth century, with many more following in the eighteenth from Switzerland and the Palatinate.

When compulsory military service was introduced in Prussia, the Mennonites accepted the offer of Empress Catherine to settle in Russia in closed colonies, beginning in 1788. The freedoms granted them "forever" were withdrawn in the nineteenth century, leading nearly twenty thousand to migrate to Canada and the western United States. Those who stayed in Russia were caught up in the maelstrom of the forced collectivization of the 1920s under the Communist regime. Mennonites still exist in the Soviet Union, but are ordinarily counted along with the Baptists by the state.

Modern missionary activities in the nineteenth and twentieth centuries emanating from the Netherlands and North America have created Mennonite congregations on the continents of Africa, Asia, and in the Pacific. The latest census of Mennonites shows a total of 450,000, more than half of whom are in North America. There are nineteen branches of Mennonites in North America, but

[20] Quoted in Wenger, *Even Unto Death*, p. 51.

four of them—the (Old) Mennonite Church, the General Conference Mennonite Church, the Mennonite Brethren Church, and the Old Order Amish—include seven-eights of the total within their own membership. Representatives from most of the areas of Mennonite population gathered in Amsterdam in July 1967 for the eighth of a series of world conferences planned to "bring the Mennonites of the world together in regularly recurring meetings of brotherly fellowship." The theme was "The Witness of the Holy Spirit."[21]

The Hutterian Brethren

Hans Jakob Grimmelshausen created the classic account of the Thirty Years' War in his picaresque novel, *Simplicissimus*. In curious contast to his story of the barbarous conduct of all parties in this war is his description, based on personal observation, of an idyllic community of "noble, blessed life" which seemed "more angelic than human." If it had not been for its deviant religious belief, the Roman Catholic author asserted, he would have joined it.

> In the first place they had large treasure and an abundance of provisions which however were by no means used extravagantly or unnecessarily. No profanity, no dissatisfaction, no impatience was observed among them, yea, one heard no unnecessary word. There I saw the craftsmen working in their shops as though they were under contract. Their school teachers taught the youth as though they were their own children. Nowhere did I see men and women together but everywhere each sex was performing its own work apart from the other. . . . There was no anger, no jealousy, no vengeful spirit, no envy, no enmity, no concern about temporal things, no pride, no vanity, no gambling, no remorse; in a word, there was throughout and altogether a lovely harmony.[22]

This was a colony of the Hutterite Brethren or Hutterites, descendants of Anabaptists from Switzerland and Germany, but especially from Austria. The fact was that when Grimmelshausen

[21] Cornelius J. Dyck, ed., *Eighth Mennonite World Conference* [Program Booklet] (Nappanee, Ind.: Evangel Press, 1967), p. 1. See also "World Membership Total Near 450,000," *Mennonite Weekly Review* (May 4, 1967).
[22] Quoted in John Horsch, *The Hutterian Brethren* (Goshen, Ind.: Mennonite Historical Society, 1931), pp. 67–68.

visited them in the seventeenth century, the community was in a state of decline. In religious convictions they held to the same principles as other Anabaptists, with one exception. Whereas the Swiss Brethren allowed believers to hold private property as stewards, always in readiness to share what they had with needy saints, the Hutterites took as their model the Christian communism portrayed in the second chapter of the Acts of the Apostles.

Christian love for the brother finds its true communion, they affirmed, only if unhindered by possessions. "It means having everything in common out of sheer love for the neighbor." As expressed in their authoritative statement of faith: "Thus all those who have fellowship with Him likewise have nothing for themselves, but have all this with their Master and with all those who have fellowship with them, that they might be one in the Son as the Son is in the Father."[23]

The Hutterian Brethren were fond of the metaphor of the elements of the communion as an analogy to their life together. (The first known expression of this image is found in the *Didache,* or *Teachings of the Twelve Apostles* written about A.D. 120.) In the same way that the kernel of grain must be crushed and broken so that there may be bread, said the Hutterites, and the single grape must be crushed together with others for wine, so must "those who want to celebrate the Lord's Supper be broken and ground by the millstone of God's word, and must give up their own will and purpose."[24] As forbidding and austere as this expectation may seem, the fact is that the life of the communal body established on this basis in 1528–1529 stretches across four centuries to the present despite internal conflicts, wars and plagues, concerted and cruel persecution, and repeated exile and migration. There is no more astonishing chapter in the long history of the Christian church than the saga of this branch of Anabaptism.

THE FIRST ORGANIZATION

As the violent suppression of Anabaptists increased in intensity across Europe at the close of the 1520s, the only hope for more

[23] From "The Five Articles . . ." quoted in Harold S. Bender, ed., *Hutterite Studies: Essays by Robert Friedmann* (Goshen, Ind.: Mennonite Historical Society, 1961), p. 83. The second quotation is from Peter Riedemann's *Account,* quoted in George H. Williams, *The Radical Reformation* (Philadelphia: Westminster, 1962), p. 433.
[24] From Andrew Ehrenpreis' *Sendbrief,* quoted in Bender, *op. cit.,* p. 177.

and more of them lay in reaching asylum in Moravia. Although this land came under Habsburg rule in 1526, the Moravian nobility had a long tradition of independence in both religious and political matters. The Austrians were determined to crush all dissent from the Roman faith, but their actual success in implementing their will by threat of force was sporadic. Moreover, the Hussite wars of the previous century had decreased the population and many a noble (and an occasional prelate) was prepared to wink an eye at religious error if settlers could thereby be won to bring life and income to desolated villages and farms.

Nikolsburg, a possession of the lords of Liechtenstein, became the center of the Anabaptist influx. Here two separate groups formed. The leader of the more moderate party was Hubmaier, who won over a Lutheran congregation there and even baptized his patron, Lord Leonard. Hubmaier consistently maintained that a Christian could be a magistrate and that defensive war was permissible. A more radical group, led by Jacob ("One-eyed Jacob") Wiedemann and inspired by the eschatological teachings of Hut, condemned mingling of church and state, and held out for complete nonresistance. The war issue was at the forefront because of the impending threat of Turkish invasion. The Hubmaier faction was nicknamed the "men of the sword" (*Schwertler*) and Wiedemann's faction the "men of the staff" (*Stäbler*). The pacifist Anabaptists could often be distinguished from other men by their practice of bearing staffs instead of weapons as they traveled from place to place. (The staff had been the symbol of the Minor Party of the Unity of Brethren in their debate with the Major Party, a controversy analogous to that which occurred in Nikolsburg.)

The differences came to a head in May 1527 with a disputation between Hut and Hubmaier.[25] Reconciliation was not possible and the Wiedemann group began a separate congregation. Alarmed by Hut's radicalism, Lord Leonard imprisoned him, but also was unable or did not wish to prevent Hubmaier's capture by the Austrians who took him to Vienna for trial and execution. The Liechtenstein lord asked the Wiedemann party to leave Nikolsburg because he felt them to be unnecessarily factious. When

---

[25] The most thorough study of the debate, Torsten Bergsten, *Balthasar Hubmaier* (Kassel: J. G. Oncken Verlag, 1961), pp. 459–460, raises the question of the fairness of Hubmaier in attributing statements to Hut not actually his own.

some two hundred did leave, the lord had a change of heart, rode after them and asked them to return. They refused. Their pacifism was such that they could not live in good conscience in the lands of a ruler who was willing to use force to protect them.

They camped in a ruined village, homeless and with limited funds, refugees once again. Then they chose leaders to guide their fortunes: "At that time these men spread down a cloak before the people, and every man did lay his substance down upon it, with a willing heart and without constraint, for the sustenance of those in necessity, according to the doctrines of the prophets and apostles."[26] Although the principle of communitarianism had been much discussed before, the group now put it into effect. This act marks the beginning of Hutterite history.

Representatives sent ahead to Austerlitz found the lords of Kaunitz more than ready to receive them, extending special privileges for the first years and promising "to leave their conscience free and unhindered" on military service and war taxes. Their Hutterite settlement in Austerlitz in 1529 became the first *Brüderhof* or colony of brothers, a distinguishing mark ever since. They agreed upon a twelve-point confession, of which the key affirmation was: "Every brother and sister should utterly devote himself to the community, body and soul, in God, receive all gifts from God and hold them in common, according to the practice of the first apostolic church and community of Christ in order that the needy in the community might be sustained like the Christians in the time of the apostles."[27] The utilitarian emphasis here was later to be elaborated more theologically.

THE CONTRIBUTION OF JACOB HUTTER

The process of perfecting community life was anything but easy. The trials of establishing a sound economic basis were compounded by the coming of new refugees from Austria and division among the leadership. Wiedemann was accused of autocratic methods. Some charged unequal distribution of the community's goods, and even shameful neglect of children when parents were ordered to communal labor. It was owing to the strong leadership of one person that the community did not fail. This was Jacob Hutter (d. 1536), named for his hatmaking trade. Born in South

---

[26] From the Hutterite *Chronicle*, quoted in Williams, *op. cit.*, p. 230.
[27] *Ibid.*, p. 232.

Tyrol, Hutter became the leading figure in Austrian Anabaptism after the execution of Blaurock and other Swiss Brethren missioners. He heard of the religious freedom in Moravia and went there first in 1529 to investigate possible resettlement of his persecuted Austrian followers.

A large group found conditions so intolerable at Austerlitz that they moved to Auspitz. The Austrians there called on Hutter, whom they respected, to come again from Austria to set things in order. He returned for a visit and found that the leadership in Austerlitz bore the most blame for the division. In 1533 Hutter came to Moravia once again, this time determined to remain until the continuing disputes were solved once and for all. He was thoroughly convinced of his apostolic calling to lead the divided flock. His evident organizational skills and piety won him a large following, and after several confrontations he was able to take the leadership. This was not without schism, as three deposed elders departed, each taking with him a small number of followers. Some of these eventually found their way back. In a fashion not unlike that which happened with Menno Simons, the movement was later to be called by Hutter's name, although he was not the original leader.

Hutter was able to stay in Moravia but two years. In 1535 the debacle of Münster provided the occasion for renewed pressure by the Austrians upon the Moravian nobles. This time the Hutterites were forced to leave their Brüderhofs. Hutter appealed to the governor for tolerance, insisting that they could not "be prohibited from the earth, for the earth is the heavenly Father's, may he do with us as he will."[28] The governor answered by placing a heavy price on Hutter's head.

His concerned followers insisted that he return to the Alpine valleys, which he did, his pregnant wife with him, only to be captured immediately. The Tyrolese recognized the importance of their prisoners, and went to great length to make him reveal the names and hiding places of his fellows. One treatment involved immersing him in icy water until his skin cracked open, then pouring alcohol into the wounds and igniting it. He remained steadfastly silent until his death at the stake in February 1536. His wife escaped but was later captured and killed.

[28] Quoted in William R. Estep, *The Anabaptist Story* (Nashville: Broadman Press, 1963), p. 89.

THE GOLDEN PERIOD

Back in Moravia, the homeless Hutterites split up into smaller groups and slowly found places to live. Ten years later, however, renewed persecution forced them to flee once more. For years they barely existed in the forests and in extensively excavated underground retreats. It was not until 1555 with the Peace of Augsburg that they were relatively safe. From 1565 until the end of the century they enjoyed a period of peace and prosperity which their historians called the "golden period." Under the able leadership of men like Peter Walpot (1518–1578) and Peter Riedemann (1506–1566), they founded at least one hundred Brüderhofs, with a total membership estimated at thirty thousand (earlier sources claimed seventy thousand).

The brotherhood was organized under one "bishop" (*Vorsteher*) living at the Neumühl near Nikolsburg. Under him in each colony were the ministers of the word (*Diener des Wortes*) and the ministers of service (*Diener der Notdurft*); the former were concerned for the spiritual health of the group, the latter for the economic progress. Each Brüderhof was largely self-sufficient under its efficient management. Many different shops and mills provided not only for their own colony, but also goods to be sold to others. Certain wares including pottery and cutlery were noted for their perfection, and now are museum pieces.

Both men and women were assigned work in the colony according to their abilities; children were cared for in nurseries. An excellent school system was organized. The Hutterites are said to have been completely literate, a remarkable achievement for that day and place. Early school regulations demonstrate advanced understanding of child psychology, merging firmness with freedom, and enjoining strict sanitation. Hutterite medicine was so esteemed that even the heretic-hating Emperor Rudolf II called a Hutterite physician to Prague in 1582 to cure a painful malady.

Since some of the Brüderhof buildings were still standing in the twentieth century, it is possible to get a good idea of the physical arrangement. Two-story buildings of substantial sun-cured brick housed common rooms and shops on the ground floor, and individual sleeping rooms for married couples above. One Brüderhof had forty-seven different buildings. Storehouses, mills, and shops completed the colony.

More impressive even than the showplace model communities was the mission concern of the Hutterites. Carefully planned and administered, and persistent, the Hutterite program sent missioners across Europe from what has been called "perhaps the greatest missionary center of the sixteenth century."[29] An extensive correspondence linked the travelers with the home base; more than four hundred of these letters have been preserved. The leading historian of the Hutterites, Robert Friedmann, calls these epistles the "finest and most genuine expression of the Anabaptist genius."[30] Many of the *Sendbriefe* were long (one of them 189 pages) and intended as defenses and expositions of the Hutterite faith, as well as a means of strengthening the internal life of the fellowship. This is seen clearly in the writings of Peter Riedemann.

While imprisoned in the Marburg area, Riedemann penned an *Account of Our Religion, Doctrine and Faith* (1540) meant for the landgrave of Hesse. This was adopted by the Hutterites as a definitive statement of faith, their most important writing next to the Bible. The *Account* consists largely of a compilation and harmony of more than eighteen hundred biblical references. The first part is arranged on the pattern of the Apostles' Creed; a shorter second section describes and defends Hutterite beliefs. The book is a classic of religious expression and has found a recent, English translation.[31]

It was also at this time that Hutterite historiography began. Caspar Braitmichel (d. 1573) was assigned the task of preparing a chronicle to relate the important events in the life of the brotherhood. The result is a basic source not only for Hutterite history, but also for all branches of the Anabaptist movement, because of the reports contained in it from the far-flung Hutterite missioners. The chronicle begins with the Garden of Eden, and comes down through the centuries in the confident belief that the Hutterites are the inheritors and continuators of primitive Christianity. Bulky manuscript copies of this "Great Chronicle" (*Gross Geschicht-Buch*) were taken along as their greatest treasure by the Hutterites on their many migrations. A sequel, the so-called "Small Chronicle" (*Das Klein-Geschichtsbuch der Hutterischen Brüder*), comes

---

[29] Littell, *The Anabaptist View of the Church*, p. 120.
[30] Robert Friedmann, in Bender, *op. cit.*, p. 158.
[31] Kathleen E. Hasenberg, trans., *Account of our Religion, Doctrine and Faith* (London: Hodder and Stoughton, 1950), for the Society of Brothers.

down to 1802, repeating briefly the contents of the earlier chronicle. The compiler was John Waldner (1749–1824), who wrote it in Russia.[32]

THE PERIOD OF TRIBULATIONS

The Great Chronicle lists 2175 martyrdoms, one index of the road of sorrow trod by the Hutterites during the Counter-Reformation. Suppression came upon them in full force at the close of the sixteenth century under the hand of Cardinal Francis von Dietrichstein, an implacable enemy although he had a Hutterite as his personal physician. The cardinal was aided in his campaign by several priests and some turncoats who mounted a public program of slander against the Hutterites. The title of one of the books written by the priest Christopher Fischer is indicative: *The Hutterite Dove-Cote, in Which Is Recounted All of the Mess, Manure, Filth, and Dirt, That Is Their False, Stinking, Filthy, and Horrible Doctrine* (1609).

Their enemies were also able to play with good advantage on the economic grievances of poor peasant neighbors, who were jealous of the nobility's preference for and protection of the heterodox colonists:

> They have the preference of managers of estates, be it dairy or wheat farms, mills, tile yards, gardens, or anything else. They are appointed by them to high positions in the castles, such as manager, steward, and keeper. . . . The lords give the Anabaptists such great freedom that in certain offices they do not even require an account from them. It is displeasing to God that the lords do tolerate them and entrust the estates to them. It is contrary to Christian love. . . .[33]

Because of the Hutterite reputation of wealth they were a favorite target for taxation. Their refusal to pay war levies led to

[32] See the comprehensive article by Robert Friedmann, "Hutterite Chronicles," in Bender, *op. cit.*, pp. 151–156 (taken from the *Mennonite Encyclopedia*, II: 589–591). It was a sensation for European scholars when they learned in the twentieth century that these chronicles still existed in the Hutterite colonies in North America. The *Great Chronicle* was published by Rudolf Wolkan in modern German in 1923. A. J. F. Zieglschmid edited a letter-perfect edition in 1943, with elaborate notes and bibliography. This same editor also published the *Small Chronicle* in 1947, in contemporary German.

[33] From Christopher Fischer, *Fifty-Four Important Reasons Why the Anabaptists Should Not Be Tolerated in the Land* (1607), quoted in Estep, *op. cit.*, p. 99.

seizure of their goods. In 1605 the Turks invaded Moravia, destroying sixteen colonies and devastating the rest.

After 1620 all non-Catholics were at the mercy of the imperial troops. The chronicler grimly reported that "the year 1621 began with much tribulation. The robbing, plundering, and burning of houses carried on by the soldiers continued throughout this and the following year." Women were attacked and the men tortured. "Such things were openly practiced by the imperial soldiery who believed themselves to be the best of Christians."[34]

In 1622 all Protestants in Moravia had been killed, driven out, or forcibly Catholicized. The Hutterite survivors, perhaps one thousand, flocked to daughter colonies in Slovakia, and one in Transylvania founded in 1621 upon the invitation of Gabor Bethlen. Little capital was at hand to finance a new start. Their last reserves of money had been seized by trickery. A strong leader, Andrew Ehrenpreis (1639–1662), labored tirelessly to hold the group together. He produced extensive regulations, much like a monastic rule, which covered every aspect of their communal life; they are still being followed. The very number and wording of the regulations is mute testimony to the extent of the deterioration of community discipline. Evidence is found of desire for private property and slackening in moral tone. From this time also is dated the compilation of written sermons (*Lehr und Vorred*) presently used in the colonies. "One may safely say that the Hutterian Brethren of today continue the Ehrenpreis tradition at least as much if not more than earlier tradition (e.g. that of Jacob Hutter)."[35] Yet twenty years after the death of Ehrenpreis, the communal economy was dropped.

The cause of the abandonment was the repeated invasions by the Turks (a menace to Central Europe since 1521) who found the concentrated communities to be easy looting. Two Quakers who visited the colonies in 1662 described the tribulations of the Hutterites, referring to the Brüderhofs as "Families." They reported that in one area where there had been "nine Families there is but one remaining, and the rest were burned with the Value of many Thousands in them, and about two Hundred of the Men were slain and taken captive."[36] The Hutterites reasoned that if the property

[34] Quoted in Horsch, *op. cit.*, pp. 54–55.
[35] Robert Friedmann, in Bender, *op. cit.*, p. 46.
[36] From Joseph Besse, *A Collection of the Sufferings of the People Called*

were divided up among the families there would be less provocation for attack and more chance of survival. They consequently developed a kind of cooperative, sharing labor but dividing property.

With 1683 and the defeat of the Turks before Vienna by the Austrian forces, the terror of invasion was removed, but the Hutterites were now faced again with Catholic proselyting. Varying subtle with severe techniques, the Jesuit-led campaign eventually succeeded in stamping out organized Hutterite religious practice. The Church confiscated Hutterite books, took children from their parents to be raised in Catholic homes and orphanages, imprisoned leaders in monasteries, coerced attendance at Catholic mass. These Hutterite Catholics became known as Habaner (likely from the term *Haushaben*). Traces of their Hutterite background were still noticeable down to World War II in their community organization.

The Brüderhof in Alwinz in Transylvania remained the only intact colony and there the membership dwindled to less than thirty, perhaps as low as sixteen. However, new life came into the nearly extinct movement when a band of Lutherans, forced from their Carinthian homes because of their faith, settled in nearby Creutz in 1756. The newcomers accepted the Hutterite way and shaped their life accordingly. (Many of the contemporary Hutterites stem from these Austrians.) By 1767 the pressure of Catholicization reached Transylvania, and the Hutterites were forced to flee once more, just before all of their children were to be seized. A caravan of sixty-seven went over the mountains to Wallachia (present-day Romania), pushing on despite exhaustion in their anxiety to stay ahead of their pursuers. The chronicle relates that they found they could sleep while walking.

Once out of the empire, they found themselves in the maelstrom of the Russo-Turkish war and were buffeted about until a Russian field marshal offered them land on his estate under generous terms. There they stayed until 1802 when the heirs of the Russian tried to force them into serfdom. When they appealed to the Tsar, they were given crown lands nearby. The security which this

Quakers (London: 1752), pp. 420–432, quoted in Victor Peters, *All Things Common: the Hutterian Way of Life* (Minneapolis: University of Minnesota Press, 1965), p. 28.

brought led some to wish to break up the community and live privately. When their Brüderhof building burned down in 1819, communal life was abandoned. This did not lead to great prosperity, and later the people applied to the government for assistance. The next step was removal to a Mennonite settlement near the sea of Azov, where the Mennonite patriarch John Cornies took them under his strong hand but discouraged the communal pattern. It was not until his death that some Hutterite leaders were able to rekindle support for the colony idea. Finally in 1856 they received permission from the government to make a new beginning. A kind of revival swept the Hutterites, and several Brüderhofs were organized.

This renaissance was abruptly shattered when the Tsarist government decided to extend the military conscription to the Hutterites and Mennonites, despite the early promises for exemption. The most a delegation from the two groups was able to secure was permission to do forest work as an alternative. Some Mennonites accepted this, but the stricter elements of both groups determined to leave the country. They looked to the New World for asylum. A delegation of Hutterites was sent in 1873 to choose a place where they could live and worship in peace.

MIGRATION TO NORTH AMERICA

The delegates found themselves the object of acute competition between land agents of the western railroad companies. These companies needed settlers along their lines to provide business, and were willing to make glowing promises. After experiencing much trouble and chicanery, the Hutterites finally settled near Yankton, South Dakota. Three different migrations were involved, all named after their leaders—the *Schmiede-Leut* (after Michael Waldner, a blacksmith), the *Darius-Leut* (after Darius Walter), and the *Lehrer-Leut* (after Jacob Wipf, a teacher). The latter group was the more liberal, and had not been communally organized in Russia, but accepted this on reaching America. Other Hutterites came and settled near the Brüderhofs, but did not join. Many of them became members of the General Conference Mennonite Church and the Krimmer Mennonite Church (Krim= Crimea).[37]

[37] An excellent, concise description of the migration and the problems of landholding in North America is found in Paul K. Conkin, *Two Paths to*

In 1917 the war hysteria in America made the German-speaking, communally-living pacifist Hutterites once again the object of persecution. Two young Hutterites died of mistreatment in Fort Leavenworth.[38] During World War II things were easier for the Hutterites, with the provision of Civilian Public Service camps and farm deferments. The primary cause for tension since 1945 has been the Hutterite need for more land to take care of an increasing membership, numbering fourteen thousand in 142 colonies (1963).

By far the most successful and oldest of communitarian Christian movements, the Hutterites are still marching to the step of the distant drummer heard by Jacob Hutter and his co-religionists in 1533. By all indications, they will be successful in perpetuating their colonies.[39]

Utopia (Lincoln: University of Nebraska Press, 1964), pp. 41ff. See also J. A. Hostetler and G. E. Huntington, *The Hutterites in North America* (New York: Holt, Rinehart and Winston, 1967).

[38] Horace C. Peterson and Gilbert C. Fite, *Opponents of War, 1917–1918* (Madison: University of Wisconsin Press, 1957), pp. 126–131; Guy F. Hershberger, *War, Peace, and Nonresistance* (Scottdale, Pa.: Herald Press, 1953), pp. 111–114. The Austrian Rudolf Wolkan in *Die Hutterer* (Vienna: 1918), writing during World War I, mused: "In America they were permitted free exercise of their religion, and, in addition, were to be freed forever from military service. Has President Wilson recognized these privileges? I do not know. It is, however, certain that the brethren will not bow to measures of force and would rather accept hard prison terms than to be untrue to their beliefs. . . ." (p. vii).

[39] Paul S. Gross, *The Hutterite Way* (Saskatoon, Can.: Freeman Publishing Co., 1965).

· IV ·

Separatist Puritans

In his classic study of the rise of Puritanism in England, William Haller asserted that this reform movement which culminated in civil war was "nothing new or totally unrelated to the past but something old, deep-seated, and English, with roots reaching back into medieval life." Appropriately, therefore, he began his story with Chaucer's parson. This paragon provided a noble example to his flock in that "first he wroghte, and afterward he taughte." The same idea Haller expressed has received scholarly reinforcement through localized studies which demonstrate that dissent blossomed in former strongholds of medieval Lollardy.[1]

Nonetheless, it is quite true that the dynamic for English Puritanism was provided by the Continental Reformation. When the Catholicizing policies of "Bloody" Queen Mary (reigned 1553–1558) drove English churchmen abroad, they were profoundly impressed by the reformers in the Rhineland and by the model city of Geneva, fashioned and guided by John Calvin's authoritative if indirect hand. Upon return to their homeland under the milder rule of Queen Elizabeth, they were eager to reshape the national church after the Frankfurt and Geneva patterns. "Popish" accretions of liturgy, polity, vestments, and church life were to be stripped away to allow pristine Christianity to shine in the light of day.

To the chagrin of the would-be reformers they found that popular Queen Bess was more concerned for the unity of the realm and her intricate foreign policy than for thoroughgoing religious refurbishing. The "Elizabethan Settlement"—a typically British amal-

---

[1] William Haller, *The Rise of Puritanism* (New York: Columbia University Press, 1938), pp. 3, 5. Henry W. Clark, *History of English Nonconformity*, second ed. (New York: Russell & Russell, 1965), I: 69–74; A. G. Dickens, *Lollards and Protestants in the Diocese of York* (London: Oxford University Press, 1959).

gam of Roman Catholicism and Protestantism—was designed to encompass the bulk of English religionists. Extremists, either old-line Roman Catholics on one end of the scale, or stubborn Puritans on the other, would either acquiesce or be squelched by sanguine means.

By the end of the sixteenth century, two factions had formed within Puritanism. The first was hopeful that a Church of England reformed after biblical authority could be secured within the existing order. Scotland under the dour John Knox provided an example close at home of what could be done. The second party, convinced that obedience to Christ demanded "reformation without tarrying for any" (Browne), began to call for separation from the establishment. If the church did not provide devout ministers, small groups of Christians could and must meet for mutual edification. Their spirit is well expressed in the testimony of those arrested in 1567 for defying the Act of Uniformity (1559) by meeting in Plumbers' Hall in London:

> So long as we might have the worde freely preached, and the Sacraments administered without the preferring of idolatrous geare about it we never assembled together in houses. But when it came to this poynt, that all our preachers were displaced by your lawe, that would not subscribe to your apparaile and your lawe, so that wee could not heare none of them in any Church, by the space of seaven or eight wekes . . . and were we troubled & commaunded to your courtes from daye to daye, for not comming to our parish Churches, then we bethought us what were best to doe. . . . And if you can reprove . . . anie thing that we held by the Word of God, we will uelde to you, and do open penaunce at Paule's Crosse; if not, we will stand to it by the grace of God.[2]

It was but a short step from this position to the fully developed idea of the gathered church of covenanted believers. This found classic formulation in the words of Robert Browne (1550–1633) in the 1580s: "The Church planted or gathered is a company or number of Christians or believers, which, by a willing covenant made with their God, are under the government of God and Christ, and keep his laws in one holy communion: because Christ hath redeemed them unto holiness and happiness forever, from which they were fallen by the sin of Adam." Similar affirmations

[2] Quoted in John T. Wilkinson, *1662—and After* (London: Epworth Press, 1962), pp. 1–2.

made by groups of the "visible saints" laid the foundation of Independency from which modern Congregationalism sprang.[3]

The adamant refusal of the Anglican Church during the Stuart dynasty to accept the changes sought so eagerly by the Puritans eventually drove even the moderate party into nonconformity and ultimately led to the Civil War and Commonwealth of 1640–1660. Some Puritans, despairing of ever gaining religious power in England, migrated to the Continent or to North America in the early seventeenth century. At the beginning of the Revolution the Presbyterian Puritans were predominant; they wished to organize a national church of the entire population by replacing the episcopal hierarchy with a national assembly, classis, and local presbyteries. Although they succeeded in overthrowing the bishops, they were blocked from setting up their own establishment by the increasing strength of the Independents (Congregationalists) and Baptists, who played leading roles in Cromwell's New Model army. The Society of Friends, or Quakers, born during the Commonwealth, represented a yet more radical form of Puritanism.

In 1662 the speaker of the House of Commons introduced a bill to reimpose the Church of England in the wake of the restoration of the Stuarts. His remarks concisely summarized the trend toward increasing radicalism which had taken place within the Puritan camp:

> We cannot forget the late disputing Age, wherein most Persons took a Liberty, and some Men made it their Delight, to trample upon the Discipline and Government of the [Anglican] Church. The Hedge being trod down, the Foxes and the Wolves did enter. . . . At length it was discerned, the . . . plot did not only bend itself to reform Ceremonies, but sought to erect a Popular Authority of Elders, and to root out Episcopal Jurisdiction. In order to this Work, Church Ornaments were first taken away; then the Means whereby Distinction or Inequality might be upheld amongst Ecclesiastical Governors; then the Forms of Common Prayer . . . were decried as superstitious, and in Lieu thereof nothing, or worse than nothing, introduced.[4]

[3] Quoted in Horton Davies, *The English Free Churches* (London: Oxford University Press, 1952), p. 33. See also G. F. Nuttall, *Visible Saints: the Congregational Way, 1640–1660* (Oxford: Basil Blackwell, 1957).

[4] Quoted in G. F. Nuttall, "The First Non-Conformists," in G. F. Nuttall and O. Chadwick, eds., *From Uniformity to Unity* (London: S.P.C.K., 1962), p. 151.

With the "Glorious Revolution" of William and Mary (1688), harassment of the dissenters by the Anglican establishment ceased in its overt forms. Despite Presbyterian efforts, the national church continued in the episcopal polity. The result was the emergence of the two-party system with the Church of England on the one side, and the nonconformists or Dissenters on the other. This line-up became a predominant shaper of English character and politics. Henceforth, "church" and "chapel" were two options, with definite implications for class and rank.

On the left wing of dissent were the Baptists and Quakers, representing seventeenth-century expressions of the Believers' Church.

The Baptists

A country gentleman with training in the law named Thomas Helwys issued in 1612 what has been called the "first claim for freedom of worship to be published in the English language"; it was titled *A Short Declaration of the Mistery of Iniquity.* Helwys penned a special inscription on the book's flyleaf for presentation to King James I, notorious for his rigid insistence on the necessity for church establishment ("No bishop, no king") and his pretensions to divine right. It read: "The King is a mortall man and not God, therefore hath not power over the immortal soules of his subjects to make lawes and ordinances for them and to set spiritual Lords over them." The bold book and the bolder dedication caused their author to be seized and thrown into Newgate Prison. He was never heard from again.[5]

Helwys (d. 1614?) was the leader of the first English Baptist congregation, established about 1611–1612. From this event on the Baptists have had a continuous history to the present. Some five years before the founding of the congregation, Helwys had sought refuge in Holland with a group of Gainesborough separatists, led by John Smyth (d. 1612), a Cambridge-educated formerly Anglican clergyman. This band was known as the Second English Church of Amsterdam, as they kept apart from the "Ancient Church" of English separatists already in residence there, because of doctrinal differences.

[5] Helwys' life is discussed in Robert G. Torbet, *A History of the Baptists,* rev. ed. (Philadelphia: Judson Press, 1963), pp. 36–39.

BAPTIST BEGINNINGS

This gap widened in 1608–1609 when Smyth became convinced that infant baptism was wrong, both from the standpoint of biblical authority and the inherent logic of the gathered church concept. If the episcopacy of the Church of England must be rejected, as the separatists all claimed, how can her baptism be preserved? Smyth proceeded to baptize himself ("se-baptism") and then those members of the congregation who were persuaded of the validity of his act, about forty persons. However, Smyth, who saw no particular virtue in consistency of religious conviction when new light was found, soon came to doubt the sufficiency of his self-baptism. This may have come through his contacts with the Waterlander branch of the Dutch Mennonites, from one of whom his congregation was renting their meeting place.

In 1610 Smyth and thirty-three followers addressed a petition to the Mennonites, seeking full membership among them. About ten of his flock objected to this step; they maintained that he had no right to repudiate the baptism he had performed upon himself and them. Thomas Helwys was the spokesman for the group. This minority even warned the Dutch Mennonites against accepting their colleagues. The cautious Mennonites took their time about accepting the Englishmen, and Smyth died in 1612 before their decision was reached. It was not until 1615 that his supporters were incorporated into the Waterlander fellowship.[6]

In the meantime Helwys led his splinter group back to England, convinced that it was wrong and unworthy to evade persecution by residence in a foreign land, especially when the tensions of refugee life helped foster internal strife. He was successful, as has been mentioned, in founding a congregation at Spitalfields near London. Other men including John Murton and Leonard Busher came forward to provide leadership when Helwys was imprisoned. Like Helwys, Busher also was moved to address the king, affirming that "through the unlawful weed-hook of persecution, which your predecessors have used, and by your majesty and parliament is still continued, there is such a quantity of wheat plucked up,

---

[6] The best survey of Baptist-Mennonite relationships written recently is Ernest A. Payne, "Contacts Between Mennonites and Baptists," *Foundations*, IV (January 1961), 39–55.

and such a multitude of tares left behind, that the wheat which remains cannot yet appear in any right visible congregation."[7]

This congregation and the others which formed from it, remained in communication with the Dutch Mennonites through letters and personal visits. Several times the English proposed outright union with the Dutch but differences in conviction on church-state relations prevented agreement. The Baptists believed that Christians could serve as magistrates and that taking oaths of allegiance demanded by the state was permissible, both denied by the Mennonites. There were also doctrinal differences.

By 1644 this movement numbered forty-seven congregations and had become known as the General Baptists. The name came from their Arminian theology, that is they believed in the general atonement (Christ died for all men) as taught by the Dutch theologian Jacob Arminius. The wave of the future for Baptists was to come from another group known as the Particular Baptists. They held a strictly Calvinist position on atonement (Christ died for the elect only) and also contended for baptism by immersion to symbolize the burial to sin and rebirth of the regenerate man.

The Particular Baptists arose in 1638–1640 from within an Independent congregation begun by Henry Jacob in Southwark, London. Jacob was a Puritan pastor who had spent some years in Zeeland before returning to England in 1616 to begin the Separatist church. Some of the Southwark members became convinced that believers' baptism by immersion was the only valid practice. This led to an amicable division.

Hearing that there was a society of Christian believers in the Netherlands who practiced such a baptism, they sent over one of their number, the Dutch-speaking Richard Blunt. He visited these Collegiants, a pietist group with close Mennonite connections, at their center at Rhynsburg near Leiden. Blunt was baptized there and upon his return he baptized a Mr. Blacklock; then in 1642 they both proceeded to baptize "the rest of their friends that were so minded" to the number of fifty-one. (Some historians hold that Blunt was baptized in England after he returned.) In 1644 there were already seven congregations of these Particular Baptists.

Recent scholarship has demonstrated a partial dependence by the Particular Baptists upon the writings of Menno Simons in the

[7] Quoted in A. H. Newman, "Baptists," *New Schaff-Herzog Encyclopedia of Religious Knowledge*, I: 460.

formulation of their Confession of Faith of London (1677), a fundamental doctrinal statement patterned upon the Presbyterians' Westminster Confession and the Congregationalists' Savoy Confession. The Baptist rootage in Calvinism is quite evident and close relationships were maintained with Congregationalists through the seventeenth century.[8]

BAPTIST DEVELOPMENT

The rise of the Baptists within English Independency makes natural their characteristic emphasis upon the authority and autonomy of each local congregation. Yet they were from the first eager to make common cause with like-minded churches. In 1644, for example, the seven Particular Baptist meetings agreed upon a common confession of faith. Although they rejected creeds as tests of faith, the formulation of such confessions of faith was very common. Both Smyth and Helwys were involved in confession-drafting in Amsterdam. By 1689 eight major Baptist confessions were in existence. They served to create unity of doctrinal matters, and to provide a basis upon which churches could be organized and disciplined.

Connections between congregations were handled by "associations," perhaps inspired by those developed to raise funds for military needs in the Civil War. The General Baptists favored a more structured association, with annual meetings and centralized organs of national character. The Particular Baptists were content with more informal gatherings of those congregations in the same general geographical area and with exchanges of correspondence.

During the Commonwealth period, Baptists enjoyed considerable freedom under the toleration policy of Oliver Cromwell. The high percentage of Baptists in the Roundhead army, some of whom rose to high rank, ensured the favor of the Lord Protector, whose own son-in-law was a Baptist. When the army purged the parliament of Presbyterians, a key figure in the "Rump Parliament" was Praise God Barebones, who had Baptist connections. Several Baptists served Cromwell on the "Tryers," a government Board of Examiners to pass on the qualification of pastors for endowed parishes, although other Baptists considered this to be a

[8] See the careful discussion in Glen H. Stassen, "Anabaptist Influence in the Origin of the Particular Baptists," *Mennonite Quarterly Review*, XXVI (October 1962), 322–348.

violation of their basic principle of separation of church and state.

A few Baptists during the interregnum were caught up in the millennial excitement of the Fifth Monarchy Men, whose views harkened back to the Münsterite aberration. When King Charles II was restored to the throne, the Baptist leadership immediately sent a petition to the monarch disavowing any formal connection with the heretical rebellion. Their pleas had little effect, and Baptists felt the harsh hand of repression when the Anglican establishment was reintroduced. The series of laws—Act of Uniformity, Corporation Act, Conventicle Act, Five Mile Act, Test Act— passed after 1661 hampered severely but did not halt the growth of Baptist witness.

The most famous Baptist victim of the Restoration's religious restriction was the tinker John Bunyan (1628–1688), one of the "mechanic-preachers" who combined handcrafts with powerful sermonizing. Following his baptism in 1653, Bunyan became known as an effective and eloquent preacher despite his lack of formal education. It was this activity which caused his arrest. The indictment read that he "devilishly and perniciously abstained from coming to [the Anglican] church to hear divine service, and is a common upholder of several unlawful meetings and conventicles, to the great disturbance and distraction of the good subjects of this kingdom." During his twelve years in jail he wrote the allegory *Pilgrim's Progress* about Christian's journey, with the notice to the reader:

> This book is chalketh out before thine eyes
> The man that seeks the everlasting prize:
> It shows you whence he comes, whither he goes;
> What he leaves undone; also what he does;
> It also shows you how he runs, and runs,
> Till he unto the Gate of Glory comes.[9]

DECLINE AND RENEWAL

After 1689 and the Act of Toleration, Baptists enjoyed legal protection, though with many restrictions. They had to subscribe to at least thirty-four of the thirty-nine articles of Anglicanism. Allegiance and fealty were to be sworn to the king; tithes and taxes had to be paid to the state church. Many of the restrictions

[9] John Bunyan, *The Pilgrim's Progress from this world to that which is to come* (Philadelphia: Leary & Getz, 1854), p. 6.

were not lifted until the late nineteenth century. Dissenters did not enjoy the privilege of study at Cambridge or Oxford, for example, until 1871.

The eighteenth century was one of relative stagnation for the Baptists. Many of the General Baptists drifted into the Arian and Socinian camps. Particular Baptists wrangled over doctrinal issues and became hyper-Calvinistic. More attention was placed upon building church edifices than upon building the church. The first generation of university-trained men who had become convinced Baptists died off, and makeshift educational arrangements failed to produce outstanding leaders.

It was not until the Wesleyan revival swept England that new life came to the Baptists. A New Connexion was organized among the General Baptists in 1770, but the major activity came from the Particular Baptist side. The theologian Andrew Fuller (d. 1815) tempered the extreme Calvinism which had thwarted an earlier generation. A notable group of able pulpit men, including Robert Robinson at Cambridge, Andrew Gifford, and John Ryland, brought both members and prestige to the church. This heritage was brilliantly continued in the nineteenth century by Robert Hall and especially by Charles Haddon Spurgeon (1834–1892) who preached regularly to seven thousand hearers in London.

But it was the shoemaker-pastor William Carey (1761–1834) who takes front rank among the renewers of the Baptists. Influenced by Methodists and prayer meetings held by a fellow workman, Carey was baptized in 1783 by Ryland's like-named father. While earning his living by his trade and by schoolteaching, Carey became an active preacher. The missionary imperative grew upon him as he followed a systematic schedule of study and biblical exegesis. He was impressed by the reports of the voyages of Captain Cook and the labors among the American Indians of John Eliot and David Brainerd, as well as the far-flung mission efforts of the Moravians.

Carey published his thoughts in *The Enquiry into the Obligations of Christians to Use Means for the Conversion of the Heathen* (1791). A year later he preached at an association meeting at Nottingham on the theme "Expect great things from God; attempt great things for God," using Isaiah 54:2–3 as his text. The upshot was the formation of what came to be known as the Baptist Missionary Society. Carey proposed that the work be supported by personal subscriptions of as little as one penny per week. Fuller and others swung their weight behind the scheme and it soon gained momentum. The foremost historian of missions wrote about Carey: "He seems to have been the first Anglo-Saxon Protestant either in America or in Great Britain to propose that Christians take concrete steps to bring the Gospel to all the human race. . . . William Carey and the society which arose in response to his faith were in fact the beginning of an astounding series of Protestant efforts to reach the entire world with the Christian message."[10]

Carey himself was one of the first missionaries to be sent abroad and he spent a distinguished career in India. Soon the Baptists were sending missionaries to many other foreign lands. Their mission to Jamaica had unforeseen results when William Knibb returned to England in 1832 from his work there to crusade for the abolition of the slave trade after seeing its effects in the West Indies. He is given credit for galvanizing public opinion which led to the act of parliament of 1833 outlawing slavery. In this and other ways the mission effort begun by Carey led to a renewal of the church in England.

BAPTISTS IN AMERICA

At much the same time that Baptist congregations were forming in Great Britain, a similar development took place in North America. The founder of Rhode Island, Roger Williams (1603–1683) is usually considered to be the father of American Baptists. Actually he was associated with them for only a few months, ending his days in the ranks of the Seekers who were doubtful of the final truth of any organized religious body. In 1639 he received in his colony several Baptists, and was rebaptized by one of them. Thereupon he baptized his baptizer and ten others to form the First Baptist Church of Providence. The congregation first leaned toward Particular Baptist views, but was reorganized in 1652 with General Baptist orientation.

More deserving of the title of father of the American Baptists is John Clarke (1609–1676), a well-educated physician and linguist. Clarke had come from England to Massachusetts, only to be driven out for championing the cause of Anne Hutchinson in the

[10] Kenneth S. Latourette, A *History of the Expansion of Christianity* (New York: Harper & Brothers, 1941), IV: 68–69.

Antinomian controversy. Sometime in the 1640s a group under his leadership in Newport accepted Baptist views. It was Clarke who played a leading role in one of the early tests of religious liberty in America. He and several colleagues were thrown into jail when they preached in Lynn, Massachusetts, thereby violating a law against the presence and activity of "Anabaptists." Although his own fine was paid, an associate, Obadiah Holmes, was severely scourged because of his conscientious refusal to pay. Clarke published a narrative of the incident and his views on religious freedom in *Ill Newes from New-England*, which had considerable impact back in England. He sailed there with Roger Williams to obtain a royal charter for Rhode Island ensuring religious liberty, and stayed on for several years until he succeeded in his task.

Another early *cause célèbre* in New England was the case of Henry Dunster, respected president of Harvard College. Dunster was forced to resign because he refused to allow his infant child to be baptized. The conversion to Baptist principles of this intellectual and pillar of society made it more difficult to pass off the Baptists as merely a collection of lower-class enthusiasts. Although many Baptists in fact were unlearned, they early turned to higher education. They founded the College of Rhode Island (later Brown University) in 1764.

The growth of Baptists in the seventeenth century was slow, with ten churches and perhaps three hundred members by 1700. The center of Baptist activity then shifted from New England to the Middle Colonies. In 1707 five congregations from Pennsylvania and New Jersey formed the Philadelphia Baptist Association. This grew to include Delaware, New York, Connecticut, Maryland, and Virginia. The association concerned itself with ministerial supply and standards, fellowship, doctrinal orthodoxy, education, and extension of the Baptist message.

The most rapid growth of the Baptists came after the Great Awakening of the 1740s. Many "New Light" Congregationalists joined the Baptists when the revival fires touched them. In the southern colonies there was impressive expansion under the leadership of men such as Shubael Stearns and Daniel Marshall, who worked in the Carolinas and in Virginia. By 1800 there were thirteen hundred congregations in the South. The last decades of the eighteenth century saw a phenomenal increase in the number of the Baptists along the new frontiers and also along the sea-board. In 1780 there were twelve Baptist associations, in 1790 triple that number. The Baptist farmer-preacher, the democracy of their polity, the simple form of worship, their championship of religious liberty—all these helped to allow the Baptists to become one of the two largest denominations in American church life in the nineteenth century.

LATER DEVELOPMENTS

From these beginnings in Britain and America, the Baptists spread around the world. American Baptist missionary activity began in 1814 when two missionaries sent out by the Congrega-tionalists, Adoniram Judson and Luther Rice, were convinced of the scriptural validity of believers' baptism during their long ocean voyage to Asia. The Baptist Missionary Society organized to sup-port them and set the pattern for many other societies.

Baptists returned to Europe during the nineteenth century. A central figure was John G. Oncken (1800–1884), a German who had come in contact with Free Churches during his stay as a youth in Great Britain. From his base in Hamburg, Oncken worked after 1823 as an agent for a British Bible society. In 1839 he became interested in the Baptist position. His actual baptism in 1834 by a visiting American professor, followed by the baptisms he con-ducted himself, caused great scandal. Repeated interventions by the authorities, prison sentences, and mob violence continued until the midpoint of the century. The Baptist movement spread to Berlin and throughout Germany, everywhere meeting with mis-understanding and outright persecution.[11] Oncken also traveled tirelessly in Scandinavia and into eastern Europe as far as Russia, baptizing and organizing congregations. Others came to aid him, so that by 1900 most European countries had at least modest numbers of Baptists. A remarkable increase occurred in Russia, where in the decade after 1914 the membership skyrocketed from one hundred thousand to one million.

Today Baptists number about twenty-three million in 110 coun-tries. In the United States eighteen and a half million are distrib-uted among the seven major Baptist bodies and many smaller ones. There are an estimated 1,200,000 in Europe, 640,000 in

[11] The painful process of their fight for recognition is found in Rudolf Donat, *Wie das Werk begann* (Kassel: J. G. Oncken Verlag, 1958).

Asia, and perhaps 500,000 in the Soviet Union. An international link is the Baptist World Alliance, begun in 1905, which is designed to promote fellowship and service. The World Alliance has been especially active in making representations to governments of countries in which full religious freedom for Baptists and others is not enjoyed. Beginning in the early seventeenth century as a handful of English separatists, the Baptists are now the largest non-Roman Catholic religious body in existence.[12]

The Quakers

A flippant way of summarizing the course of English church history in the sixteenth century begins by subtracting from the Roman Catholic Church the papacy, the mass, and five sacraments, to achieve the Church of England. If the rule of presbyters is substituted for bishops, and the liturgy simplified, the Presbyterians emerge. Independency (Congregationalism) comes by replacing the national church by autonomous congregations. By removing infant baptism and making membership conditional upon regenerate church membership, the Baptists are revealed. Take away all church sacraments, all liturgy, all church offices, and what is left—the Quakers.

A more sober way to express the same thought is to claim the Society of Friends as the logical consequence of Puritan belief, in much the same way as Anabaptism is held to be the extension and completion of the Reformation. The most recent study of Quaker beginnings contends: "Most of their insights in ethics and worship were in fact the same as those of the puritans. Even characteristically Quaker teachings were often puritan attitudes pushed to severe conclusions."[13]

This point of view is criticized by those who find more accurate Troeltsch's judgment that "the Society of Friends represents the final expression in its purest form of the Anabaptist Movement."[14] They point to the violent exception which early Quaker leaders took to the Puritanism of their time and the repeated

[12] W. M. S. West, "Baptisten," in F. H. Littell and H. H. Walz, eds., *Weltkirchenlexikon* (Stuttgart: Kreuz Verlag, 1960), pp. 125–126.
[13] Hugh Barbour, *The Quakers in Puritan England* (New Haven: Yale University Press, 1964), p. 2.
[14] Ernst Troeltsch, *The Social Teaching of the Christian Churches*, trans. O. Wyon (London: George Allen & Unwin, 1931), II: 781.

protestations that Quakerism in fact was "Primitive Christianity Revived." In the words of George Fox: "The Quakers are of the seed of Abraham, of that seed in which all the nations are blessed, and of the faith of Abraham and never came from the several Protestants nor Papists neither from their evil root nor stock. . . ."[15]

It is not correct to picture the Friends on the extreme left of the English religious horizon. More radical yet were the Ranters, the Fifth Monarchy Men, and other sects now forgotten, against whom the early Quakers pitted themselves in mortal spiritual combat because of their opponents' chiliasm, antinomianism, and individualism. At the same time the Quakers were contending with the people "in the mixture" on the other front. Perhaps it is fair to say that despite the Quakers' spirited opposition to Puritanism in their view of the scriptures, the church, worship, sacraments, and man's freedom, they can only be understood against the backdrop of Puritanism. As has been said in another context, an adolescent is never so much his father's son as in the ways he chooses to rebel against the parent.[16] It is very difficult to distinguish any direct continuity with the earlier continental expressions of the Radical Reformation or with the older mystical tradition despite evident similarities.

What is clear from the contemporary records is that many "seekers" became "finders" as they were gripped by the Quaker message after prolonged pilgrimages through all of the religious options in the turbulent Commonwealth period. A typical story is that of John Gratton (1645–1712), who recorded his search for the true church. These excerpts are important both for their criticism of the English churches as well as for the testimony of what he found among the "Children of Light":

> I cried unto the Lord that he would tell me what he would have me do, and that he would shew me, who were his people that worshipped him aright. . . . The Episcopalian Priests came in their white surplices and read common-prayers. . . . I saw they had the

[15] One of William Penn's books was *Quakerism a New Nickname for Old Christianity*. The quotation is from Lewis Benson, *Catholic Quakerism* (Gloucester, U.K.: the author, 1966), p. 9. The first chapter of this small book contains an excellent concise discussion of the current views on the place of Quakers in history.

[16] John Howard Yoder, *The Christian Witness to the State* (Newton, Kan.: Faith & Life Press, 1964), p. 88.

form without the power . . . their worship to be in ceremony and outward things without life. The Presbyterian priests, whom I had so much esteemed and admired, made their farewell sermons and left us. . . . They ought not be silent at man's command if the Lord had sent and commanded them to preach. . . . So I left them. . . .

I went to Chesterfield to seek out and meet those people called Independents for I like the name, seeing nothing at all in man as man to depend on, but they depended only upon the death and sufferings of Christ in his own body and did not come to see him nor his appearance in themselves to be their life, so they were dead professors and dry trees not bringing forth fruit. . . .

I found a people called Anabaptists. . . . I thought they came nearest the Scriptures of any I had yet tried. . . . After they came out of the water . . . I saw no appearance of the spirit of newness of life or power . . . their baptism being only with water which cannot wash away the filth of the flesh. . . . After some time I heard of a [Friends'] meeting at Exton . . . and when I came I was confirmed that they were in that truth whereof I had been convinced, though they were so much derided by the world. There was little said in that meeting, but I sat still in it, and was bowed in spirit before the Lord, and felt him with me and with Friends, and saw that they had their minds retired, and waited to feel his presence and power to operate in their hearts. . . . And there arose a sweet melody that went through the meeting and the presence of the Lord was in the midst of us and more true comfort, refreshment and satisfaction did I meet with from the Lord in that meeting than ever I had in any meeting in all my life before.[17]

In the 1650s and 1660s an astounding number of Englishmen made the same discovery as Gratton. In what has been termed an explosion of religious fervor, comparable to the Great Awakening in America or the Wesleyan revival, thousands were brought into the Society of Friends.[18] To churchly contemporaries, this upsurge seemed to be explicable only by demonic forces; an anti-Quaker tract of 1660 was titled *Hell Broke Loose; or, an History of the Quakers.*

The nickname itself is eloquent testimony to the impact of the

[17] Quoted in Harold Loukes, *The Quaker Contribution* (New York: Macmillan Company, 1965), pp. 12–13, and Howard Brinton, *Friends for 300 Years* (New York: Harper & Brothers, 1952), pp. 12–13.

[18] See the first chapter of D. Elton Trueblood, *The People Called Quakers* (New York: Harper & Row, 1966), pp. 1–19.

movement. They were called Quakers because some of their speakers or "Publishers of the Truth" called on all men to tremble before the Lord; also many Friends were seen to shake and quiver as they spoke. "The priest scoffed at us and called us Quakers. But the Lord's power was so over them, and the word of life was declared in such authority and dread to them, that the priest began trembling himself; and one of the people said, 'Look how the priest trembles and shakes, he is turned a Quaker also.' "[19]

QUAKER ORIGINS

The year 1652 has been observed as marking the origin of the Society of Friends, but to speak of one founding date of a movement of this nature is misleading. It was then that the first recognized Quaker community formed in Preston Patrick, Westmorland, in the north of England—the "Quaker Galilee."[20] Those gathered came from a loosely associated group of "Seekers," earnest searchers for religious truth who found no peace in existing ecclesiastical structures. They found it mutually helpful to meet regularly for prayers and Bible study, waiting expectantly for light to come.

The catalyst which transformed the passive seekers into aggressive possessors was the powerful message of George Fox (1624--1691). He had come to the chapel where the meetings took place, taking a seat by the door. The customary leader was somehow unable to begin, standing several times with open Bible but constrained from speech. After a pregnant silence, Fox "stood up in the mighty power of God and in the demonstration thereof was his mouth opened to preach Christ Jesus, the Light of Life and the way to God, and Saviour of all that believe and obey him, which was delivered in that power and authority that most of the auditory which were several hundred were effectually reached to the heart, and convinced of the truth that very day . . ."[21] Earlier Fox had a vision, while standing on Pendle Hill, of a people "thick as motes in the sun, that should in time be brought home to the Lord."[22] This was to him a corroboration of his divine leading.

---

[19] Norman Penney, ed., *The Journal of George Fox* (London: J. M. Dent, 1924), p. 57.
[20] The phrase is Barbour's; see chapter three, *op. cit.*, pp. 72–93.
[21] Quoted from an eyewitness' report in Brinton, *op. cit.*, p. 10.
[22] Found in W. Penn's "Character Sketch," in Penney, *op. cit.*, p. xvi.

Though often called the founder of Quakerism, George Fox was in fact but one of several charismatic leaders who roamed restlessly around the British Isles, driven by inward callings. His abilities, nevertheless, were so pronounced, and his sense of mission so strong, that he early became the focal point of the tempestuous movement. The nobleman William Penn the Younger (1644–1718), the most notable Quaker convert and a close associate, reported that he had never seen Fox in any situation—whether facing a rabid mob, in conversation with the Lord Protector Cromwell, in "threshing meetings" in large cities, on extended and hazardous travels in Europe or America—when he was "out of his place or not a match for every service or occasion."[23]

Fox was born in the English Midlands, the son of a sturdy weaver dubbed "Righteous Christer" by his half-scoffing, half-admiring neighbors, and a pious mother. As an adult Fox credited his early concern for religious righteousness to the influence of his devout puritan home. "In my very young years I had a gravity and stayedness of mind and spirit not usual in children; insomuch, that when I saw old men carry themselves lightly and wantonly towards each other, I had a dislike thereof raised in my heart, and said within myself, 'If ever I come to be a man, surely I shall not do so, nor be so wanton.' "[24] This spirit brought him to an acute crisis as a young man, when a relative and a friend challenged him to a drinking bout. This frivolity on the part of professed Christians so grieved him that he determined to break with society.

He sought counsel from priests and adherents of Christianity, only to conclude that "they did not possess what they professed." He also decided that formal theological learning would be useless "for the Lord opened to me that being bred at Oxford or Cambridge was not enough to fit and qualify men to be ministers of Christ." In a terrible agony of spirit reminiscent of Luther's struggle for certainty, Fox fasted, lived alone, and walked about, in his expression, as a "man of sorrows."

At the extremity of his despair, when all outside aid had proved unable to help him, release came: "And when all my hopes in them and in all men were gone, so that I had nothing outwardly to help me, nor could I tell what to do, then, Oh then, I heard a voice which said, 'There is one, even Christ Jesus, that can speak to thy

[23] *Ibid.*, p. xxii.
[24] *Ibid.*, p. 1.

condition.' And when I heard it my heart did leap for joy."[25] He was convinced that his testing had come from God so that he would not be tempted to give anyone else credit for his breakthrough except Jesus Christ alone. "And this I knew experimentally." The last sentence is a key to Quaker life. Fox's was not to be a religion of creed, or ceremony, or of cultic practice, but one of experience. His very struggles were meant to enable him to aid others who were undergoing similar crises.

Intense mystical visions brought him "openings" of complete unity with creation, as he reported later. "All things were new, and all that creation gave another smell unto me than before, beyond what words can utter." By 1647 Fox was embarked on a personal mission to "bring people off from all the world's religions, which are vain, that they might know the pure religion, might visit the fatherless, the widows, and the strangers, and keep themselves from the spots of the world." Vain traditions, "Jewish ceremonies," "windy doctrines," and "beggarly rudiments" were keeping men from the true empirical faith, and must be swept away.[26] This accounts for the consistent iconoclasm which led Fox and other Quakers to condemn church buildings as "steeple houses," to interrupt services with their own testimonies, to refuse "hat honor," to discard the swollen courtesies of the day in favor of plain speech, and to reject the heathen names of days of the week and of months. They were engaged in all-out warfare with the ways of the world, content with nothing less than unconditional surrender of pagans and professors, puritans and princes, to the way of the Lord.

The military metaphor may seem paradoxical for a company now best known as pacifists. It is, however, the most accurate way to describe both their aims and their methods. They were as little embarrassed in using martial images as St. Paul or the early Christians. One early record tells of the visit of two "public Quakers" to Bristol in 1654:

> John Camm began to speak tenderly, and in great zeal, directing [men] to the heavenly grace of God, and testifying against Sin. . . . John Audland, who very much trembled . . . stood up full of dread and shining brightness in his countenance, lifted up his Voice as a Trumpet, and said: "I proclaim Spiritual War with the Inhabitants

---

[25] *Ibid.*, pp. 3–8.
[26] *Ibid.*, pp. 17–22.

of the Earth, who are in the Fall and Separation from God." [He] went on in the mighty power of God. . . . But ah, the seizings of souls, and prickings at heart, which attended. . . . Some fell to the ground, others crying out, under the sense of the opening of their states [of soul][27]

A favorite expression was the "Lamb's War." Edward Burroughs wrote: "The Lamb hath called us to make War in Righteousness for his name's sake, against Hell and death, and all the powers of darkness. . . . And they that follow the Lamb shall overcome, and get the victory over the beast, and over the Dragon and over the gates of Hell." James Nayler explained that the Lamb's War must first be waged within each man against his carnal nature. "The *Lamb wars* . . . in whomsoever he appears and calls them to join with him therein . . . with all their might . . . that he may form a new Man, a new Heart, new Thoughts, and a new Obedience . . . and *there is his Kingdom.*"[28]

QUAKER GROWTH

It is against this backdrop that the Quaker expansion of 1650–1690 can be grasped. In what has been called the fastest-growing movement of western history, Friends swarmed over Great Britain, the Continent, Asia Minor, the Atlantic seaboard, and the West Indies, determined to bring their gospel to the entire world. The missioners were likened in Quaker writings to "spiritually weaponed and armed men going forth to fight and conquer all nations and bring them to the nation of God."[29] From one of his eight imprisonments, George Fox sent this mandate: "This is the *word* of the Lord God to you all and a charge to you all in the presence of the living God, be patterns, be examples in all countries, places, islands, nations, wherever you come; that your carriage and life may preach among all sorts of people and to them; then you will come to walk cheerfully over the world, answering that of God in every man."[30]

Here is a central thrust of the Quakers—the call to "walk cheerfully over the world" confidently expecting that the "seed" or

[27] Barbour, *op. cit.*, p. 57.
[28] *Ibid.*, pp. 40–41.
[29] Quoted from Fox's Journal in Frederick B. Tolles, *Quakers and the Atlantic Culture* (New York: The Macmillan Co., 1960), p. 23.
[30] Quoted in Loukes, *op. cit.*, p. 33.

"inner light" planted by God in every human would respond to a witness unafraid. Quakers went to confront the Sultan of Turkey and were heard courteously; they went to convert the pope at Rome and were jailed. Fox sent a message to the Emperor of China announcing: "Friends, there is a Power over all Powers, and this power is making itself manifest." Humble men and women traveled thousands of miles in obedience to their "leadings." Only slightly unusual is the record of Mary Fisher who visited the West Indies in 1655, New England in 1656, the Indies again in 1658, Constantinople in 1660, before her death in South Carolina.[31]

An Anglican sent to North America by the Society for the Propagation of the Gospel in Foreign Parts reported to his board in 1700 how difficult such people made his work:

> The Quakers compass sea and land to make proselytes; they send out yearly a parcel of vagabond Fellows that ought to be taken up and put in Bedlam. . . . Their preaching is of cursing and Lyes, poysoning the souls of the people with damnable errors and heresies, and not content with this in their own Territories of Pensylvania, but they travel with mischief over all parts as far as they can goe; over Virginia and Maryland, and again through Jersey and New York as far as New England.[32]

REACTION

The response of the civil authorities in England and New England is quite understandable. From their point of view these Quaker travelers were presumptuous troublemakers, nonordained fanatics. Occasionally Quakers in the early years walked naked through the town streets in imitation of the Old Testament prophets, as a sign of the spiritual barrenness they observed about them. The most notorious case involved James Nayler (1617–1660), second only to Fox as an eloquent leader, who allowed himself to be led into a town by a bevy of admiring female followers chorusing "Hosannah." Although he explained that this implied no blasphemous identification of himself with Jesus, but rather was a sign of Christ's second coming, an outraged Parliament investigated the incident and punished Nayler severely. He

---

[31] Fox's quotation is found in Barbour, *op. cit.*, p. 68. The missionary voyages of Mary Fisher are discussed in Tolles, *op. cit.*, pp. 26–27.

[32] Tolles, *op. cit.*, p. 25.

died soon after, but not before composing one of the most moving statements of Christian experience ever written.

Quaker zeal strained even Cromwell's official toleration policy, and local townspeople, often enough egged on by their pastors, mobbed Quakers who came without invitation to give their witness. The journals of Fox and other Friends are filled with reports of beatings, stonings, whippings, duckings, judicial browbeatings, and jailings. A typical incident involved Fox in Tickhill:

> When Friends were in the meeting, and fresh and full of the life and power of God, I was moved to go out of the meeting to the steeple-house. . . . So I went up to them and began to speak; but they immediately fell upon me; and the clerk up with his Bible, as I was speaking, and struck me on the face with it so that it gushed out with blood, and I bled exceedingly in the steeplehouse. Then the people cried: "Let us have him out of the church!" and when they had got me out, they beat me sore with books, fists, and sticks, and threw me down and over a hedge into a close, and there beat me and threw me over again. . . . After a while I got into the meeting again amongst Friends; and the priest and the people coming by the house, I went forth with Friends into the yard, and there I spake to the priest and people. . . . My spirit was revived again by the power of God, for . . . I was almost mazed and my body sore bruised but by the power of the Lord I was refreshed again, to him be the glory.[33]

After 1662, when the full effect of the Restoration laws against Dissenters were felt, the Quakers bore the brunt. They never resorted to secrecy or duplicity, but continued to hold their meetings with calm defiance. In at least one instance, when all of the adult members were dragged off to prison and their place of meeting burned, the children continued the regular meeting amid the ruins. The Presbyterian Richard Baxter, no friend of the Quakers, wrote:

> The fanatics called Quakers did greatly relieve the sober people for a time for they were so resolute, and gloried in their constancy and sufferings that they assembled openly and were dragged away daily to the Common Gaol, and yet desisted not, but the rest came the next day nevertheless, so that the Gaol at New Gate was filled with them. Abundance of them died in prison, and yet they continued

[33] Penney, *op. cit.*, pp. 56–57; the last sentence is taken from a more recent edition of the *Journal* by J. Nickalls.

their assemblies still—yea many turned Quaker because the Quakers kept their meetings openly and went to prison for it cheerfully.[34]

Before toleration came in 1689, some fifteen thousand were jailed, often under unspeakably vile conditions; four hundred and fifty died either in prison or as a result of their imprisonment. Another 243 were sentenced to transportation to penal colonies overseas, although only a handful were actually deported. Many others were ruined financially by fines and confiscation of property.[35]

ORGANIZATION AND DEVELOPMENT

A direct result of these conditions was the emergence of Quaker organization. Meetings on Sufferings were formed to record the extent of persecution, to draw up lists of those who needed support, and to succor the families in need. This became an executive committee and has remained such in England. The earliest Friends kept in loose contact with one another through Swarthmore Hall, the home of Margaret Fell, who married Fox in 1669. In 1653 local meetings were advised to select one or two of those "most grown in the Power and Life" to take responsibility for maintaining the group, arranging meetings, and exercising discipline. A system of general meetings, held at monthly, quarterly, and yearly intervals, was developed to deal with necessary matters. Clerks were chosen to guide these sessions and to record the "sense of the meetings," for formal votes were never taken.

Though the Quakers rejected the ordination of ministers, they did develop a practice of recording or recognizing the gifts of those who had special facility in ministering by the spoken word. The "public Friends" traveled often to other Quaker meetings, and by this process did much to keep unity, making Quakers on both sides of the Atlantic one body.

From the beginning the Quakers were amazingly productive in publications; they had issued over 2750 tracts as early as 1715. William Penn was one of the most articulate of the early leaders. His books, *No Cross, No Crown* and *Some Fruits of Solitude* had great circulation; his *Frame of Government*, upon which he based his "Holy Experiment" in Pennsylvania, was widely influential. A

---

[34] Quoted in Trueblood, *op. cit.*, p. 26.
[35] The statistics are taken from the careful computation of Barbour, *op. cit.*, pp. 70, 207–233.

well-trained Scot named Robert Barclay (1648–1690) wrote the classic defense and systematic treatment of Quaker belief as a young man of twenty-seven. Barclay's *Apology,* written first in Latin and then in English, while anti-Calvinistic, is a striking parallel in both form and motivation to the *Institutes* of John Calvin.

Following their release from government harassment in 1689, the Quakers entered upon a period of consolidation. This has been variously categorized as the era of "Quietism," a time of "guarding the light," or the "Quaker as bourgeoisie."[36] There was definite dampening of the evangelistic zeal, and cautious care for tending the inward life of the group. Strict disciplines of plain dress, speech, and conduct were attended to by elders and "weighty Friends." The necessity for dealing with the oncoming generations led to the practice of "birthright membership" for children of members. Many Friends were cut off from membership for marrying those not of their persuasion.

This shift in Quaker life is clearly seen in the incident when the American Quaker, John Woolman (1720–1772), appeared at the London Yearly Meeting in 1772. The aging Woolman was led to the strenuous journey by his concern to give witness in England against slaveholding and slave trading, as he had done so effectively among Quakers in North America. The genteel London Quakers—many of them prosperous merchants—were put off by the eccentric dress of the visitor, who wore only undyed homespun clothes as a testimony against the exploitation of Negroes in the manufacture of textiles and colored dyes. He was coolly given to understand that he could be excused from his mission and could return home forthwith. Happily, Woolman's genuine spirituality and integrity were soon recognized. He was received warmly by English Quakers before his death, which came while he was still sojourning in Great Britain.

For all the criticism that has been leveled against this period of Quaker history, it is true that some of the most noted Quaker humanitarian activity arose from it. The work of Quakers in mental health, prison reform, improvement of labor conditions, education as well as abolition, is known to all.

The nineteenth century was marked, especially in America, by

[36] Brinton, *op. cit.,* pp. 181–187; Loukes, *op. cit.,* pp. 58–71; John Sykes, *The Quakers* (Philadelphia: J. B. Lippincott, 1959), pp. 162–243.

several schisms. Evangelical impulses on the one side and rationally tinged traditionalism on the other caused sharp tensions and finally separations. In the United States, many of the midwestern and western Quakers adopted the usual Protestant practices of salaried pastors, set forms of worship, and even conservative theological positions. The twentieth century brought a reawakening under the stimulation of such men as Rufus Jones and Henry Cadbury. The American Friends Service Committee, founded in 1917, won international esteem for Quakers by its innovative and wide-gauge program of ministry to human need.

By the time of the Fourth World Conference of Friends, held July 24–August 4, 1967, in North Carolina, world membership neared two hundred thousand. There are presently 123,000 Quakers in North America, six thousand in South and Central America, twenty-four thousand in Europe, forty thousand in Africa (Kenya has the largest Yearly Meeting), fifteen hundred in Australasia, and seventeen hundred in Asia.[37]

---

[37] *Friends Around the World* (Philadelphia: Friends World Committee, [n.d.]).

· V ·

Free Church Pietists

"BETTER with the Church in hell than with pietists, of higher or lower type—in a heaven which does not exist." This fulmination attributed to Karl Barth typifies the current assessment of Pietism among theologians, who find it a handy label for individualism, subjectivism, legalism—indeed, anything they particularly dislike.[1]

In fact, this late-seventeenth and eighteenth-century movement of reform and revival which swept through Christendom from eastern Europe to the North Atlantic coast was the seedbed from which sprouted some of the most creative institutions and personalities Protestantism has known. The judgment of Horst Stephan is by far a more accurate estimate of its impact: "The stream of religious revival, which we designate with the label Pietism, flows in a nourishing manner through the areas of church, theology, and the general culture. It proved itself to be a powerful bearer of progress, not only insofar as it destroyed that which was out of date, but also in that it lent unsuspected fertility to seeming arid soil." Modern Protestant missionary activity, educational reform, wide-gauge philanthropic activity, much of the current theological enterprise, the ecumenical movement—all these can trace their roots to Pietism.[2]

[1] Quoted in Andrew Drummond, *German Protestantism Since Luther* (London: Epworth Press, 1951), p. 79; Barth later softened his criticism of Pietism. See the discussions of recent theological appraisals in Dale W. Brown, "The Problem of Subjectivism in Pietism" (unpub. Ph.D. dissertation, Northwestern University, 1962), pp. 150–158, and his "The Bogey of Pietism," *The Covenant Quarterly,* XXV (February 1967), pp. 12–18. See also John H. Yoder, *The Christian Witness to the State* (Newton, Kan.: Faith & Life Press, 1964), pp. 84–90.

[2] Horst Stephan, *Der Pietismus als Träger des Fortschritts in Kirche, Theologie und allgemeiner Geistesbildung* (Tübingen: J. C. B. Mohr, 1908), p. 58. A similarly favorable judgment is awarded by John T. McNeill, *Modern Christian Movements* (Philadelphia: Westminster Press, 1954), pp. 49-74.

What was it? In 1689 the first recorded public statement using the word "Pietist" was made by Joachim Feller, a Leipzig professor: "The name Pietist is now known all over the city. What is a Pietist? One who studies God's Word, and leads a holy life in accord with it."[3] Pietism was a reaction against an increasingly sterile Protestant scholasticism, which in striving to defend the legacy of Luther with symbolic books and strident disputations, forgot his wise saying that "the heart of religion lies in its personal pronouns."[4] Pietism was concerned with a reformation of life to complete the earlier reformation of doctrine. Its ethical intent was needed in a Europe still reeling morally from the degradation of the Thirty Years' War, recently portrayed so graphically in Brecht's *Mother Courage*.

Pietism can best be understood by looking at its characteristics. It was experiential, emotional, individual, biblically centered, and ethically minded. Where the orthodox Protestant asked of man: "Is he sound?" the Pietist asked: "Is he saved?" One of its central figures, August Hermann Francke (1663–1727), maintained that he valued a "drop of true love more than a sea of knowledge." Since he was a leading orientalist and a distinguished professor at Halle, this appraisal may not be explained away by anti-intellectualism. Instead of inquiring about the relationship of the individual to the institutional church and its clergy, Pietism asked about the personal relationship to Christ, about conversion.[5]

Pietism asserted the "primacy of feeling in Christian experience" (Walker). This brought renewed attention to the individual, but the individual was very much a part of a group. The setting up of conventicles or study cells, such as those begun in 1670 by Philip Jacob Spener (1635–1705) in Frankfurt/Main, became a hallmark of the movement. It was Spener's introduction to a new edition of the devotional writings of John Arndt (*True Christianity*) which marks the beginning of Lutheran Pietism in Germany in 1675.

Ordinarily Pietism is defined as that reform effort within the German Lutheran church led by Spener and Francke. But this was

[3] Johann Georg Walch, *Historisch und theologische Einleitung in die Religions-Streitigkeiten der evangelisch-lutherischen Kirchen* (Jena: 1730–1739), I: 548.
[4] Quoted in Drummond, *op. cit.*, p. 52.
[5] *Ibid.*, p. 60.

really part of a larger stream, which preceded their efforts and was not limited to one country. The Reformed Churches of the Lower Rhine and in the Netherlands had been caught up by it even earlier and they had been influenced by yet earlier developments in England. McGiffert and other recent writers are correct in placing within the broader spectrum of Pietism both the evangelical revival of England and the Great Awakening in America in the eighteenth century.[6]

Although Pietism in the first instance was a reform movement *within* the church, several independent bodies sprang from it. One of them was the Church of the Brethren in Germany. Twenty years later came the Renewed Moravian Church, which took remnants of the Unity of Brethren and vitalized them into a small but dynamic Christian movement. The Moravians provide a direct link to what has become the most influential outgrowth of Pietism, that is Wesleyan Methodism. Although John Wesley was to break with the devotional and theological style of the Moravians, it was to them that he owed decisive aid in several critical junctures of his spiritual pilgrimage. Through the shaping impact of the Wesleyan societies, the message of Pietism has been inextinguishably stamped upon the religious life of North America.

The Church of the Brethren

> In the year 1708 eight persons agreed to establish a covenant of a good conscience with God, to accept all ordinances of Jesus Christ as an easy yoke, and thus to follow after their Lord Jesus—their good and loyal shepherd—as true sheep in joy or sorrow until the blessed end. . . . These eight persons united with one another as brethren and sisters in the covenant of the cross of Jesus Christ as a church of Christian believers.[7]

The eight were led by Alexander Mack (1679–1735), a miller stemming from a well-situated burgher family near Heidelberg. After reaching their decision, they proceeded to an act of baptism,

[6] Arthur C. McGiffert, *Protestant Thought Before Kant* (New York: Charles Scribner's Sons, 1949), pp. 155–185; James H. Nichols, *History of Christianity, 1650–1950* (New York: Ronald, 1956), pp. 80–93; John Dillenberger and Claude Welch, *Protestant Christianity* (New York: Charles Scribner's Sons, 1954), pp. 122–140.

[7] Alexander Mack, Jr., quoted in Donald F. Durnbaugh, ed., *European Origins of the Brethren* (Elgin, Ill.: Brethren Press, 1958), p. 121.

very much like the earlier initiatives of John Smyth and followers in Amsterdam and Roger Williams and friends in Rhode Island. By this action they placed themselves squarely within the Anabaptist tradition, although they had come to this through their involvement in Pietism.

Their course had begun simply. In several areas of Europe people had become dissatisfied with the routine church functions. They wished to come together privately for sessions of Bible study, prayer, and mutual admonition. Many lived in the Palatinate, where religious life was at low ebb. Not only had the official state religion alternated eight times in one hundred and fifty years between the three recognized faiths (Roman Catholic, Lutheran, Reformed), but the recent French invasions and occupations had caused great confusion. Much of the clergy's time was spent in bickering and even violence over the possession of church buildings. A government ruling in 1698 provided that all three groups should share in their use, but given the state of tension it may well be true, as observers assumed, that the main intent of the compromise was to heighten difficulties. The conduct of the pastors was an open scandal, as attested to by the frequent calls for reform coming from the consistories. These conditions were worsened by a profligate court life conducted by the Elector Palatine, ruinous taxes, and forced labor. So many subjects of the Palatinate opted to migrate to escape their lot that "Palatine" became a generic term for all Germans entering the North American colonies.

The people who came together privately for their meetings were liable to prosecution which led to jail, confiscations, and eventually expulsion. What actually happened in their meetings is revealed in the records of the hearings they were subjected to after being arrested. A typical account is this one of 1709:

> When they come together they sing two or three hymns, as God moves them; then they open the Bible and whatever they find they read and explain it according to the understanding given to them by God, for the edification of their brethren. After they have read, they fall to their knees, raise their hands to God and pray for the authorities, that God might move them to punish the evil and protect the good; then they praise God that He has created them for this purpose.[8]

---

[8] *Ibid.*, p. 73.

The reference to the authorities sounds like special pleading, but it is consistent with other uncoerced expressions of their attitude toward the state.

When the state officials persisted in suppressing them, the Pietists were confirmed in their opinion that religion should be divorced from the state. The inability of the clergy to understand the sincerity of their religious quest stiffened them in their convictions. They had not begun with any intention to separate themselves from the churches of their childhood. But when put to the test of turning their backs upon their newly won insights or giving up their homes and church membership, they chose the latter and went into exile.

There were in fact very few places where religious dissenters could find shelter in Germany. One of these areas of asylum was the tiny county of Wittgenstein, northwest of Frankfurt/Main in the hills between the Lahn and Eder rivers. The counts who ruled the enclave had first offered homes to religious refugees when the Huguenots were expelled from France in 1685. Genuine religious piety, as well as the calculation that their land (which had lost many of its inhabitants in the Thirty Years' War) could use new blood, induced the Wittgenstein counts to risk the wrath of the Holy Roman Empire. Imperial laws forbade such toleration. However, by the time the ponderous machinery of the imperial bureaucracy got around to investigating the denunciations of the "fanatical and heretical people of low and knavish extraction" who seemed to be repeating the "history of Jan van Leyden, Knipperdölling, and Thomas Müntzer and consorts," as one outraged nobleman expressed it, the dissenters had already left for the more hospitable climes of the Netherlands.[9]

The "Brethren" as they called themselves, or the "New Baptists" as they were labeled by their peers, had been influenced by the historical work of Gottfried Arnold (1666–1714). He had lovingly detailed in several books the life and beliefs of the early church, for he held them to be normative for all later Christians. It was Arnold's writings that were meant when the Brethren described how "they found in trustworthy histories that the early Christians during the first and second centuries were planted into the death by crucifixion of Jesus Christ, according to the com-

[9] Ibid., p. 133.

mandment of Christ, through triune immersion in the water bath of holy baptism."[10]

They had also been influenced by the Mennonites in Germany and Holland, the successors of the Swiss Brethren or evangelical Anabaptists. The Brethren seriously considered asking for baptism from the Mennonites whom they visited in "heartfelt love," but thought that the quiet, secluded Mennonites were not fully faithful to the rugged faith of their ancestors. They had accepted the role as the "quiet ones in the land" in return for an uneasy tolerance. This seemed to the Brethren to mean a loss of their "first love." Despite this judgment, they praised the moral conduct of the Mennonites and remained in close contact with them.

CRITICISMS OF THE BRETHREN

The first baptisms brought the Brethren into conflict on two different fronts. The first was, of course, with the state church, backed up by government officials, for whom rebaptism was a crime punishable under imperial law. To be true, no longer were those found guilty of "Anabaptism" killed outright, but they were to suffer a range of punitive possibilities. The other front was found in the antagonism of the Radical Pietists in whose ranks the Brethren had stood for a time. Like their forerunners the Spiritualists of the sixteenth century, the Radical Pietists considered any churchly organization, no matter how informal, to be a sign of the fall. (This situation repeats that of the Quakers between government and the radical left of England.) Men such as E. C. Hochmann von Hochenau (1670–1721), who had greatly influenced many who became Brethren by his fervent preaching and warm spiritual counseling, and John George Gichtel (1638–1710), the foremost exponent at the time of the teachings of Jacob Böhme, attacked the Brethren for what they felt to be sectarianism and narrowness. They predicted that when the wealth of Mack was completely dissipated by his payment of fines and aid to needy members, the new experiment would die.

The most articulate literary opponent of the Brethren was the former Württemberg Lutheran pastor, Eberhard Lewis Gruber (1665–1728). He had moved to the Marienborn area (where a count had also granted limited religious freedom in order to at-

[10] *Ibid.*, p. 121.

tract settlers) after being dismissed from two parishes for his radical religious views. In 1713 he challenged the Brethren with forty "Basic Questions"; these queries and Mack's answers were published as the first printed record of Brethren beliefs. The first question and its answer were: "Do you maintain that for over one thousand years there has been no true and genuine baptism, and consequently, no true church on earth?" "We maintain and believe that at all times God has had His church which always observed the true baptism and ordinances. This, however, was always hidden from the unbelievers and often consisted of but few members. Despite this the gate of hell could not prevail against the church of the Lord Jesus. It can also be proved from the histories that God has caused His ordinances to be revealed as a witness to the unbelievers at all times."[11]

One year later Gruber returned to the attack with a writing called *Conversations Concerning the True and False Separation*. This was a warning against those who had separated from the state church only to proceed to initiate a new brotherhood. True separatists, he contended, begin no new sect. Rather, they go "into the inward sanctuary, in their heart, and serve God there." Ironically, before that year was out Gruber himself became the leader of a cult, the sensational "New Prophets," or the Community of True Inspiration. This was built around the charismatic testimonies of "tools of the spirit" like Gruber, who were thought to be direct channels of the Holy Spirit; their utterances in trance-like states were taken down as Holy Writ. The descendants of these Inspired still practice their faith in the formerly communitarian colonies of Amana, Iowa.[12]

THE MOVEMENT EXPANDS

Before the baptism in late summer, 1708, the Brethren in Wittgenstein sent an open letter to the Pietists of the Palatinate, many of whom they knew personally. The letter described how their conviction had ripened that they should be baptized in apostolic fashion. They understood that obedience to the Great Commission of Matthew 28 and the injunctions of I Peter 3 clearly called for this: "As Christ our head and keeper lowered Himself

[11] *Ibid.*, pp. 325–326.
[12] Donald F. Durnbaugh, "Brethren Beginnings" (unpub. Ph.D. dissertation, University of Pennsylvania, 1960), pp. 66–67.

into the water, so must we of necessity, as His members, be immersed with Him." The letter invited others to join with them in the initiatory step:

> So, then, if some more brethren wish to begin this high act of baptism with us out of brotherly unity according to the teachings of Christ and his apostles, we announce in humbleness that we are interceding together in prayer and fasting with God. . . . If we then begin in the footsteps of the Lord Jesus to live according to His commandment, then we can also hold communion together according to the commandment of Christ and His apostles in the fear of the Lord.[13]

Quite a number followed this urgent appeal. So many came to the Brethren meetings in Schwarzenau in Wittgenstein, that no building could contain the crowd at one time. Residents still point out the lawn called the "Anabaptist garden," where they met. Members were sent out at once to take the message to other territories. Surviving records, while not complete, indicate that these travels extended into several western European countries, and involved great personal risk.

One of the men was Christian Liebe (1679–1751), who was caught by the city fathers of Bern, Switzerland. He readily admitted that he had come "to visit the local brethren, to minister, to solace, and to baptize someone if the occasion arose." Their answer was to sell him as a galley slave to the King of Sicily, along with some Mennonites. (During the same month that this incident took place, the Bernese authorities were engaged in a vigorous diplomatic campaign to denounce the French for their practice of sentencing French Reformed subjects to the galleys.) Though several of the Liebe party died either on the long trek over the mountains to Italy or at the oars, he and the remaining survivors were liberated by the combined efforts of Dutch Mennonites, Swiss Pietists, and an English bishop.[14]

After Schwarzenau, the largest number of Brethren converts gathered in Marienborn near the beautiful medieval town of Büdingen. A contemporary account of the Brethren initiative there summarizes:

> At this time a special awakening arose in the hearts of many among

---

[13] *Ibid.*, pp. 57–58.
[14] Durnbaugh, *European Origins*, pp. 217–240.

the friends in this land, who did not wish to remain longer in such division and indifference. They therefore began to unite in prayer and edify one another from the holy Word. They were called New Baptists because they practiced, among other well-seeming ordinances, baptism of adults by immersion. They were mostly single-minded and good souls. They displayed at first a great earnestness and zeal in their behavior and conduct, through which many were moved and were drawn into their circle.[15]

A succession of baptisms, in which both new settlers and established subjects were involved, alarmed the Marienborn count, who directed that thorough investigations be made. Although he had promised religious freedom, he intended this to be restricted to private exercises in individual homes. Public actions, such as he deemed the baptisms to be, were not to be tolerated. When the flamboyant Inspired also became active, the count decided that the Brethren had to leave as well. Alexander Mack appealed for clemency on behalf of a widow and her daughter, but without success. Sympathetic officials provided passports for the Brethren in 1715, certifying that "they have so conducted themselves in their civil lives that no one can reasonably bring anything against them" and recommending "to everyone to aid them in their undertaking" of migration.[16]

The Marienborn Brethren found a place to stay in Krefeld on the Lower Rhine. This had become an important textile manufacturing center thanks to the skills of some Mennonites who had settled there earlier. The economic advantages they had contributed caused the authorities to wink an eye at their religious beliefs and to shrug off the angry denunciations of the Reformed clergy. However, when the Brethren came and began to attract to their ranks some of the local Reformed parish members, the fury of the pastors rose to a crescendo. It was bad enough to have the heretical Mennonites around, but at least they tended to their own business and restricted their teachings to their own families.

A small congregation of Brethren at nearby Solingen was raided early in 1719, and six of the men marched off to jail. When the best efforts of the clergy failed to persuade them to return to one of the accepted faiths, the case was turned over to three theological faculties for advice. The Roman Catholic faculty recom-

[15] *Ibid.*, p. 180.
[16] *Ibid.*, p. 188.

mended execution, the Lutheran the galleys, and the Reformed life imprisonment at hard labor. The milder suggestion of the Reformed faculty was the one adopted. The six Solingen Brethren were sent to the fortress of Jülich on the Dutch border to begin serving their sentence.

They soon were so trusted that they were allowed to go into the town to buy necessities, so long as at least one of the group was inside the prison. The authorities knew that the Brethren would never desert their fellows. Further proselyting attempts upon them here also proved fruitless, although the prisoners understood that immediate release from their hardships could be secured by accepting a state church.

The exhausting work and abominable living conditions in dank dungeons told on their health. Scurvy weakened them further. After three years they were visited by some Dutch travelers, who had accidentally heard of their incarceration solely on religious grounds. The report of the Dutchmen back at The Hague resulted in diplomatic pressure being placed upon the Elector Palatine. The Dutch government made it clear that important negotiations in progress with the German ruler would be blocked until he agreed to release the six prisoners. This took place, after some delay, in November 1720, a few months short of four years' confinement. A full record of their prison experiences which one of their number wrote has circulated in manuscript among Pietist conventicles in Germany and Holland to this day.[17]

Similar circumstances obtained in the other areas where Brethren groups formed, in Switzerland, the Palatinate, and Hamburg-Altona. Perhaps five hundred had joined the movement by the tenth anniversary of the first baptism.

MIGRATION

By 1719 the combination of state harassment and economic necessity caused the Brethren to weigh the possibility of migrating to the New World to find a place where they could exist in peace, and practice their faith without interference. The earlier travels of William Penn in Germany and descriptive tracts and booklets circulated by Penn's agents from the Netherlands made Pennsylvania seem the best site. Those living in Krefeld had direct contact

[17] *Ibid.*, pp. 240–280.

with the descendants of the first mass migration of Germans (1683), the pioneers of Germantown above Philadelphia. A large number of Brethren, therefore, left Krefeld for Germantown in 1719.

The Schwarzenau congregation found it advisable to leave Wittgenstein in 1720 before the imperial government closed in upon them. They moved to a village in Frisia near Leeuwarden. An eighteenth-century American historian who talked to some of them about their decision to move once again to North America, wrote:

> Since they could never gain strength enough in Europe to eat their own bread, although in Holland good friends were moved to assist them and actually did show them great love, they were continually longing for a place, where by the blessing of God, they might be able to maintain themselves by the labor of their hands, and to pass the rest of their lives in perfect liberty of conscience, which nowhere in Europe they could enjoy together.[18]

This contingent migrated in 1729 under the leadership of Alexander Mack. By 1735, the great majority of Brethren had completed the migration. Those who remained in Europe died out or merged with other groups like the Mennonites. The latest references to intact groups in Europe are found in the 1740s.

DEVELOPMENT AND SCHISM

After the first (1719) party of Brethren had established themselves in and around Germantown, they took steps to organize a congregation. This was completed on Christmas Day, 1723, after they had first consulted by letter with their co-religionists still in Europe. They chose Peter Becker (1687–1758) as their first minister in America, and it was he who carried out the first baptism near Germantown and presided at the first love feast. This is the Brethren term for a communion service which consists of the washing of feet (John 13), an agape meal, and the partaking of the eucharistic elements.

Following this baptism, Brethren expansion was rapid. The entire male membership of Germantown embarked on a mission into the back country, and several new congregations resulted. A re-

---

[18] Samuel Smith, *History of the Province of Pennsylvania*, ed. W. Mervine (Philadelphia: J. B. Lippincott Co., 1913), p. 189.

vival spirit prevailed. A Lutheran writer of the early nineteenth century, looking back at the course of religion among the German groups in North America, described this as the "first ardent awakening to cause great excitement" among the Germans, the harbinger of many succeeding waves.[19]

In the new Conestoga congregation in present-day Lancaster County, the leading spirit was Conrad Beissel (1690–1768). He had come to America hoping to join the hermitage established near Germantown by the followers of John Kelpius. This, however, was no longer extant upon his arrival. After a brief stay in Germantown he went into the wilderness to live as a hermit, until he was baptized by the Brethren and became the leader at Conestoga. It was not long until he broke the relationship with the Germantown Brethren and gathered a following of admirers, out of which grew the famed Ephrata Community.

This combination of celibates and married "householders" composed what Voltaire called the "most inimitable Christians." At its peak the community reached a level of economic and cultural productivity unequaled in eighteenth-century America. Their mills, printing press, handcrafts, manuscript illuminations, and schools have rightly been the objects of intensive scholarly research. Thomas Mann included an extensive discussion of the uniquely beautiful choral music of Ephrata in his novel *Doctor Faustus.*[20]

With the death of the brilliant but imperious Beissel, the Community leveled off in growth and influence and soon began to decline. This was hastened by the onset of the Revolutionary War. After the Battle of Brandywine the brothers and sisters at Ephrata took in and tended the wounded troops. Typhoid fever broke out and swept away many of the community as they labored selflessly. Buildings had to be burned to stop the contagion. Ephrata never recovered from this blow. Married members of the Ephrata Community, however, did continue their religious observances through the nineteenth century. More recently the remaining buildings have become a historic shrine cared for by the Commonwealth of Pennsylvania. A daughter colony near Waynesboro, Pennsylvania,

---

[19] "Gestalt des Reichs Gottes unter den Deutschen in America," *Evangelisches Magazin*, III (April, May, and June 1814), 3: 131.

[20] Voltaire's remark is in "Église," in *Oeuvres complètes*, XVIII (Paris, 1878), p. 501.

continued for a longer period and a handful of these German Seventh-Day Baptists still worship in the church at Snow Hill.

The mainstream of Brethren survived the Ephrata schism. Congregations were established in the south in the Shenandoah Valley and then in the west as the frontier was pushed back in the late eighteenth century. A Philadelphia editor of an 1810 edition of the writings of Alexander Mack wrote of the "repeated removals into different parts of the continent, where societies have since been formed, namely in the interior of this state, in New Jersey, in Maryland, Virginia, North Carolina, Kentucky, and in the state of Ohio, where instead of the fathers are the children, who are risen up as their successors to bear witness to the truth of those principles, in which many of their predecessors lived joyfully and died triumphantly."[21]

In 1880–1882 a three-way split occurred when a conservative party ("Old Order"), which opposed any changes in church practice, broke off and a liberal party ("Progressive") was ejected from the denomination for moving ahead too rapidly. The moderate party, known as the German Baptist Brethren, and since 1908 as the Church of the Brethren, now numbers over 215,000 adult members, predominantly in North America. Members overseas are the result of mission programs in India, Nigeria, and Ecuador.[22]

The People Called Methodists

The Evangelical Revival in England was to the Church of England as Churchly Pietism was to the Lutheran Church. Wesley and Whitefield were the Anglo-Saxon counterparts of Spener and Francke. Many of the criticisms leveled at the German church—rationalism, clericalism, scholasticism—were repeated by the English reformers in their own situation. The jeremiads aimed at society's ills by the field preachers in England remind one of exhortations by the earlier Pietists.

Although there is a tendency of writers to paint a black picture of the state of the English nation and the national church in order

[21] [John Schlingluff], ed., *Rights and Ordinances . . . by Alexander Mack* (Philadelphia: John Binns, 1810), p. 16.
[22] *Church of the Brethren Yearbook 1967* (Elgin, Ill.: General Brotherhood Board, 1967), p. 10.

to allow the reform movements to shine forth the more brilliantly, impartial historical judgment does indicate that all was not well. Not even the defenders of the eighteenth-century Anglican establishment attempt to show that this period was a high point in the long career of the church. The onslaughts of Deism had been weathered, but the defenders, such as Bishop Butler in his *Analogy*, accepted the rationalistic presuppositions of their opponents. Partisans of the Church were at pains to demonstrate the utter reasonableness of Christian claims. "Enthusiasm" was the worst epithet they could hurl. An anti-Methodist polemic by a Professor Joseph Trapp catches up the typical stance: *The Nature, Folly, Sin and Danger of Being Righteous Overmuch, with a View to the Doctrines and Practices of Certain Modern Enthusiasts* (1739).

Hannoverian England notoriously made up for the enforced discipline of the Puritan era, with the court leading the way. It was there that the *bon mot* circulated that legislation was needed to remove "not" from the places it occurred in the Ten Commandments and insert it in appropriate positions in the Creed. R. H. Tawney summarized the predominant understanding of religion by those disposed to it as "morality tempered by prudence, and softened on occasion by a rather sentimental compassion for inferiors."[23]

The locus for a change from this tepid attitude were the private societies—loose organizations of the religiously concerned which began to be formed in the late seventeenth century. The first was called into life by a student of Spener's, Anthony Horneck, a transplanted Rhinelander who became an Anglican priest. The society was a club of gentlemen who met once a week to discuss matters of their faith, their own spiritual progress, and ways of aiding others. The two most important were the Society for Promoting Christian Knowledge (1699) and the Society for the Propagation of the Gospel in Foreign Parts (1701). The S.P.C.K. and the S.P.G. were heavily involved in the development of Anglicanism in America. More generally, the society approach provided the pattern for the voluntary agency which became so typical of American church life in the nineteenth and twentieth centuries.

The first known reference in English history to "Methodism"

came in 1639 when a controversialist harangued the "Anabaptists and pike-staff Methodists who esteem all flowers of rhetoric in sermons as no better than stinking weeds."[24] This is a harbinger of Wesley's desire for "plain truth for plain people." Methodism came into its own in the 1730s as a label for the elite gathering of Oxford scholars, who practiced a systematic and rigorous discipline of study, prayer, philanthropy, sacramental observance, and personal piety. Other terms given them by witty collegians were even less complimentary: "Bible Moths," "Supererogation Men," the "Holy Club." Methodist was the tag which stuck. Though a source of irritation for Wesley, he adopted it as if it were an honor, and challenged all of his detractors to become Methodists. This he defined as those who believe and live in the "common principles of Christianity."[25]

Beginning as a small and self-conscious clique of privileged students, Methodism swept through a lightly churched or completely unchurched population in Great Britain and North America to become one of the most powerful and populous of Protestant bodies.

JOHN WESLEY

The early history of Methodism is largely a collection of biographies of John Wesley (1703–1791) and a few close colleagues. Wesley is a complex personality. A devout and loyal presbyter of the Church of England who fought schism all his life, he was the organizer of a leading nonconformist Free Church. A defender of the necessity of apostolic succession for the proper administration of the sacraments, he ordained "superintendents" on his own hook and sent them to America to ordain others. A man who was spitting blood at the age of twenty-five, he lived to be eighty-eight and testified that he only began to feel old at eighty-five. A cool, almost pedantic personality, he calmly recorded the numbers of his listeners who were struck down writhing at his feet by his sermons. The founder of a denomination hailed as the foremost representation of the democratic spirit, he ruled a far-flung flock with an iron hand until his death. Although constantly on the

[24] Noted in Henry W. Clark, *History of English Nonconformity*, new ed. (New York: Russell & Russell, 1965), II: 211.
[25] John Wesley, "The Character of a Methodist," in Fosdick, *op. cit.*, pp. 505–513.

move, he wrote or edited four hundred and forty books for the edification and instruction of his followers. A firm defender of infant baptism, he demanded evidence of a regenerate life as guarantee of one's true faith. Classed by recent biographers variously as a Pietist, a Lutheran, an Anglican, or Moravian, he was hailed by the historian Lecky as having "a wider constructive influence in the sphere of practical religion than any other man who has appeared since the sixteenth century."[26]

John Wesley and his younger brother Charles (1707–1778), "the Other Wesley," were the sons of a pious but bellicose Anglican rector of Epworth, England, and a strong-willed mother descended from a line of distinguished dissenting clergymen. The boys were respectively the fifteenth and the eighteenth of a family of nineteen children, and, but for the timely death of a sovereign of England, might never have been born! It happened that Mrs. Wesley objected on religious grounds to saying "Amen" to the family devotions of her husband Samuel when he prayed for King William III. The rector departed for London, thundering: "If we are to have two kings, we must have two beds."[27] Propitiously for the Wesley family if not for the dynasty, the monarch died a few months later, and the couple were reconciled. The first fruit of their renewed marital harmony was John, followed four years later by Charles.

Their childhood was dominated by the mother, who managed to find time for each child in order to direct his moral and general education. She gave special attention to John after his dramatic escape from the blazing rectory in 1708 when it was fired by disgruntled parishioners. The parents and servants rescued all of the children when the fire was noticed, except John in an upstairs nursery. With presence of mind, the five-year-old stood near a window, from which he was snatched by a quick-thinking onlooker on top of a human ladder. To Susanna Wesley and to the lad himself, it seemed that he was a "brand plucked from the burning" and hence singled out by the Lord for a special mission.

The Wesley boys followed family tradition by attending Oxford. John excelled as a scholar and was eventually appointed a Fellow at Lincoln College. Apparently he was destined for an academic career. He seemed popular with his peers who said: "Who could

[26] Quoted in Fosdick, *op. cit.*, p. 494.
[27] Quoted in Rupert E. Davies, *Methodism* (Penguin Books, 1963), p. 44.

be dull where Jack Wesley is?"[28] A condition of the fellowship was that he take holy orders as an Anglican deacon. This, and his father's wish that John succeed him at Epworth, caused young Wesley to consider religion more seriously. The reading of the early fathers of the Church, and devotional books by Thomas à Kempis, Jeremy Taylor, and especially by William Law occasioned about 1727 the first of a number of conversion experiences which changed his life. It was in 1734 that Wesley wrote to his father: "God deliver me from a half-Christian," a motto which would guide his future life.[29]

John Wesley's first attention was directed inward, toward the achievement of a satisfactory assurance of his own salvation. This was the motivation for his adherence to the Holy Club or Methodists, described above. His brother Charles had taken the initiative in beginning the group, when John was home in 1729 assisting his father with parish duties. Upon the older brother's return he became the acknowledged leader. Oxford was at a low ebb of scholarship and piety at the time, and the earnest exercises of these men brought quick ridicule and scorn. Edward Gibbon, hardly to be accused of zealotry, characterized the university faculty as "easy men who supinely enjoyed the gifts of the founder. . . . Their conversation stagnated in a round of College business, Tory politics, personal anecdotes of scandal; their dull and deep potations excused the brisk intemperance of youth."[30]

Attacks coming their way in this setting did not discourage the Methodists from pursuing their personal salvation. Their ingrown spirit is caught in the excerpt from the long answer that John Wesley sent to his father, whose rapidly failing health caused him to urge his son to return to Epworth to take up parish duties permanently:

> My one aim in life is to secure personal holiness, for without being holy myself I cannot promote real holiness in others. In Oxford, conversing only with a chosen circle of friends, I am screened from all the frivolous importunities of the world, and here I have a better chance of becoming holy than I should have in any other place. . . . [There] I should be of no use at all: I could not do any good to

[28] Quoted in Clark, *op. cit.*, II: 210.
[29] Cited in Ronald A. Knox, *Enthusiasm* (Oxford: Clarendon Press, 1950), p. 243.
[30] Quoted in Davies, *op. cit.*, p. 47.

those boorish people, and I would probably fall back into habits of irregularity and indulgence.[31]

In 1735 an opportunity came to Wesley which seemed to promise an avenue of service to others, at the same time allowing him to find his religious peace. This was to go to the colony of Georgia as a missionary to the Indians, whom he expected to find in a kind of Rousseau-like paradise. As they reacted with simple honesty and candor to his teaching, he would himself gain a clarity difficult to attain in the sophisticated university setting. He hoped to "learn the true sense of the gospel of Christ by preaching it to the heathens."[32] The philanthropist James Oglethorpe fathered the colony with the idea of providing a way out of the vicious circle for those who were imprisoned in England for debt and then kept in prison so·that they had no way of earning money to repay the debt. It seems that Oglethorpe in inducing Wesley to go to Georgia did not take too seriously the Oxonian's concern for preaching to the natives. Oglethorpe's main interest was in providing spiritual sustenance for the settlers from England. Charles Wesley went along also as his secretary.

The mission to Georgia ended as a fiasco for Wesley. He was never able to contact the Indians in his some two years' residence. An unfortunate courtship led to personal and social calamity. When he tried to impose a high-church discipline upon the residents of Savannah, a virtual rebellion drove him back to England, a defeated and distraught man.

THE ALDERSGATE EXPERIENCE

His American adventure, nevertheless, set him on the path to the religious certainty he sought so assiduously. On the ship to America in 1735 he had met a party of Moravians, and had learned German in order to converse with them. During a perilous moment on the voyage when all other passengers panicked, the Moravians calmly sang and prayed. This so impressed Wesley that he entered into close contact with them and their American leader, August Gottlieb Spangenberg (1704–1782). The Moravians confronted Wesley with his relationship with Jesus Christ: "Do you know he has saved you?" Wesley responded: "I hope He has died

---

[31] *Ibid.*, p. 51.
[32] Emory S. Buckle, ed., *The History of American Methodism* (New York: Abingdon Press, 1964), I: 54.

to save me." "Do you know yourself?" Wesley answered: "I do," but noted in his journal later: "I fear they were vain words."[33] On returning to England, Wesley was aided by another Moravian, Peter Böhler, who was on his way to America. Böhler's advice was to "preach faith until you have it and then because you have it, you will preach faith."

This Wesley attempted. The break-through came on May 24, 1738, a day still commemorated by Methodists. That evening he went to the meeting of a society at Aldersgate, sponsored by Anglicans but influenced by the Moravians. There he heard read Martin Luther's preface to Romans: "About a quarter before nine, while he was describing the change which God works in the heart through faith in Christ, I felt my heart strangely warmed. I felt I did trust in Christ, Christ alone, for salvation and assurance was given me that He had taken away my sins, even mine, and saved me from the law of sin and death."[34]

This often-cited event is usually considered the turning point in the life of John Wesley, but it should be seen in the context of his earlier conversion under the influence of Law's *Serious Call to a Devout and Holy Life* and subsequent experiences. Later that same year, Wesley was profoundly affected by reading the account of Jonathan Edwards concerning the revival in New England. The importance of his Aldersgate insight was that it freed him from the crushing burden of striving to achieve his salvation by his own efforts. As did Martin Luther with his "justification by faith alone," Wesley saw that the most rigorous regimen could not bring peace of soul. The unmerited grace of God—"Free Grace," to use a characteristic phrase of later Methodists—was available for *him*. This brought liberation from a crippling concern for his own salvation and enabled him to turn his great energies toward aiding others to find the same peace. When he empirically found that he had the ability to help others, this reinforced his own conviction. Though there would be setbacks following Aldersgate, the direction for his life was now clear.

In the summer of 1738, he journeyed to Germany to visit the Moravians at their headquarters in Herrnhut, on the estate of Count Zinzendorf. He was impressed enough to exclaim that he

---

[33] Davies, *op. cit.*, p. 54.
[34] *Ibid.*, pp. 57–58.

would gladly spend the rest of his life there. Yet, he did notice some things which caused him disquiet. These he wrote down in a letter addressed, but never sent, to his German friends. Their great emphasis on justification by faith, which seemed to cut the ethical nerve, an overdependence on Zinzendorf, a temptation to lightness of conduct—these he found worthy of criticism. They presaged an increasing estrangement from the Moravians which would eventually lead to a definite rupture of relationships.

When he returned to England, John Wesley and his brother Charles preached as they found opportunity in London. Those reached by their messages begged for the chance to counsel privately with them. When the burden of this grew too great, someone suggested that those wishing advice should agree to gather at specified times every week. "Thus arose, without any previous design on either side, what was afterward called *a Society*, a very innocent name, and very common in London, for any number of people associating themselves together," Wesley wrote in describing the beginnings of Methodism.[35]

EVANGELICAL REVIVAL

Even before this, the Evangelical Revival was under way. It was George Whitefield (1714–1770) who first created the movement which would culminate in Methodism. The son of innkeepers, he secured a university education by becoming a servant for wealthy students at Oxford. Although aware of and sympathetic with the concerns of the Holy Club, he hesitated to make himself known to them because of the gap in social standing. By accident they came to know him and he was quickly drawn into the circle. When Wesley left Oxford it was Whitefield who took the leadership.

An austere discipline caused Whitefield's physical breakdown in 1735, which in turn led to a thoroughgoing conversion. "I was delivered from the burden that had so heavily pressed me. The spirit of mourning was taken from me, and I knew what it was to truly rejoice in God my Saviour." He was allowed to receive ordination in the Church of England despite his youth, and made a reputation for eloquence and power with his first sermon. By 1736

[35] "A Plain Account of the People Called Methodists," in Fosdick, *op. cit.*, pp. 500–501.

the results of his preaching became so remarkable that this year is reckoned the beginning of the Evangelical Revival. He did not claim intellectual brilliance, but he did possess a moving voice, evangelistic passion, and genuine concern for people. As Clarke describes:

> There broke out the first outbursts of that marvellous eloquence which swayed multitudes, melted the hard-hearted, clove away for its message to the hearts of the poor and ignorant and struck the scoffers nearly always into silence and ofttimes into something better still; and there flamed up in Whitefield's soul that passion for evangelizing which would not let him settle either in the academic atmosphere of Oxford or in the curacy of a country parish . . . but forced him to compass sea and land in order to win men to a faith like his own.[36]

Whitefield was the first trans-Atlantic personality, equally famous on both sides of the ocean. He traveled to North America seven times, spending fully two years of his short life at sea, and died there on his last visit. His life finally flickered out like the candle he held in his hand when he forced himself to speak, though desperately exhausted, to those waiting to hear the night before his death in Newburyport, Massachusetts.

When hundreds of people swarmed around an English church in which he was speaking, to hear through the windows, Whitefield hit upon the idea of preaching in the fields. Wesley described his shock at the innovation, thinking it a sin to convert people outside of the walls of a church building. Only with great reluctance did he accept this method after Whitefield's repeated urging. The significance of the field preaching was not only the throngs, numbering up to twenty thousand, who were reached. It was also in the shattering of the traditional parish system. Wesley's often repeated statement that he took the world as his parish is not in the first instance a call to world missions. It was a declaration that the urgency for preaching the Word should not be bound by an archaic parochial system. The shift in English population, brought on by changes in agriculture and the rise of industrialism, the frequent absence of bishops from their dioceses, and the shortcomings of those employed to carry out the work of the local church, made the Anglican system clearly inadequate. Faced with

[36] Clark, *op. cit.*, II: 217.

this obvious need, Whitefield, and Wesley following him, were willing to break with traditional church polity.[37]

As they pressed into areas where the gospel had hardly been known before, bearing a message phrased in understandable and dramatic form, the revivalists set free tremendous emotional forces. Sometimes this took the form of weeping, prostrations, outbursts of joy, frenzied scenes. A recent author has mined the descriptions of these outbreaks noted by Wesley as evidence that this was a kind of "brainwashing."[38] John Wesley was alert, however, to the dangers of the stress upon feelings and placed great emphasis upon the training and guiding of those "awakened" by the itinerant preaching. It was not enough to take the message; the converts must be organized. "I am more and more convinced that the devil himself desires . . . that the people of any place should be half-awakened and then left to themselves to fall asleep again. Therefore I determine, by the grace of God, not to strike in any place where I cannot follow the blow."[39]

ORGANIZATION

Wesley has been called a second Loyola in the skill and thoroughness with which he organized. Bands, classes, societies, conferences became the outer framework of the people called Methodists. Many of these ideas came from the Moravians, but they were put to use in new ways and with new effectiveness by Wesley.[40] He saw this as a major part of his work. "Press the *instantaneous* blessing," he wrote to his brother Charles, "then I shall have more time for my regular calling, enforcing the *gradual* work."[41]

He himself described the beginning of the Methodist system as resulting from the suggestion of a member on how to raise money to pay for a meeting place. The idea was to form groups of twelve which would be visited weekly by the local leader in order to collect a penny from each member. Wesley seized on the plan as

[37] See Albert C. Outler, ed., *John Wesley* (New York: Oxford University Press, 1964), p. 72.
[38] William Sargant, *Battle for the Mind* (Garden City, N.Y.: Doubleday & Co., 1957).
[39] Buckle, *op. cit.*, I: 19.
[40] See Clifford W. Towlson, *Moravian and Methodist* (London: Epworth Press, 1957), pp. 174–247.
[41] John Wesley to Charles Wesley, June 27, 1766, in Outler, *op. cit.*, p. 82.

the vehicle for answering the problem of church discipline: "I called together all the leaders of the classes (so we used to term them and their companies), and desired that each would make a particular inquiry into the behaviour of those whom he saw weekly. They did so. Many disorderly walkers were detected. Some turned away from the evil of their ways. Some were put away from us. Many saw it with fear, and rejoiced unto God with reverence."[42] Communist cells seemingly owe a debt to the Wesleyan organization, possibly mediated through English socialism which has had strong linkage with Methodism. Signed tickets, issued quarterly for admission to the classes, provided an effective means of church discipline.

As the movement expanded Wesley found it hard to keep in touch with his co-workers. He took Whitefield's idea of an annual conference as a means of instruction, coordination, and assignment of areas of labor. As not enough ordained clergymen rose to the occasion, Wesley was forced to resort to laymen. Though he did not take to this lightly, his essentially experiential orientation soon led him to feel that the work demanded all those with evident gifts, whether they had normal theological training or not: "Give me one hundred preachers who fear nothing but sin, and desire nothing but God, and I care not a straw whether they are clergymen or laymen; such alone will shake the gates of Hell, and set up the kingdom of heaven upon earth."[43] Circuits were set up for such men, to be covered regularly. After one or two years at the most, men were shifted to different circuits, on the assumption that their different talents should supplement one another, and that by that time the chief work of a man should have been accomplished.

CONFLICTS

In an age of intense doctrinal rivalry between the various Christian bodies, John Wesley raised an appeal for toleration and harmony. "Think and let think," was one of his mottoes. A more extended expression of the same concern was the following which characteristically placed Christian deeds above creeds:

I will not quarrel with you about my opinions; only see that your

[42] "A Plain Account," in Fosdick, op. cit., pp. 503–504.
[43] Quoted in Horton Davies, The English Free Churches (London: Oxford University Press, 1952), p. 133.

heart is right toward God, that you know and love the Lord Jesus Christ; that you love your neighbor, and walk as your Master walked, and I desire no more. I am sick of opinions; am weary to bear them; my soul loathes this frothy food. Give me solid and substantial religion; give me a humble, gentle lover of God and man; a man full of mercy and good faith, without partiality and without hypocrisy; a man laying himself out in the work of faith, the patience of hope, the labor of love. Let my soul be with these Christians wheresoever they are, and whatsoever opinion that are of![44]

Of course, anyone who claims that he will give his hand to any other if the other's heart is right "as my heart is with thine" is taking a definite theological position. Others who placed greater weight on doctrinal clarity and correctness of polity must take exception. Despite Wesley's disclaimers, his position was a direct affront to many who considered themselves to be as devout Christians as Wesley himself. Although he took the world as his parish, there were those who considered that they had responsibilities for at least some of that territory. Bishop Butler was voicing the opinion of many when he pronounced: "Sir, the pretending to extraordinary revelations and fits from the Holy Ghost is a horrid thing—a very horrid thing. You have no business here; you are not commissioned to preach in this diocese. I therefore advise you to go home."[45]

Wesley also found himself in serious disagreement with those who were the closest to him. He first broke with the Moravians, especially that branch in England which advocated quietism. Wesley suspected that the Moravians with their emphasis upon the atonement of Jesus and the grace of God were guilty of antinomianism, that is of considering themselves above the law of Christ because of their sanctified state.

A more critical clash came with Whitefield and his followers. Here the issue paralleled the split between the Particular and the General Baptists of a century before. Whitefield adhered to the Calvinistic doctrine of predestination, whereas Wesley, more logically for those engaged in evangelism and mass conversion, avowed Arminianism. He even named his leading periodical *The Arminian Magazine*. This struggle caused sharp tensions between

[44] Quoted in Fosdick, *op. cit.*, p. 129.
[45] Quoted in H. Davies, *op. cit.*, p. 129.

the two leaders of the revival movement, but not a complete and final break. They agreed to disagree on the point. It did result in two different denominational groups, the Wesleyan Methodists and Lady Huntingdon's Connection, named after the most prominent supporter of Whitefield.

But it was with the Church of England that the most troublesome and most protracted conflict occurred. On the one side was Wesley, who loudly and consistently heralded his loyalty to the established church. The year before his death he reaffirmed: "I live and die a member of the Church of England."[46] On the other side were the Anglicans who saw that the whole direction of his movement was bound to lead to separation. Wesley's insistence on converted, committed, regenerated Christians tightly organized into voluntary societies was in direct opposition to a church of baptism and creed, sacraments and priests. "In fact, the clergy of the Church detected by a true instinct—what Wesley himself failed to detect—that Methodism was in reality a sign of the Nonconformist spirit's intrusion into their jealously guarded preserves."[47] One can read the history of early Methodism as the gradual unfolding of the logic of Wesley's basic position, leading to separation, despite his own reluctance to accept the development.

Before his death, he took two actions which sealed the schism. The first was the "Deed of Declaration" of 1784, by which he set aside one hundred men to serve as "The Conference of the People Called Methodists." More serious was Wesley's action in ordaining Dr. Thomas Coke to go to North America to ordain others there. He justified his action by pointing out that America had no bishops, as had England. Practical necessity outweighed any niceties of canon law:

> Here therefore my scruples are at an end: and I conceive myself at full liberty, as I violate no order and invade no man's right by appointing and sending laborers into the harvest. . . . If anyone will point out a more rational and scriptural way of feeding and guiding the poor sheep in the wilderness, I will gladly embrace it. . . . [The American Brethren] are now at full liberty simply to follow the Scriptures and the primitive church.[48]

[46] Quoted in Knox, op. cit., p. 506.
[47] Clark, op. cit., II: 228.
[48] "To 'Our Brethren in America,' " in Outler, op. cit., pp. 83–84.

His shocked brother Charles replied with the poetic gift which had created so many hymns and had won so many to Methodism:

How easily are bishops made, by man or woman's whim.
    Wesley his hand on Coke hath laid, but who laid hands on him?

And so Wesley died in 1791, "leaving behind nothing but a good library of books, a well-worn clergyman's gown, a much-abused reputation, and—the Methodist Church."[49]

METHODISM IN AMERICA

Laymen are the principals in the drama of the Methodist beginning in America. Robert Strawbridge (d. 1781), a fiery and improvident Irishman, settled in Frederick County, Maryland, by the early 1760s and immediately began to travel about and preach. He had no compunction about administering the sacraments to those who lacked a pastor, although he had never been ordained. In New York, it was another immigrant from Ireland, Philip Embury (d. 1775), who began to preach in 1766 among a group of his compatriots. These people were of German descent, who had first settled in Ireland after fleeing the unhappy conditions in the Palatinate. A cousin, Barbara Heck, challenged Embury to do something about the decline in morals among the immigrants, "lest we all go to hell together" as the tradition relates. A class was formed and meetings were held, which grew rapidly in numbers when a portly one-eyed British officer named Captain Thomas Webb (d. 1796) joined them. Webb's practice was to place a sword across the pulpit and then exercise his gifts as an eloquent Methodist lay preacher.

These people sent appeals to England for aid. In 1769 Wesley asked for volunteers, advising that the New York class was "in great want of money, but much more of preachers."[50] The first two to respond were Joseph Pilmoor and Richard Boardman. By far the most important Methodist preacher to answer the Macedonian call was Francis Asbury (1745–1816), who did for North America what Wesley had performed for Great Britain. This "Prophet of the Long Road," as a biographer called him, made all of America his home in his continuous travels. His journal covers

---

[49] Quoted in Fosdick, *op. cit.*, p. 497.
[50] Quoted in Buckle, *op. cit.*, I: 81.

some forty-five years, in which time the Methodists developed from a struggling group of scattered societies to one of the two most popular American denominations.

The achievement is the more remarkable when it is recalled that during the Revolution the Methodists were widely regarded as Tories. There was no doubt that John Wesley was, and his several publications favoring the British government made him an embarrassment to his American followers. One observer predicted that by the end of the Revolution all of the Methodists on the western side of the Atlantic could be accommodated in a smallish corn-crib. However, extensive growth attended the work in the 1770s of men such as Devereux Jarrat, an Anglican preacher in Virginia, from whose converts came many Methodists.

Asbury had been made co-superintendent with Coke by Wesley, but refused to accept the appointment without the concurrence of the Methodist preachers. These men were hurriedly assembled at the Lovely Lane Chapel in Baltimore in December 1784. The conference held there gave birth to the Methodist Episcopal Church, actually the first organized Methodist church anywhere. Under Asbury's leadership and personal engagement, the Methodist system of circuit riders, classes, and conferences was shaped to meet the surging needs of the expanding American population on the frontier. Hundreds of young preachers burned themselves out in heroic attempts to bring the gospel to the last settler in the last clearing, and that for sixty-four dollars a year. Two-thirds of the Methodist ministry never survived the twelfth anniversary of their ordination. Half of them died before they were thirty-five. But their combination of stem-winding sermons, full-throated hymns, and exhortations to the upright life had done its work. By the Civil War the Methodists were numerically the leading denomination; one of five American Christians was a Methodist. The Methodist doctrines of free grace, Christian perfection, and active piety seemed ideally suited to American needs. The tightly organized church polity enabled it to plan its expansion like a military campaign.

Today, Methodists number some twenty million in more than fifty countries. There are fourteen and a half million in North America, one million in Europe, one and a half million in Africa, two and a half million in Asia, and half a million in Australia. Three different Methodist bodies which divided at the Civil War period were reunited in 1939, and in 1968 they united with the Evangelical United Brethren, itself a merger of two Methodist-like denominations which formed among the German element in the United States. Plans call for reunion of the British Methodists with the parent Church of England in the 1970s. It remains to be seen whether the voluntaryistic principle incorporated in such an interesting way in the early Methodist societies can be successfully reintegrated with Anglicanism.

· VI ·

New Testament Restorationists

KENNETH SCOTT LATOURETTE, the dean of American church historians, calls the 1800s the Great Century. To him the "growing repudiation" of religion caused by Marxism, the intellectual revolt, and increasing secularism is more than matched by "abounding vitality and unprecedented expansion." Three of the seven volumes of his history of the expansion of Christianity are devoted to the years between 1815 and 1914.[1]

A major reason for this assessment is the upsurge in missionary activity, seen by him as the chief barometer of religious interest. Another can be seen in the rise of free churches in Great Britain and on the Continent in areas where establishment had always been the pattern, and the tremendous expansion of church life in the United States, where the voluntary principle of membership came into its own after the Revolution. In 1776 about five percent of the population were church members, in 1900 nearly forty percent. Gunnar Westin's analysis of the trend stated:[2]

Throughout the century the ideas concerning the free church, the gathered church, won wide acceptance throughout the entire world; tens of thousands of new churches were organized with millions of new members joining. This free church march of victory during the last 150 years has been favored both by the irresistible process of secularism developing in the cultural areas of the nations of the Western Hemisphere, with a tendency for a real free church within the established state churches, and the giant expansion of Protestant

---

[1] Kenneth S. Latourette, A History of Christianity (New York: Harper & Brothers, 1953), p. [1061].
[2] Franklin H. Littell, From State Church to Pluralism (Garden City, N.Y.: Anchor Books, 1962), pp. 30–33: "During the years from the camp meeting of the Cane Ridge Revival (1801) . . . to the 1960 census more people joined the Christian Church than ever before in her history" (p. 33).

world missions with the building of the minority churches (younger churches) in the non-Christian countries.[3]

Many of the free churches formed in the nineteenth century resulted from the growing determination of Christians not to be patronized and controlled by the state. Several of the German free churches and those in Scotland, for example, had this motivation. Doctrinally, they remained staunchly Lutheran or Reformed. Others reflected the impact of Anglo-Saxon missionary efforts flourishing on the mainland of Europe. The Free Church of Vaud, Switzerland, and the Methodists and Baptists in Germany would be cases in point. Often the foreign Bible societies played major roles in the formation of these churches.[4]

A different basis is found in the groups stressing restoration of early Christianity. One, the Disciples of Christ, which began about 1810 on the American frontier, had over a million members by 1900. Another, the Plymouth Brethren, has remained fairly small numerically, and moreover has been divided into eight different branches, but has had a theological influence much larger than its membership would indicate.

The nineteenth century was favorable for an appeal to a return to scriptures. Individualism and liberalism were the reigning impulses. Seen in terms of religion, there was a confident expectation that each man could approach the documents of Christianity, particularly the New Testament, and find for himself that which was needful for his own salvation. The absolute dependability of the Scriptures was as yet undoubted, and it provided the appropriate resource from which to challenge ecclesiastical and theological authority. Actions of synods, ecumenical creeds, traditional beliefs —all had to be weighed upon the scales of private interpretation of the Bible.

Times were ripe for new religious formations, and they came in great numbers. From among those which could be chosen, the Disciples of Christ and the Plymouth Brethren present themselves as characteristic examples of the restorationist mood of the nineteenth century. Both advocated Christian unity on a platform of New Testament Christianity.

---

[3] Gunnar Westin, *The Free Church Through the Ages*, trans. V. Olson (Nashville: Broadman Press, 1958), p. 224.
[4] *Ibid.*, p. 223ff.

Disciples of Christ

An American Religious Movement is the descriptive title of a book on the Christian Churches (Disciples of Christ) written by its most highly esteemed interpreter. Others have claimed it as numerically the largest indigenous American communion. In its strengths and weaknesses it is characteristically American.[5] Yet, every narrator of the Disciples of Christ starts by discussing the religious movements in Great Britain which helped shape it. All students of Disciples' history agree that the philosophical base is to be found in the writings of John Locke. Three of the four founding fathers were born and educated in Ireland or Scotland, and the fourth was born a member of the Church of England and became a Presbyterian pastor. It is, therefore, essential to begin the story of the Disciples of Christ by describing the rise of the small Restorationist sects in the British Isles.

With the coming of government recognition and moderate toleration in 1689, the nonconforming denominations took their ease in Zion. One answer to the lethargy was the Wesleyan revival already described. Another was the emergence of small groups of dissenters from dissent. These, hardly noticed by the larger nonconformist bodies, turned their attention to restoring the forms, ordinances, and cultus of their independent congregations according to what they conceived to be the original Christian pattern.

One such was a small gathering founded by John Glas (1695–1773), a university-trained minister of the Church of Scotland whose ordination was taken from him in 1727. His misdeed was to publish his conviction that the New Testament church had neither the state connections enjoyed by the Kirk nor a synodical frame of church government. The congregation which rallied around his leadership attempted to establish a church purely along the lines of early Christianity. In their search of the scriptures they concluded that instead of one pastor's leadership there should be a plurality of elders; instead of a monthly or quarterly communion

[5] Winfried E. Garrison, *An American Religious Movement: a Brief History of the Disciples of Christ* (St. Louis: Christian Board of Publication, 1945). The assessment of Garrison as the leading historian of the Disciples is found in David E. Harrell, Jr., *Quest for a Christian America* (Nashville: Disciples of Christ Historical Society, 1966), p. 18.

this should be observed each Lord's day; instead of theological training at a university, lay ministers should be acknowledged by the congregation for their practical demonstration of piety and biblical mastery. Glas's son-in-law, Robert Sandeman (1718–1771), gave systematic treatment to these beliefs along rationalistic lines. The teaching that brought him most sharply into conflict with the Wesleyans, whom the "Sandemanians" otherwise resembled, was an assertion that faith was based on intelligent belief. Man had no need for waiting passively in a mournful state for a sudden converting action from God. Human reason, once confronted by the scriptural evidence of revealed truth, sufficiently enabled acceptance.

Perhaps a dozen churches in England and half that many in North America were organized around these teachings. They practiced foot washing, the kiss of charity, and the love feast, all of which they based on New Testament teaching. Sandeman himself came to America and preached in Connecticut, dying in Danbury, which became the center of the small movement in the colonies now extinct. The most noted member in England was Michael Faraday, the scientist, a faithful adherent of the London meeting of the Old Scotch Independents, as they were known. Some in Scotland who practiced immersion baptism were referred to as "Old Scotch Baptists."

A second movement—of great importance for the history of evangelism on the continent as well as in America—centered about two Scots. These were the brothers Robert Haldane (1764–1842) and James Alexander Haldane (1768–1851), both raised as members of the Church of Scotland. Robert served briefly in the navy, then retired to the family estate to spend his leisure in biblical study. Influenced by the early teachings of his devout mother, he decided to devote his remaining life to the cause of evangelization, and sold his estate to obtain means to do so. The younger brother James Alexander was a ship's captain in the East India trade. He first became seriously concerned with the state of religion when he attended a general assembly of the Church of Scotland which formally voted to *reject* the resolution "that it is the duty of Christians to send the gospel to the heathen world."[6]

The Haldanes began to preach, distribute tracts, and hold out-

[6] James DeForest Murch, *Christians Only* (Cincinnati: Standard Publishing Co., 1962), p. 16.

door meetings, although neither was ordained. They contacted an Anglican evangelist named Rowland Hill (1744–1833) and employed him to preach in a large tabernacle they built for the purpose in Edinburgh. In 1799 they withdrew from the established church of Scotland. Those who followed them were organized into a congregation. Its orientation is seen clearly in the title of a book written by James Alexander Haldane in 1805: A View of the Social Worship and Ordinances of the First Christians, Drawn from the Scripture Alone; Being an Attempt to Enforce Their Divine Obligation and to Represent the Guilty and Evil Consequences of Neglecting Them.

Hindered from carrying out several missionary ventures they initiated, the brothers Haldane set up a training school for ministers in Glasgow under the guidance of Greville Ewing. It was through Ewing that Alexander Campbell came into the orbit of the Restorationist movement, when he was delayed one winter while on the way to North America to rejoin his father, Thomas Campbell. The younger Campbell was to become the most vigorous exponent of the Restoration idea in the New World.

THE CAMPBELLS

Thomas Campbell (1763–1854) was a well-educated clergyman of one of the branches of Seceder Presbyterian Church, with a parish in County Armagh, Ireland. The original secession from the Church of Scotland came about in 1733 when the independence-loving Scots protested a move which took away their right of electing pastors in the local parishes and gave it to the large landowners under a patronage system. Other divisions later split the Seceder movement on minute points of church-state relations. Campbell was dismayed by this disunity and worked without success to reunite the several bodies. He was influenced in his drive for unity both by the revival message of the Haldane type which deplored schism among Christians, and also by his deep attachment to the religious ideas of John Locke, especially as developed in the Letters Concerning Toleration and Essay on Human Understanding. Locke's position is illustrated in this excerpt from his first letter on toleration:

> Since men are so solicitous about the true church, I would only ask them here, by the way, if it be not more agreeable to the Church of

Christ to make the conditions of her communion consist in such things, and such things only, as the Holy Spirit has in the Holy Scriptures declared, in express words, to be necessary to salvation?[7]

Thomas Campbell educated his son Alexander (1788–1866) along these same lines, and prepared the son by intensive tutoring to assist him in the academy he created in Rich Hill. In that area lived an Independent pastor, John Walker (later involved in the beginnings of the Plymouth Brethren), who influenced the young Campbell's thinking. Thomas Campbell decided in 1807 to seek his further way in America, following in the path of many other Scotch-Irish before him. By good fortune he arrived in Philadelphia during a synodal meeting of the Seceder Presbyterians and was immediately given a charge in Washington County in western Pennsylvania.

Before long he was in trouble with the synod. The ostensible reason was his generosity in permitting non-Seceder Presbyterians to commune. Actually, a more serious issue arose when Campbell announced that the "church has no divine warrant for holding Confessions of Faith as terms for communion," i.e. using the Westminster Confession as the basis for church discipline. Although he was partially vindicated by the synod, the local presbytery refused to permit him to use any of the pulpits under their control.

Not daunted, he continued to preach when and where invited. He organized with his hearers the Christian Association of Washington in 1809. They did not consider themselves to be a congregation or a church, but rather "voluntary advocates for church membership." Theirs was to be a "Second Reformation." To provide a more systematic expression of the views and motives of those joining with him, Campbell wrote and had printed the celebrated *Declaration and Address*, now not only considered to be a basic document of the history of the Disciples but also of the modern ecumenical movement.

The watchword of the Association was: "Where the Scriptures speak, we speak; where they are silent, we are silent." With this in mind he called upon all Christians to join in the "restoration of primitive Christianity":

[7] Quoted in Winfried E. Garrison and Alfred T. De Groot, *The Disciples of Christ: a History* (St. Louis: Christian Board of Publication, 1948), p. 42.

Dearly beloved brethren, why should we deem it a thing incredible that the Church of Christ, in this highly favored country, should resume that original unity, peace, and purity which belong to its constitution and constitute its glory? Or, is there anything that can be justly deemed necessary for this desirable purpose, both to conform to the model and adopt the practice of the primitive Church, expressly exhibited in the New Testament? . . . Were we, then, in our church constitution and managements, to exhibit a complete conformity to the apostolic Church, would we not be, in that respect, as perfect as Christ intended we should be? And should not this suffice us?

Following a discussion of the motives for making the appeal, Campbell listed thirteen propositions which he felt flowed from the restorationist base. The first contended that the "Church of Christ upon earth is essentially, intentionally, and constitutionally one; consisting of all those in every place that profess their faith in Christ and obedience to him in all things according to the Scriptures. . . ." Other theses maintained that no creeds were necessary, and that the New Testament provided just as perfect a constitution for the present church as did the Old Testament for the Jewish people. In all areas where no clear scriptural injunction was found, there should be freedom of opinion. A simple profession of faith was held adequate for church membership.[8]

In the meantime (1808), Thomas Campbell had summoned his family to join him. The ship upon which they embarked was wrecked off the coast of Ireland, without harm to the family. While waiting for another passage Alexander Campbell used the delay to pursue studies at the University of Glasgow. It was here that he was befriended by the Haldane group and studied the writing of Sandeman and others of his persuasion. He was estranged from the Presbyterian church by his new convictions. The fear he felt in informing his father of this change was swept away when he found his father had, independently, made a similar pilgrimage. According to tradition, Thomas Campbell had the first printed sheets of the *Declaration and Address* in his saddlebags when he rode to meet his family on their way from Philadelphia to the western part of Pennsylvania.

---

[8] The most recent (partial) publication of the *Declaration and Address* is in H. S. Smith, R. T. Handy, and L. A. Loetscher, eds., *American Christianity* (New York: Scribners, 1960), I: 578–586.

BRUSH RUN AND THE BAPTISTS

Alexander Campbell settled down in his new home to intensive study of theology. He first preached in 1810, met with favorable response, and was invited to preach one hundred times in the course of the following year. In May 1811, the Washington Association changed its status to that of a congregation, after the Presbyterians refused to take it into their synod. The Association chose Thomas Campbell as elder, and licensed Alexander to preach. Before long, it was the eloquent son who took up the leadership of the movement, and the father resumed his teaching. The congregation was known as the Brush Run Church.

Soon after its organization, several members requested baptism by immersion. Thomas Campbell performed the service although he had some doubts about its validity. When an infant son was born to Alexander Campbell and his wife, the daughter of a wealthy farmer from what is now West Virginia, the question demanded resolution. Was infant baptism scriptural? Intensive study led the Campbells to conclude that it was not. They accepted the consequences of their decision and were baptized by immersion along with their wives, in June 1812, by a Baptist minister.

This action brought them into fellowship with the Baptists. The Brush Run Church joined the Baptist Association of Redstone. For the next seventeen years, the Campbell-led movement was linked with the Baptists. Alexander Campbell became a belligerent defender of immersion baptism; in 1823 he founded a periodical, *The Christian Baptist*. Yet, tensions grew because of the Baptist use of official confessions of faith, considered to be creeds by Campbell. By 1830 the uneasy alliance was broken, but even before this the "Reformers" or "Disciples," as Campbell's followers were called, were clearly a separate entity.

During this period Campbell gained a national reputation by his adroit performance in several well-publicized debates. They began with arguments over the manner and practice of baptism. More newsworthy yet was his defense of organized Christianity against the liberal freethinker and philanthropist Robert Owen, in the United States to develop his communitarian settlement at New Harmony, Indiana. Campbell won renewed attention in debating the Catholic Bishop Purcell in Cincinnati in 1837.

Campbell's life was a full one. He administered the large farm given him by his father-in-law at what became Bethany, West Virginia, published his paper, wrote books, acted as local postmaster, and organized Bethany College in 1840. In 1825 he published a translation of the Bible, notable for using "immerse" where most translations used "baptize" (hence "John the Immerser"). Four years later he was a delegate to the Virginia State Constitutional Convention, where he attacked the predominance of the tidewater politicians and won recognition for his oratorical brilliance.

His religious stance reflected deistic natural theology. This was particularly evident in his iconoclastic attacks on churchly traditions and customs. He upheld the natural rights of man, the ability of individuals to think and decide for themselves on religious matters. With withering scorn he attacked the desire of clergymen for titles and honors, and blasted away at "priestcraft" with the zeal of a Thomas Paine, whose writings he knew though he considered them to be in error on revelation. A characteristic critique is the following:

> Instead of the Apostle's doctrine, simply and plainly exhibited in the New Testament, we have got the sublime science of Theology, subdivided into Scholastic, Polemic, Dogmatic, and Practical Divinity. Instead of the form of sound words . . . we have countless creeds, composed of terms and phrases, dogmas and speculations, invented by whimsical Metaphysicians, Christian Philosophers, Rabbinical Doctors, and Enthusiastic Preachers.[9]

The objects of his criticism retaliated, calling "Campbellism" a new sect. A Sunday School scholar listed the names of the tribes opposing Joshua as "Canaanites, Amorites, Jebusites, and Campbellites."[10]

BARTON STONE AND THE CHRISTIANS

Even before Campbell's activity, there were several similar movements in America, known as the "Christian Churches." The first came out of Methodism in Virginia and North Carolina. At issue was the polity of that rapidly growing denomination. Some

[9] Robert F. West, *Alexander Campbell and Natural Religion* (New Haven: Yale University Press, 1948), p. 31.
[10] Garrison and De Groot, *op. cit.*, p. 304.

democratically oriented Methodist lay preachers resisted the authoritative episcopal system, as practiced by Francis Asbury. James O'Kelly was their leading spokesman. When the annual conference refused to accept their call for the right of appeal from the bishop's rulings, they withdrew in 1793 and organized the "Republican Methodist Church." In belief they were identical with the Methodist Episcopal Church.

One year later they took the name "Christian Church." Their position was that "the primitive church government, which came down from heaven, was a republic, though 'Christian Church' is its name."[11] Congregations enjoyed complete liberty in running their own affairs, in calling pastors, and in doctrinal matters. By 1810 they had gathered an estimated twenty thousand members in the South and the then-settled West, Kentucky and Tennessee.

A second group formed along the frontier in New England. Independently of each other, two young Vermonters came to question the predestinarian teaching of the Particular Baptists. One was Elias Smith (1769–1846), who was ordained as a Baptist preacher at the age of twenty-three. He was gradually convinced through his own biblical study that the Baptists had strayed from the intent of the early church. Abner Jones (1772–1832) organized the first independent "Christian" church in Vermont in 1801 after hearing Smith preach. He established more congregations the next year and persuaded Smith to join him. Smith for his part founded the *Herald of Gospel Liberty,* an influential periodical which continued into the twentieth century. There is evidence of nearly one hundred such "companies of free brethren" in New England by 1827. Their position was: "We mean to be New Testament Christians, without any sectarian names connected with it, without any sectarian creeds, articles, or confessions, or discipline to illuminate the Scriptures. . . . It is our desire to remain free from all human laws, confederations, and unscriptural combinations; and to stand fast in the liberty wherewith Christ has made us free."[12] Many of these churches remained independent until 1931, when they joined the Congregationalists to form the Congregational Christian Churches.

The last of the "Christian" movements to develop came from the Great Revival in Kentucky and adjoining states. Although not

[11] Garrison, *op. cit.,* p. 43.
[12] Quoted in Garrison and De Groot, *op. cit.,* p. 90.

the leading figure in the early stages, the dominant personality in its evolvement was Barton W. Stone (1772–1844). Born of a long-established Maryland family, Stone was profoundly influenced while still a student by the revivalistic preaching of the Presbyterian James McGready. However, he could not accept the idea that man could do nothing for his own salvation, and was put off by the portrayal of God as a wrathful avenger. A visiting minister who preached on the theme of a loving God provided the occasion for Stone's conversion. He was licensed as a Presbyterian minister, although not completely convinced of the trinitarian formula of the Westminster Confession. Later at his ordination, he accepted the confession with the reservation "as far as I see it consistent with the word of God."[13]

After early trials at preaching in Virginia and the Carolinas, Stone went west to Kentucky, dodging hostile Indians on the way. He became the pastor of two congregations at Cane Ridge and Concord in northern Kentucky, in 1796, just before the camp-meeting revivals began to sway the population. Stone was an interested and sympathetic observer of the intense emotional reactions to revivalistic preaching but was not heavily involved in their leadership. The climax of the camp-meeting crusade came at the Cane Ridge revival of 1801, located near his own church, with some twenty thousand in attendance. The chief result of the meetings for Stone was to cause him to preach "free grace" in opposition to the Presbyterian emphasis on the elect. "Christ died for all," he now believed.

Traditionalist Presbyterians looked askance at the camp meetings. They were opposed to the doctrinal deviations, were repelled by the outbreaks of passion and emotion, and were determined to uphold the educational standards of the ministry. They haled the Presbyterians involved in the revival before the synod of Kentucky. Two of those accused, joined by three colleagues (including Stone), decided to break with the synod before they were expelled. They renounced its jurisdiction and called into life an organization of their own, the Springfield Presbytery.

The rupture with the synod took place in September 1803, and before a year was over the five members decided to dissolve the

[13] See the discussion in William G. West, *Barton Warren Stone* (Nashville: Disciples of Christ Historical Society, 1954), p. 17.

presbytery. They now considered presbyteries to be unscriptural in principle. The whimsically phrased but deadly serious announcement of the dissolution was called "The Last Will and Testament of the Springfield Presbytery." The signers wished to dramatize their rejection of the "power of making laws for the government of the church, and executing them by delegated authority." Just as the earlier "Christian" churches had decided, they now placed the authority for conducting the life of the church and calling ministers into the hands of each congregation. The actual ability to preach and convert rather than doctrinal correctness was to become the touchstone for ministers. These men would be supported henceforth by free-will offerings, not by pledges.

"We *will*, that this body die, be dissolved, and sink into union with the Body of Christ at large, for there is but one body, and one spirit, even as we are called in one hope of our calling." This was the first provision of the testament. The name "Christian" was intended to underscore their dislike of sectarian controversy. A later motto would state that they did not claim to be the only Christians, but aspired to be "Christians only."[14]

By late 1804, about twenty of the Christian churches had been started in Kentucky and Ohio; numbers of Presbyterians friendly to the revivals joined their ranks. Some of the members of older Christian bodies coming west joined them. Leadership was a problem, for one of the five founders became a Shaker, and others returned to the Presbyterian church. Barton Stone alone remained loyal to the new movement, and was soon recognized as their intellectual and spiritual spokesman in his own right. "There was a firmness, a sweetness, and a saintliness in Stone's character that gave him a growing influence among his brethren."[15] Never financially successful like Alexander Campbell who died the richest man in West Virginia, Stone persisted under great handicaps. An important medium for his leadership was his periodical, *The Christian Messenger*, founded in 1826. He reported in this journal two years later that the "Christians" numbered fifteen hundred congregations with a membership of 150,000. Because of

[14] The text of the "Will" is available in Smith, Handy, and Loetscher, *op. cit.*, I: 576–578. W. West has demonstrated that the author was Richard McNemar, *op. cit.*, p. 77.

[15] Garrison and De Groot, *op. cit.*, p. 123.

the loosely linked nature of the movement, this could be no more than an informed estimate, and undoubtedly included all three of the Christian bodies.

UNION OF THE DISCIPLES AND CHRISTIANS

In 1832 the followers of Campbell and the followers of Stone joined forces. They agreed that their common beliefs outweighed the differences, and since both stressed the evils of sectarianism, the differences should not be allowed to interfere. They shared the conviction that denominationalism was wrong, that creeds were unnecessary, that predestination was in error. Salvation was possible through the acceptance of the biblical evidence, although Stone favored evangelistic and revivalistic techniques, to bring men to this realization; not so Campbell. The chief evangelist of the Disciples was Walter Scott (1796–1861), who developed a simple and effective five-step approach to salvation; this involved faith in God, repentance, baptism, remission of sins, and reception of the Holy Spirit.

Leading members of the Disciples and Christians meeting in Lexington, Kentucky, in 1832 sent out a team to take the message of union to the individual congregations, each of which would need to decide for themselves. Gradually most of them accepted the idea, although both church names continued to be used. Alexander Campbell himself was surprised by the union, and not completely pleased, but soon saw its value.

Rapid numerical growth marked the Disciples' course in the nineteenth century. Their democratic church polity, use of lay elders, and reasonable appeal to the scriptures struck a responsive chord on the frontier. By the Civil War they counted 200,000 members, a figure which was doubled by 1875. Though without overhead organization, they were often in the forefront in bringing the gospel to newly settled areas. An example would be the later settlement of the Oklahoma territory. Before statehood was reached, the Disciples had a congregation in each county and in every town of more than one thousand population. When the Cherokee territory was opened in 1893, a Disciples minister from Guthrie secured a Kentucky racing horse. Within thirty-nine minutes after the starting gun had started the run, he had staked out a claim for a church lot in what was to become the chief city of the territory.

STRAIN AND SCHISM

The first major test of unity came to the Disciples in 1849 when a conference was called to organize for foreign missions. Those attending organized the American Christian Missionary Society, and sent abroad a missionary, but many opposed the move. They claimed that an annual meeting for this purpose would develop into denominational machinery. Campbell favored the innovation. He wrote that "in all things pertaining to the public interest, not of Christian faith, piety, or morality, the church of Jesus Christ in its aggregate character is left free and unshackled by any apostolic authority."[16] Opponents, however, quoted his own earlier strictures on organized mission societies against him. Later divisions among Disciples could be said to fall between those who emphasized Campbell's earlier period of iconoclasm against ecclesiastical structure, and those who appealed to his later thought. The call for restoration was pitted against the plea for Christian unity.

Slavery, abolition, and finally the outbreak of the Civil War brought serious crises to the unity-loving communion. Leaders avoided outright schism between north and south, although most of them lived in the south and many were pacifists. Most attempted to take a neutral stand, claiming that there were no specific scriptural precepts on the question of abolition; hence this should not be made a test of church allegiance. Also the lack of a national assembly, which had authority to speak for the Disciples as a whole, made partisanship more difficult. Nevertheless, northern sympathizers used a meeting of the missionary conference of 1863 to pass a resolution of Union support, which grieved the southern element. The Disciples in the north came out of the war with a heightened denominational consciousness and a concern for social action, whereas the southerners were stiffened in their separatist church stance.[17]

These tensions found final expression in 1906 when a large number of conservatives declined to be listed with the Disciples in the federal government's religious census. Since then there has been the Churches of Christ in addition to the Christian Churches (Disciples of Christ). The two factions polarized around several church periodicals. In the life of the Disciples, it is commonly

[16] *Ibid.*, p. 245.
[17] See the thorough discussion in Harrell, *op. cit.*, pp. 139–174.

said, editors have played the role that bishops fill in other denominations. In the absence of overall structures in which to discuss church policies, the columns of the papers afford the only platforms. Issues hotly debated before the split of 1906 were the scriptural validity of church instruments for worship (which the conservatives saw as the opening wedge for other innovations) and the admission of non-immersed persons to church membership and communion. There was also intense difference of opinion about the wisdom of associating with other Christian bodies in the conciliar movement (Federal Council).

A second major division can be dated from 1955, when a conservative party among the Disciples began to publish a separate list of ministers. This group had begun holding separate conventions as early as 1927—the North American Christian Conventions. The practice of "faith missions" as opposed to missionaries sent out by church agencies was a key issue for these conservatives. One Disciple historian calls them "Churches of Christ Number Two."[18]

In September 1966 the Disciples initiated a plan (to be passed on finally in 1968) which would change the decentralized, congregationalist polity into a highly structured and representatively administered denomination. The name was changed, significantly, from the Christian *Churches* to the Christian *Church*. One reason for the shift was their participation in the Consultation on Church Union. "Who could unite with eight thousand autonomous congregations and 127 separate agencies?" a defender of the plan asked.[19]

By 1964 it was reckoned that four million members were included in the Disciples-Christian family. What had started out as an urgent call to supplant denominations had become several itself. But the keen desire for unity persists, as attested by the dedication in the World Council of Churches publication which reads: "To the Disciples of Christ whose untiring ecumenical spirit has once again been manifest in the generous provision of

[18] Albert T. De Groot, *New Possibilities for Disciples and Independents* (St. Louis: Bethany Press, 1963).
[19] "From Churches to Church," *The Christian Century* (October 12, 1966), 1231–1232; "The Disciples in Dallas," *Christianity Today* (October 14, 1966), 52.

the funds which have made possible the writing and publication of this History of the Ecumenical Movement."[20]

The Plymouth Brethren

In the early nineteenth century, Great Britain was wracked by political and economic turmoil which necessarily created unrest among religious bodies. The successive enactments of Parliament which changed the electoral base and removed the Test Act and other restrictions on political activity by Roman Catholics and dissenters shook the state-church establishment. Devoted clergymen worried about the church's future. Two contradictory tendencies developed, both appealing to the past. One was the Tractarian or Oxford Movement led by John Keble, Edward Pusey, and John Henry Newman. These men called Anglicanism back to her churchly antecedents, to the pre-Reformation heritage. They held the writings of the church fathers to be authoritative. Liturgical reforms, monastic orders, resistance to state-sponsored changes in church life—these were the major planks of their platform. The Oxford movement persisted, surviving the defection to Roman Catholicism of Newman and others who decided that the Church of England was schismatic, to become the Anglo-Catholic wing.

Some of their colleagues in the church, like them also of the middle and upper classes, chose a different path. They also looked to the early church as a pattern, but sought authority in the scriptures and not in patristic literature. For them the "Bible was the textbook of revolution."[21] As individuals of this persuasion became known to one another, small groups were formed which gradually, or occasionally rapidly, took on more organized structure. They were called the Primitive Methodists, the Catholic Apostolic Church ("Irvingites"), and especially the "Brethren from Plymouth" or Plymouth Brethren. The latter disliked denominational labels, and referred to themselves as "Brethren," "Saints," or "Believers." They were the most rigorously consistent in their primitivism, the most evangelistic, and have certainly had the most influence upon modern church life of all these bodies.

[20] Ruth Rouse and Stephen C. Neill, eds., *A History of the Ecumenical Movement* (London: S.P.C.K., 1954), [v].
[21] The phrase is Horton Davies, *Worship and Theology in England* (Princeton, N.J.: Princeton University Press, 1962), IV: 141.

THE FIRST "BRETHREN" MEETINGS

By the nature of the case it is difficult to pinpoint precise dates and places where the Plymouth Brethren began. In widely scattered locales, little conventicles gathered to read the Bible and discuss its meaning for their lives. In many instances this occurred in the drawing rooms of the respected well-to-do, replacing the genteel entertainment which otherwise would have been customary for their station in life. Quite often ordained Anglican clergy participated. The meetings were similar in intent and method to the Pietist conventicles of an earlier century.

The direct beginnings of the Plymouth Brethren may be traced to such meetings in Dublin, Ireland. There a group centered about Anthony Norris Groves (1795–1853), who gave up a prosperous practice as a dentist in England in 1825 to prepare himself for the mission field. To do this he entered theological studies at Trinity College. He met a number of people, "chiefly members of the establishment who . . . desired to see more devotedness to Christ and union among all the people of God," and who met with some regularity to discuss how this might be done.

Two years later Groves announced his conviction from study of the Bible that "believers, meeting together as disciples of Christ, were free to break bread together as their Lord had admonished. . . ." This should take place each Sunday. When the Church Missionary Society, under whose auspices he wished to work, told him that he would need to be ordained to administer the sacraments as a missionary, he reconsidered his whole view of the ministry. He concluded that in fact ordination was not necessary for true ministry. "This I doubt not is the mind of God concerning us—we should come together in all simplicity as disciples, not waiting on any pulpit or ministry, but trusting that the Lord would edify us together by ministering as He pleased and saw good from the midst of us."[22] These two concepts—the weekly observance of the breaking of bread and the ministry of all believers—came to be the foundation of Brethren practice.

A similar meeting in Dublin was begun by Edward Cronin, a medical student. Raised a Roman Catholic, he left the Church as a young man. Many Protestant denominations in Dublin welcomed

[22] Quoted in Clarence B. Bass, *Backgrounds to Dispensationalism* (Grand Rapids: Wm. B. Eerdmans, 1960), pp. 65–67.

him warmly when he visited their services. Several pressed him to join them, but he was perplexed and uneasy about the divisions within the Church. Finally he decided that they were not ordered according to biblical teaching and kept himself aloof, studying the Bible on his own. A pastor of an independent chapel denounced him from the pulpit as irreligious, an unjust charge which led one of the congregation, the secretary of a Bible society, to join Cronin. The two began the regular observance of the Lord's supper and meetings for prayer; two of Cronin's cousins met with them.

The two groups, that of Groves and that of Cronin, deciding they had common motivations, began meeting together in 1829. They began on the basis that participants would be free to commune in and attend parish churches or dissenting chapels. As soon as 1830, however, they were meeting in a hired hall at the same time as the church services, and making public announcements inviting attendance. The only requirements they laid down for entrance into the fellowship were a simple statement of faith in Jesus Christ and the demonstration of a manner of life which commended itself as Christian. Any member could speak in the meetings, held Quaker style except for the hymns which were sung. Those attending came from all classes, and distinctions of rich and poor were "lessened by holy, loving fellowship and unity." One of the members gave this description:

> The meetings of the assembly were calm, peaceful, and hallowed; their singing soft, slow, and thoughtful; their worship evinced the nearness of their communion with the Lord; their prayers were earnest for an increased knowledge of God, and the spread of his truth. Their teaching showed their deep searching of the Scripture under the guidance of the Holy Spirit, while the exercise of the varied ministry, under the power of the Holy Spirit, testified to the blessedness of the teaching of God's Word on each important subject. . . . The fruits of the Spirit were in evidence.[23]

Besides Groves and Cronin, the leading men were Edward Wilson, Henry Hutchinson, William Stokes, John Parnell (later Lord Congleton), John G. Bellett, and John Nelson Darby. It was the last named who came to be the outstanding theologian and patriarch of the Brethren.

[23] *Ibid.*, p. 71.

JOHN NELSON DARBY

Any movement which looks to the Bible as its basic authority may find itself in need of an authoritative scriptural interpreter. For the Plymouth Brethren that person was John Nelson Darby (1800–1882). So important did he become for the life of the movement that in many areas it is referred to as "Darbyism."

He was a member of a highly placed family. His grandfather was Lord Nelson of Trafalgar fame and his uncle the Admiral Darby noted for his exploits on the Nile. Young Darby was a precocious student. He entered the university when fifteen years old, and graduated with honors in law in the summer of 1819. His family connections and personal attainments made a brilliant legal career seem inevitable, but he decided against law practice. He underwent a long and difficult conversion, about which he later said that the only passage of the Bible which gave him comfort at the time was Psalm 88, precisely because there was "not a ray of comfort in it."[24]

In 1825 he was ordained a deacon in the Church of England and made a curate in the County of Wicklow in Ireland. For over two years he threw himself assiduously into his difficult parish work among the poor and proud Roman Catholic residents. He described them as being almost as wild as the mountains in which they lived. At this time he was a convinced high churchman; he fasted regularly, upheld the apostolic succession, and looked with tolerance but pity on those who claimed to be Christians without benefit of connection with the Church of England. A contemporary witness of his work wrote:

> Every evening he sallied forth to teach in the cabins, and roving far and wide over mountains, and amid bogs, was seldom home before midnight. By such exertions his strength was undermined, and he so suffered in his limbs that not lameness only, but yet more serious results were feared. . . . [This] inflicted on him much severe deprivations; moreover, as he ate whatever food offered itself . . . his whole frame might have vied in emaciation with a monk of La Trappe. Such a phenomenon intensely excited the poor Romanists,

[24] The principal source for his early involvement with the Brethren is Darby's letter to Prof. Tholuck in Halle, published in H. A. Ironside, A Historical Sketch of the Brethren Movement (Grand Rapids: Zondervan, 1942), p. 182. See also Napoleon Noel, The History of the Brethren, ed. W. F. Knapp (Denver: W. F. Knapp, 1936), I: 34–43.

who looked on him as a genuine "saint" of the ancient breed. The stamp of heaven seemed to them clear in a frame so wasted by austerity, so superior to worldly pomp, and so partaking in all their indigence.[25]

The work of Darby and those like him bore fruit. He reported that between six hundred and eight hundred Catholics joined the Church every week. Then the archbishop of Ireland demanded that all converts take the oaths of allegiance and supremacy for he feared a shift of political alignment through their influx. This effectively stopped the conversions, for it seemed to the Irish that they would have to reject their patriotism to become Anglicans. The archbishop's frank appeal to the state to buttress the church's position outraged Darby. He wrote an indignant pamphlet and circulated it among the clergy, insisting that it was unworthy for the cause of Christ to look to the secular arm for support.

An injury forced Darby to spend time in Dublin, and while there he was brought into touch with the Plymouth Brethren through Bellett, a friend of university days. Their point of view, as he studied the Bible during his convalescence, struck him as having more integrity than that of the state church. He reflected that under the current structure, St. Paul himself would not be permitted to preach in the Church if he were not ordained, whereas a "worker of Satan" could, if he had holy orders. "This is not mere abuse, such as may be found everywhere; it is the *principle* of the system that is at fault."[26] Ministry was given by the Spirit, and not by a church organization, he declared. In 1829 he published a booklet giving these views, called *Considerations of the Nature and Unity of the Church of Christ*, which was the first of what was to become the avalanche of Brethren pamphlets.

In consequence, Darby resigned as curate and associated himself with the Plymouth Brethren, but did not break completely with the Church of England until several years later. He invested the rest of his long life in the advancement of the movement, writing, speaking, traveling, and counseling. For years he lived from a suitcase. He never married and used his personal estate for the cause. Those who knew him testify to his "almost overpower-

[25] F. W. Newman, *Phases of Faith* (London: John Chapman, 1850), quoted in T. C. F. Stunt, "Two Nineteenth-Century Movements," *The Evangelical Quarterly*, XXXVII (October–December 1965), 226.
[26] Ironside, *op. cit.*, p. 184.

ing" influence upon them. His keen intelligence, biblical knowledge, dedicated drive, and personal piety were axiomatic. The least demanding of men, he was indifferent to personal pleasure. At the same time he could be ruthless in controversy. He was so completely convinced of the correctness of his views that he accused his opponents of contradicting God, not Darby. His single-mindedness and dedication gave him great power, but it was not always used wisely. Before his death he had broken with nearly all of his early friends in the movement.

The writings of John Nelson Darby were compiled and published in thirty-four large volumes (three volumes of his letters are in print). They are more notable for their earnestness and sincerity than for their clarity, as he was extremely careless in putting his thoughts into finished form. This he himself admitted, remarking that he thought on paper rather than concentrating on how the ideas would be understood by others.

EXPANSION OF THE MOVEMENT

Darby was not in Dublin long; he traveled to Limerick and thence to Plymouth. There he cooperated for a time with Benjamin W. Newton, a fellow of Exeter College, Oxford, in establishing the largest and most prestigious meeting, which had twelve hundred members by 1845. Most of the important early tracts were published there, which helped to impress the town's name upon the movement.

The Plymouth Brethren concept spread rapidly throughout England during the midcentury. Some clergymen came over to them with their entire congregations. There was great attraction in the idea of Christian unity on a simple practical basis, with a sloughing off of many of the old theological quarrels. Laymen and clergymen (who abandoned all stipends and titles) preached in halls and theaters, in the open, wherever they could gain an audience. They were commonly referred to as "Walking Bibles," in tribute to their scriptural skill.

Many of the Brethren would be recognized as outstanding Christians in any age. George Müller, a native of Germany, had come to England as a Baptist preacher. Along with a colleague, Henry Craik, Müller developed a large congregation in Bristol. It was there that he began an orphanage which grew into a huge institution along the lines of Francke's at Halle. Müller's principle was to operate on faith and prayer, without specific appeals or endowment support. By his death in 1898 several million dollars had been donated, and thousands of children aided. In the later years of his life George Müller traveled extensively, preaching and telling the story of his orphanage wherever he went.

Other noted members were: Samuel P. Tregelles, a biblical exegete and scholar; George V. Wigram, who spent a quarter of a million dollars in preparing biblical concordances; Andrew Miller, a church historian; and Sir Robert Anderson, from 1865–1901 chief of the criminal investigation department of Scotland Yard. Several of the nobility were attracted to the Brethren, as were many physicians, lawyers, military men, businessmen, and laborers.

DISTINCTIVE BELIEFS AND PRACTICES

In 1878 Darby wrote an article for a French Catholic newspaper which had asked him for a statement on Brethren beliefs. After a section on the foundations of the Christian faith which reiterated the common affirmations of Protestantism, Darby discussed "What Distinguishes Us from Others." The Word of God was their "absolute authority as to faith and practice." The Body of Christ was "composed of those who were united by the Holy Ghost to the Head—Christ in Heaven." Catholicism could not be accepted because of the separate priesthood who repeated the sacrifice at each mass, which Darby maintained was disallowed by Hebrews 10:14. Protestantism was equally unacceptable because of its division into sects and its worldliness.

The Plymouth Brethren answer to the question of church formation was trust in simple faith in the declaration that where two or three are gathered in the name of Jesus there he will be also (Matt. 18:20). All those who possessed the Spirit of God— "every true Christian believer wherever he might be found ecclesiastically"—were members of the Body of Christ. But such Christians were under an obligation: "If anyone fails openly in what becomes a Christian—in point of morality or in what concerns the faith—he is excluded. We abstain from the pleasures and amusements of the world. . . . We do not mix in politics; we are not of the world; we do not vote. We submit to the established authorities, whatever they may be, in so far as they command nothing expressly contrary to the will of Christ. We take the Lord's Supper every Sunday, and those who have gift for it preach the Gospel of salvation to sinners or teach believers. Every one is bound to seek the salvation or good of his neighbor according to the capacity which God has given him."[27]

Early meetings were held in homes and in hired halls. Later, the Brethren built for themselves chapels or "assemblies" with architecture that emphasized the priesthood of all believers, avoiding pulpits and platforms. They were determinedly plain. One sketch shows seating on three sides of a square room with a table and chairs in front, which could be used by speakers. Darby himself was opposed to men standing behind the table to speak and insisted on sitting among the others. He also opposed any prior understanding among the leading brethren about responsibility for speaking, preferring the free reign of the spirit. To deal with those members who persisted in speaking at length without edification, he counseled getting up and leaving the room! A later practice, among the more liberal Brethren, was the provision of a "stated preacher" who might even be given regular support, while avoiding the word salary. The Brethren were vocal in their criticism of the pastoral system, which they called "one-man ministry."

Meetings would proceed by those present suggesting hymns, followed by explication of the Bible ("readings") and the breaking of bread. Unlike Quaker practice, there was a strict rule against women speaking or praying in public. Early Plymouth Brethren were very strong in opposition to instrumental accompaniment for the music. "Harps and organs down here began in Cain's city when he had gone forth out of the presence of the Lord," Darby wrote. This "only spoils any worship as bringing in the pleasure of sense in what ought to be the power of the SPIRIT of God."[28] The brethren were very active, though, in writing hymns. The most commonly used hymnbook was *Hymns for the Little Flock*; another was *The Believers Hymnbook*. They were sensitive to the theological position of non-Brethren hymns used in their books, and extensively rewrote them to bring them into harmony with their own position. Sensing too much individualism

[27] *Ibid.*, pp. 188–195.
[28] Davies, *op. cit.*, IV: 151.

in Isaac Watt's hymn, they revised it to read "When We Survey the Wondrous Cross."[29]

Doctrinally, the most distinctive emphasis of the Brethren was their teaching on dispensations and eternal security. Darby's views on the sevenfold division of time into "dispensations" were first developed in a series of conferences at the palatial home of Lady Powerscourt beginning in 1830. Some Irvingites were also present, and some contend that Darby was introduced to these teachings by them. In any case, in his writings the dispensationalist interpretation of the Old and New Testaments, the present eon and future events, were worked out in great detail. Darby and the other Plymouth Brethren are held by most scholars to be the direct sources of similar views currently held by American fundamentalists.[30]

Darby is known to have influenced Dwight Moody, the great American revivalist, although they differed on the subject of free will. (Plymouth Brethren were later to play a role in the career of Billy Graham.) Darby was in the United States in 1870, 1872 to 1873, and 1874. His indirect influence was mediated through C. I. Scofield in the widely used interpretative notes on the Bible. Unlike some groups who emphasize eschatology—the doctrine of last things—the Brethren were never mesmerized by the attempt to reckon the precise date of the Second Coming. They were more concerned with living in such a style that they would be ready when that time came, fully expecting it to break in at any moment. They understood the present era as the time in which Christ is gathering his church, which would be lifted to him in the air ("the rapture") before a time of tribulation.

Eternal security—the doctrine that a person once saved is saved forever—was prominent in Plymouth Brethren teachings. This led them to further editorial work on standard hymns. "Just As I Am Without One Plea" was changed to read "Just As I Was"; Toplady's "Rock of Ages" was changed to "Rock of Ages, cleft for sin; grace hath hid us safe within!"[31] In a controversy which Darby had on this point in America, he was challenged:

[29] John S. Andrews, "Brethren Hymnology," *The Evangelical Quarterly*, XXVIII (October-December 1956), 208–229.

[30] See Bass, *op. cit.*, pp. 17–19; C. Norman Kraus, *Dispensationalism in America* (Richmond, Va.: John Knox Press, 1958), pp. 45–56.

[31] Andrews, *loc. cit.*, p. 213.

"But Brother Darby, suppose a real Christian turned his back on the light, what then?" Darby answered: "Then the light would shine on his back!"[32]

DIVISIONS AND LATER DEVELOPMENT

Paradoxically, one of the clearest of the Brethren emphases was the least practiced within their own ranks. This was the conviction that all Christians should be united. There has been scarcely another Christian movement so torn by painful divisiveness. A not-unfriendly observer commented that "the Brethren are remarkable people for rightly dividing the Word of truth, and wrongly dividing themselves." Another critic, who had opened his pulpit to Darby, deplored the self-righteousness which he observed among the several groups. He told of one of their meeting places in London, which had placed a banner across the door reading "Jesus Only." After a time the banner was damaged so that it read "us Only."[33] D. L. Moody called their separatist tendencies "eating their gingerbread all by themselves in a corner."[34]

The first major division took place within the blooming Plymouth meeting. Newton, the co-founder, was accused of deviant teaching on the human nature of Jesus Christ, and also of creeping churchiness. Some suspect that Darby, in breaking fellowship with Newton and his followers and thereby splitting the meeting, was unconsciously motivated by rivalry. An even more serious break resulted when Darby insisted that every other meeting accept the ruling that the Newton-led party was in error. He contended that since there could be only one church of Christ it was inconceivable that a person could be out of communion with one meeting of the Brethren, and be accepted by another fellowship.

Some of Newton's former members asked for membership at the Bethesda meeting in Bristol. They were accepted. The Brethren then split into the "Exclusives" led by Darby, and the "Open Brethren" led by Müller. The issue was one of internal church discipline. The Bethesda group maintained that no overall excommunication could be leveled. Those who had at one time accepted Newton's teaching but were found not to be soiled by it,

---

[32] Ironside, *op. cit.*, p. 82.

[33] *Ibid.*, pp. 110, 201.

[34] J. C. Pollock, *Moody: a Biographical Portrait* (New York: The Macmillan Co., 1963), p. 74.

could be accepted without any confession of error. Exclusivists held that members excommunicated by one meeting were excommunicated by all and hence had to be disciplined before they could be received.

Many other "divergences" followed in both the Open and the Exclusive Brethren, which make their subsequent history an unedifying series of squabbles between high-minded but often overscrupulous men. Considerable theological keenness is necessary even to penetrate the actual differences in teaching which sharply separated the groups. The latest reported schism was under way in English and Scottish towns and fishing villages in 1964, after James Taylor, Jr., a retired New York businessman, commanded the Exclusive Brethren to break off all relationship with nonmembers upon threat of excommunication. Landlords disposed lodgers, employers fired workers, and families separated because of the edict.[35]

Despite the Plymouth and Bethesda trials, Brethren growth was great between 1845 and 1875. After that it leveled off especially in England, while continuing elsewhere. Darby himself went on the first of many foreign trips in 1837. His destination was Switzerland, because he had heard of some there who professed a like faith. From Switzerland the movement spread to France, Germany, the Netherlands, and to Scandinavia.

In Germany the ground had been prepared by pietistic gatherings in Tübingen and in Elberfeld. During repeated trips to the Lower Rhine area, Darby translated the entire Bible, with the aid of some German helpers. He also translated the scriptures into Italian, French, and English. In Germany as in most other countries, a chief vehicle of evangelization has been the printed page. Literally millions of copies of tracts, booklets, pamphlets, and large volumes have been circulated, often without charge, by Plymouth Brethren writers and publishing houses. A recent compilation, admittedly incomplete, lists over eighteen hundred separate titles. More than 151 different periodicals are known. Most of the publications are issued anonymously or at the most with only the initials of the authors.[36]

Although without any organization or sponsoring agency, the

[35] "The Uncontaminated," *Time* (June 26, 1964), p. 52.
[36] Arnold D. Ehlert, "Plymouth Brethren Writers," American Theological Library Association *Proceedings*, XI (1957), pp. 49–80.

Brethren have been energetic in missions. Anthony Norris Groves, who began the Dublin meetings, went to the Near East in 1829 and later to India. Under the designation "Christian Missions to Many Lands," many Brethren worked in Asia, Africa, and South America on a "faith" basis. They were the first Protestant missionaries to Indochina. Plymouth Brethren make a point of not keeping membership rolls or statistics, but the best estimates today suggest that the world membership is between 450,000 and 480,000. The largest numbers are in Great Britain, followed by Germany, and then the United States, Canada, New Zealand, Belgium, and the Netherlands.[37]

---

[37] Kurt Karrenberg, "Der Freie Brüderkreis," in Ulrich Kunz, ed., *Viele Glieder—ein Leib* (Stuttgart: Quell-Verlag, 1953), pp. 201–229.

· VII ·

Contemporary Expressions

CHOOSING representative Believers' Church movements from the twentieth century is no easy task. Advancing secularization has forced free church status on former establishments. The turbulent tides of history which have swept over nations in modern times have also dealt cruel blows to ecclesiastical structures which had stood in respected if isolated dignity for generations. Forcible separation of church and state and the consequent need for voluntary support of the churches by their members became stark realities in much of Europe after the two World Wars. Varying degrees of accommodation and recalcitrance marked the painful reactions of clergy and laity to new regimes. In Asia and Africa as well, many a chapter of church history has been written by the so-called "younger churches" who find their path to be strikingly similar to that of the early Christian church or the dissenting movements of later epochs. It is estimated that this century has claimed more Christian martyrs than any preceding it.

The case has been made that the best expression of the Believers' Church in recent times is found in Pentecostalism. In 1958 Henry P. Van Dusen, the highly respected president of Union Theological Seminary, sounded this note in an article in a mass circulation periodical. The Pentecostalist movement, he insisted, was a third force standing on an equal basis with Protestantism and Roman Catholicism and more vigorous than either. It was a "third, mighty arm of Christendom" upon which middle-class Christianity could no longer gaze down their noses. In an interview he put it more forcefully: "I have come to feel that the Pentecostal movement with its emphasis upon the Holy Spirit, is more than just another revival. . . . It is a revolution comparable in importance with the establishment of the original Apostolic Church and with the Protestant Reformation."[1]

The numerical superiority of Pentecostal Christianity among non-Roman Catholic groups in Latin America was highlighted in 1961 when two of these bodies formally joined the World Council of Churches. The ecumenical movement, in turn, has recognized the importance of the movement by paying persistent attention to it in recent years.[2]

John Howard Yoder, Mennonite theologian, puts the movement within the context of the Radical Reformation. "Pentecostalism is in our century the closest parallel to what Anabaptism was in the sixteenth; expanding so vigorously that it bursts the bonds of its own thinking about church order, living from the multiple gifts of the spirit in the total church while holding leaders in great respect, unembarrassed by the language of the layman and the aesthetic tastes of the poor, mobile, zealously single-minded." Flaws can easily be noted in the movement, he admits, but "meanwhile, they are out being the Church."[3] The multibranched Pentecostal family has recently found its first scholarly survey treatment in the study by John Thomas Nichol. The author estimates current world membership at eight million.[4]

Arguing against their inclusion into the present discussion is the fact that the Pentecostalists have issued in large part from denom-

[1] Henry P. Van Dusen, "Third Force in Christendom," *Life*, L (June 9, 1958), 113–124; John L. Sherrill, *They Speak With Other Tongues* (New York: McGraw-Hill Book Co., 1964), p. 27. A doubter of their long-range significance is W. G. McLoughlin, "Is There a Third Force in Christendom?" *Daedalus*, XCVI (Winter 1967), 43–68.

[2] See Walter J. Hollenweger, "The Pentecostal Movement and the World Council of Churches," *Ecumenical Review*, XVIII (1966), 310–320.

[3] John Howard Yoder, "Marginalia," *Concern: a Pamphlet Series for Questions of Christian Renewal*, No. 15 ([n.p.], 1967), p. 78.

[4] John Thomas Nichol, *Pentecostalism* (New York: Harper & Row, 1966). Nichols also places the Pentecostalists in the line of the left wing of the Reformation: "Like their spiritual ancestors, the Anabaptists, Pentecostals declare (1) that the individual as well as the corporate body of believers should seek for and submit to the leading of the Spirit; (2) that there should be a return to apostolic simplicity in worship; (3) that believers ought to separate themselves from the world; (4) that believers' baptism replaces infant baptism; and (5) that believers should look for the imminent visible return of Christ who will set up his millennial reign" (p. 3). The most complete survey is Walter J. Hollenweger, "Handbuch der Pfingstbewegung," (unpubl. doctoral dissertation); copies in the United States are located in the Yale University Library, Oral Roberts University Library, and Lee College Library.

inations already portrayed, specifically the Methodists and the Baptists. In doctrinal position and church polity they parallel the Baptists. The large number of separate movements encompassed by Pentecostalism, and their presence in many countries, while attesting their vitality, make difficult a succinct description. Of their importance, few informed observers would dispute.

Other examples of the free church mentality are even more significant though they are not usually seen within this context. The most thoroughgoing and totalitarian form of secularism of the twentieth century was the Third Reich of Nazi Germany. In that crucible emerged a form of church life, sharing many of the marks of the Believers' Church, called the Confessing Church. It is true that the leaders of the Confessing Church considered and then emphatically rejected the option of becoming another of the German free churches alongside the state-controlled national church. Instead, they contended, with surprising success vis-à-vis the authorities, that they constituted the only true German church. This notwithstanding, in many aspects of their stormy and agonized life their stance was one very much like those discussed in previous chapters. Separation from the state, congregationally based polity, voluntary financial support, independent calling and ordination of their pastoral leadership—even membership cards—were all part of the life of the Confessing Church.

The quite contemporary movement of small congregations of disciplined members, active in witnessing to an acculturated church as well as to a secularized world, is a striking illustration of the way in which concerns classically associated with the Believers' Churches are today penetrating Christendom. Most publicized of these ventures have been the East Harlem Protestant Parish in New York City and the Church of the Saviour in Washington, D.C. Yet more recently the tide of "underground churches" has been sweeping the shores of church life on both sides of the Atlantic. The momentum for renewal manifested in the Protestant-Orthodox world of ecumenism has both helped to bring about the yeasty experimentation of post-Vatican II Roman Catholicism and been in turn influenced by its developments. Increasingly the ecumenical slogan of unity of "all in each place" has been adopted literally by Protestants and Catholics alike, who are disdaining to wait on their respective communions reaching formal agreement on issues that divide. Christian love must be manifested, they say, and they are searching for ways in which this can be symbolized, be it in protest demonstrations or re-enactments of the early Christian agape meals.

Confessing Church and renewal congregations, then, are taken as the representative examples of the Believers' Church mood of the modern era.

The Confessing Church

In reflecting on the staggering speed of the National Socialist seizure of power in Germany, Albert Einstein expressed his dismay about the feeble resistance of major institutions. The universities quickly fell into line despite their vaunted tradition of intellectual and academic freedom, although individual professors protested. The newspapers which had trumpeted their advocacy of decency and democracy were soon reduced to government mouthpieces. It was alone the German church, Einstein said, which "stood squarely across the path of Hitler's campaign for suppressing the truth." Whereas previously he had nothing but contempt for the institutional church, because of her courageous and persistent stand for moral freedom the church now won his unreserved praise.[5]

The Protestant *Kirchenkampf* of the 1930s was in some ways similar to but more desperate an encounter than the *Kulturkampf* waged by Bismarck against the Roman Catholic Church in Germany some sixty years before. It was above all the result of the church's determination to preserve her independence and integrity in the face of Hitler's totalitarian drive to subdue and subordinate all aspects of German life (*Gleichschaltung*). In the words of a participant: "The struggle of the Confessing Church never had another aim than to defend the ecclesiastical essence [*kirchliche Substanz*] from the political movement of National Socialism."[6] It was also a bitterly fought controversy *within* the church centering on church-state relations—to what extent could the Nazi regime

[5] Quoted from Julius Regier, *The Silent Church* (London: S.C.M. Press, 1944), p. 90, in Arthur C. Cochrane, *The Church's Confession Under Hitler* (Philadelphia, Westminster Press, 1962), p. 40.

[6] Otto Dibelius, quoted in Dietmar Schmidt, *Niemöller* (Hamburg: Rowolt Verlag, 1959), pp. 99–100. This biography appeared in English in a very freely translated and condensed version, *Pastor Niemöller*, trans. L. Wilson (Garden City, N.Y.: Doubleday & Co., 1959).

be considered the powers that be, ordained of God? A leading student of the period calls it "essentially a struggle of the Church against itself for itself."[7] On the third level it was the slowly realized conviction, leading to action, by German churchmen that their voices must be raised to condemn the crimes against mankind perpetrated in the Third Reich, first upon Germans and later upon other Europeans. Karl Barth summarized this phase by stating that the church was slow to speak out, but speak out she did.

Leading actors in the *Kirchenkampf* have been the first to point out that the record of the Protestant church was by no means a spotless one. There is no "glorious chronicle" nor "heroic or saintly story." Rather, it is the story of a "weak, stammering, endangered congregation which moved over a field of rubble called the Evangelical Church in Germany."[8] The story is complex and not easily related. Those involved left contradictory interpretations of crucial events, so that their description forces the writer to take sides himself. To write the history of the church struggle is itself a form of *Kirchenkampf*. It remains necessary to attempt to trace the "thin red line of evangelical clarity, loyalty, and courage" (K. Barth) which has increasing relevance for the contemporary scene.[9]

THE CHURCH AND HITLER'S RISE TO POWER

When Hitler and his National Socialist Party (NSDAP) came to power in January 1933—by legal means, it must be remembered—the attitude of most Protestant churchmen was not at all unfavorable. For centuries their church had been associated with the conservative elements of society. The legal disestablishment precipitated by the fall of the Wilhelmine empire in 1918 had not destroyed the psychological orientation of "throne and altar." It even intensified the patriotic stance of churchmen, and made them receptive to political leaders who promised an enhanced position for Germany in the world of nations and of the church within that renewed Germany. The church was very cool toward the Weimar

---

[7] Cochrane, *op. cit.*, p. 19; see also Ernst Wolf, *Kirche im Widerstand?* (Munich: Chr. Kaiser Verlag, 1965).
    [8] Wilhelm Niemöller, quoted in Schmidt, *op. cit.*, p. 118.
    [9] Karl Barth, *The German Church Conflict*, trans. T. H. L. Parker (Richmond, Va.: John Knox Press, 1965), p. 45.

republic, although it fared well as an institution at the hands of the
new democracy. The lament of the chairman of the first church
rally (*Kirchentag*) after World War I can stand as a gauge of
church opinion: "The glory of the German empire, the dream of
our fathers, the pride of every German is gone!"[10]

Hitler's early pronouncements seemed to augur well for the
future. In *Mein Kampf* he emphasized the confessional neutrality
of his party. Protestant and Catholic alike should stand without
discrimination shoulder to shoulder for the cause of unity. Paragraph 24 of the Nazi platform called for religious liberty and
"positive Christianity." Very few noticed the conditions of the
promised benevolence—the state must not be endangered and the
moral and ethical feelings of the German race dare not be
offended. What was seen was the affirmation that the church could
be a pillar of the German people in their new hour.

The Führer emphasized the point in an address made soon after
his installation as chancellor: "The national government sees in
the two Christian Confessions the most important factors for the
preservation of our nationality. It will respect the agreements that
have been drawn up between them and the provincial states. Their
rights are not to be infringed." But again came the conditions: "It
expects, however, and hopes that conversely the work upon the
national and moral renewal of our nation, which the Government
has assumed as its task, will receive the same appreciation." Many
in the church were open to this moral crusade, impressed as they
were by the abstemious and puritanical image projected by the
German leader. It was then widely believed that he carried a
devotional booklet with him at all times.[11]

Concurrently, as is now known, Hitler was revealing in intimate
circles his true attitude toward the churches. In evident dependence upon Nietzschean concepts, he ridiculed the idea that a good
German could be a loyal Christian:

> Religion is very important for our people. Everything depends on
> whether it will remain faithful to its Judaeo-Christian religion and
> the slave morality of pity that goes with it, or whether it will have a
> new faith—strong, heroic . . . immanent in nature, immanent in the
> nation—whether it believes in a God who is indivisible from its

[10] Schmidt, *op. cit.*, p. 86. See also Karl Kupisch, *Deutschland im 19. und 20. Jahrhundert* (Göttingen: Vandenhoeck & Ruprecht, 1966), pp. 102–103.
[11] Quoted in Cochrane, *op. cit.*, p. 85.

blood and its fate. . . . One is either a good German or a good Christian. It is impossible to be both at the same time.[12]

He was confident that clergy would readily forfeit their faith in order to keep their salaries. He proposed using the "Catholic plan" of maintaining the outward form of the cultus, but infusing it with the new beliefs. Easter would be retained, for example, but it would symbolize the rebirth of the German nation. (In later years, when the church proved to be less tractable than he had imagined, he shifted to a determination to annihilate the church, root and branch.)[13]

THE GERMAN CHRISTIANS

Even before 1933, a movement began within German Protestantism aimed at combining the faith with National Socialist ideology. These men were called the "German Christians." They summoned their first national conference in April 1933. Playing on the old theme of state and church harmony, they announced their determination to seize control of the church apparatus in order to cooperate fully with the nation: "The church is for Germans the community of believers who are pledged to a battle for a Christian Germany. The goal of the German Christian faith movement is one evangelical German national church. The state of Adolf Hitler calls the church; the church must obey this call."[14]

The call for one unified church to take the place of the twenty-eight loosely linked territorial churches was one which had been heard before. Some of the twenty-eight in fact were "United Churches," mergers of Lutherans and Reformed which had been imposed from above by rulers in the nineteenth century. There would be obvious advantages for the Nazi government to have one organization to control instead of nearly thirty. A three-man committee of church leaders took the initiative in union talks in order to head off the German Christian move. They were soon joined in their efforts to draft a new church constitution by one

---

[12] Quoted in H. H. Schrey, *Die Generation der Entscheidung* (Munich: Chr. Kaiser Verlag, 1955), pp. 138–139.
[13] Friedrich Zipfel, *Kirchenkampf in Deutschland, 1933–1945* (Berlin: Walter de Gruyter, 1965), pp. 8–9.
[14] From the final resolutions, cited in Schrey, *op. cit.*, pp. 142–143. See also Paul B. Means, *Things That Are Caesar's* (New York: Round Table Press, 1935), pp. 214–255.

Lewis Müller (1883–1945), a military chaplain and crony of Hitler. Müller was named the Führer's special consultant on religious matters. The draft constitution called for a national bishop (*Reichsbischof*), to be a Lutheran, a ministerium to aid him, and a national synod for church legislation.

Müller was the only possible choice for the post of national bishop, said the German Christians, but most of the other elements in the church united behind another man and elected him. This was Fritz von Bodelschwingh (1877–1946), director of the famous hospital and asylum of Bethel, who was universally esteemed for his charitable work and conservative, patriotic stance. The German Christians protested vehemently; when some of his original backers weakened, Bodelschwingh was soon forced to resign. The government created a commissioner of religious affairs who clamped down on the church with rigorous administrative measures. Next, a national church election was hurriedly called by the government, preventing opponents from organizing much support for an opposition slate known as "Gospel and Church." Hitler himself threw his weight on the side of the German Christians with an election-eve appeal. Thousands of nominal church members who had never darkened a church door since their confirmations surged to the polls. The result was a landslide victory for the German Christian element. Only in Hannover, Bavaria, and Württemberg did the incumbent leadership retain control.

The "SA for Jesus Christ," as the German Christians called themselves, were not dilatory in seizing control of the church machinery. Forcible occupation of church offices was commonplace. Newly elected synodal members in their party uniforms and military insignia made mockery of parliamentary procedure. A Swedish reporter published a shocked commentary on the proceedings in the Brandenburg Church Synod (Old Prussian Union) of August 1, 1933:

> The first action of the meeting in the State Assembly hall was the dismissal of the previous chairman of the synod. His successor was Dean Grell, a man in the brown-shirt uniform, of military posture and drill sergeant voice. He explained that what was now needed were a German faith and a German god. The glorious revolution has resulted in the condition that it is a joy to be alive. Revolutions are not for weaklings. Whoever could not tear himself free from the

old customs is not suited to assist in the reconstruction. His speech was greeted by the brownshirts with clamorous cries of "Heil" and Hitler salutes. . . . The meeting closed with the singing of "Deutschland, Deutschland über alles" and the ubiquitous "Horst-Wessel Lied."[15]

Soon thereafter, Müller was made *Reichsbischof* and bishoprics were instituted in the individual states.

A faction within the German Christian movement was not content with these triumphs. They were determined to expunge all of the "Jewish" features from the German church. Jewish phrases such as "Amen" and "Hallelujah" must be deleted in favor of German equivalents. This drive culminated in the notorious mass demonstration at the Berlin Sports Palace on November 13, 1933. A Dr. Krause declared all-out warfare on the decadent Jewish elements in Protestant belief, describing the Old Testament as a collection of stories about "cattle dealers and panderers." A resolution called for all persons having Jewish racial background (the "Aryan Paragraph") and those opposed to National Socialism to be banned from the pastoral ranks. One dissenting voice out of twenty thousand present was raised when these demands and others like them were submitted to a voice vote.

A storm of indignation among the faithful answered the resolutions, as many for the first time understood where the German Christian teachings were leading. Müller, as the sponsor of the meeting, was discredited. Although he remained in office for many years, from this point he became more and more an object of suspicion and derision. His opponents referred to him with contempt as the "Reibi," a disrespectful abbreviation of *Reichsbischof* and also the name of a small mop used for washing dishes.

CHURCH OPPOSITION

Three country pastors in Lower Lusatia began organized resistance to the National Socialist take-over of the church.[16] In September they took their ideas to Berlin where they won support among the concerned city pastors, especially Martin Niemöller (b. 1892), of Berlin-Dahlem. As executive of the Young Reformation

[15] *Svenska Morgenbladet*, August 1, 1933, quoted in Zipfel, *op. cit.*, pp. 37–38.
[16] See Karl Kupisch, "Zur Genesis des Pfarrernotbundes," *Theologische Literaturzeitung*, XCI (October 1966), 722–730.

movement he was in contact with the pastors and laymen across Germany. He circulated among his mailing lists the pledge drafted by the ministers thus forming the Pastors' Emergency League. Its text as edited by Niemöller was:

1. I engage to execute my office as minister of the Word, holding myself bound solely to Holy Scriptures and the Confessions of the Reformation as the true exposition of Holy Scripture.

2. I engage to protest, regardless of the cost, against every violation of this confessional stand.

3. I hold myself responsible to the utmost of my ability for those who are persecuted on account of this confessional stand.

4. In making this pledge, I testify that the application of the Aryan paragraph within the Church of Christ has violated the confessional stand.[17]

The response was phenomenal. Within one week, there were two thousand signers; within four months, seven thousand of the fifteen thousand pastors in Germany had signed. An executive committee organized to conduct the business of the League. Thus when *Reichsbischof* Müller enacted a church law in early January 1934, forbidding any discussion in the pulpits of the church controversies and insisting that pastors stick to the "pure gospel," League leaders issued a statement of refusal which was read from thousands of pulpits.

Later that month spokesmen from several church-political orientations gathered in Hitler's office with the intention of forcing Müller's ouster. An injudicious telephone conversation of Niemöller's, tapped by Hermann Göring's agents, was reported to Hitler by Göring as evidence of treason. The sudden attack disconcerted the clergy, who quickly distanced themselves from their agreed-upon action and signed a servile statement giving Müller virtually blank-check authority. Hitler and Niemöller engaged in a heated dispute. Upon departing Niemöller told him: "You have said that I should leave the care of the German people to you. I am bound to declare that neither you nor any power in the world is in a position to take from us Christians and the Church the responsibility God has laid upon us for our people." (He later said that the dictator never forgave him that remark and that this was the

[17] Cochrane, *op. cit.*, pp. 108–109. An additional statement of loyalty to Dr. von Bodelschwingh was dropped from the pledge when he declined a leadership position.

reason for his confinement in concentration camps. It is known that Hitler became infuriated at the bare mention of the pastor's name.) Niemöller was suspended and then officially retired from his parish, but he continued his work anyway with the backing of his congregation.[18]

THE CONFESSING CHURCH

Among the Reformed and United congregations in Westphalia and the Rhineland the conviction grew that new confessional statements were needed to cope with the onslaught of the National Socialists, now firmly ensconced within the church's own ecclesiastical machinery. A synod meeting at Barmen-Gemarke in January 1934 called on Karl Barth (b. 1886), a Swiss Reformed theologian who had taught at German universities since 1921, to prepare a draft of a confession for them. This they adopted. The most important thesis was that there can be no other source of revelation for the church than that of Jesus Christ. This was directly aimed against the blood-and-soil teaching of the German Christians but also against the theology of created orders, popular among the Lutheran theologians, which allowed great importance to be placed on the institutions of family, race, nationality, and government. Barth's pamphlet *Theological Existence Today*, issued in July 1933, was but the first of a series of his publications which provided the theological backbone for the active resistance of the German Church.

In late spring 1934, the bishops of Württemberg and Bavaria expressed their solidarity with the free synods of Westphalia and the Rhineland. This opened the way for the pivotal event in the whole *Kirchenkampf*—the Barmen Synod of May 29–31. Some one hundred and forty representatives of nineteen state churches (Lutheran, Reformed, and United) met to produce a new confessional statement. They had been chosen by independent congregational meetings, without reference to the *Reichskirche*. The gravity of the religious situation was thought sufficient to validate the legality of their meeting. The leading figures of the comparatively youthful assembly (the average age was under forty) were Karl Barth, who drafted the proposed statement, and Hans Asmussen (b. 1898), a Lutheran pastor of Altona, who provided theological

[18] *Ibid.*, p. 131; Schmidt, *op. cit.*, pp. 107–114.

interpretation of it. With some minor revisions, the synod accepted the Barth proposal as interpreted by Asmussen.

The preface to the Barmen Confession was an appeal to congregations and individual Christians in Germany to "try the spirits whether they are of God!" The threat posed by the controlling German Christian party was specifically named and denounced. In the classical form of confessions, the statement's six points enunciated truths and rejected false beliefs, with scriptural authority listed first of all. The affirmations are:

1. Jesus Christ, as he is testified to us in the Holy Scripture, is the one Word of God, whom we are to hear, whom we are to trust and obey in life and death.
2. Just as Jesus Christ is the forgiveness of all our sins, just so—and with the same earnestness—is he also God's mighty claim on our whole life; in him we encounter a joyous liberation from the godless claims of this world to free and thankful service to his creatures.
3. The Christian church is the community of brethren, in which Jesus Christ presently works in the word and sacraments through the Holy Spirit.
4. The various offices in the church establish no rule of one over the other but the exercise of the service entrusted and commanded to the whole congregation.
5. The Bible tells us that according to divine arrangement the state has the responsibility to provide for justice and peace in the yet unredeemed world in which the church also stands, according to the measure of human insight and human possibility, by the threat and use of force.
6. The commission of the church, in which her freedom is founded, consists in this: to extend through word and sacrament the message of the free grace of God to all people in the place of Christ and thus in the service of his own word and work.[19]

A second synod held in Berlin-Dahlem from October 19–20, 1934, dealt directly with the question of church organization already announced by Barmen. In the Barmen declaration the signers found it necessary to counter the accusation that they were

---

[19] From the translation of Franklin H. Littell, *The German Phoenix* (Garden City, N.Y.: Doubleday & Co., 1960), pp. 184–188 (Appendix B); this is found also in John H. Leith, ed., *Creeds of the Churches* (Garden City, N.Y.: Anchor Books, 1963), pp. 518–522.

forming a new church. This had in fact been urgently considered by the leaders of the Confessing Church. When Dietrich Bonhoeffer (1906–1945) returned from the National Synod (September 27, 1933) in which the German Christians were dominant, he went to a pastor of the Lutheran Free Church (established about 1850) to inquire about joining. He was told that as pastor of the state church he could be accepted into the Free Church by bringing five hundred members of his congregation with him. But when a close friend later prepared a list of ten theses making the case for establishing a free church Bonhoeffer abandoned that idea. On Easter Day, 1934, Karl Barth wrote in an attack against indecision: "What have we all been fighting about for nearly a year now? And what is the courage, what the responsibility and what the faith with which we are steering towards the Free Church of which there is more and more talk on all sides?" Earlier in his *Theological Existence Today*, Barth had called for the church to choose voluntarily to be reduced to the state of a tiny group in the catacombs, rather than compromising with the German Christians.[20]

The Confessing Church decided on another tack. They insisted that they constituted the only true German national church. "We will not abandon this our Church and become a 'free church.' We are the Church."[21] They established their own church government, collected monies for salaries, and arranged for the education and ordination of pastors. Where this stand became difficult was in the diversity of situation of members of the Confessing Church. The Lutheran bishops of Württemberg and Bavaria—the "intact churches"—were prepared to make certain compromises with the state in order to keep from losing all control. They had withstood determined efforts of the German Christian church

[20] Barth, *op. cit.*, p. 37; Cochrane, *op. cit.*, p. 103. As far back as 1924, when Bonhoeffer visited Rome as a student, the idea of a free church came to him: "Perhaps Protestantism should never have had state church intentions, but rather should have remained a large sect, as they always have fewer complications. In this way it might not be now in such a calamity. . . . It would have become a church in the Reformation sense, which it is not now." See the discussion in Eberhard Bethge, *Dietrich Bonhoeffer* (Munich: Chr. Kaiser Verlag, 1967), pp. 89–90, 361–362, 374.
[21] Hermann Ehlers, quoted in Franklin H. Littell, "From Barmen (1934) to Stuttgart (1945): the Path of the Confessing Church in Germany," *Journal of Church and State*, III (May, 1961), 41–52.

authorities to remove them from their offices by use of administrative force and public propaganda and saw their battle as hanging on to the provincial church administrations.

Reformed and United church offices in northern Germany had been taken over by the Nazis. These were the "disrupted churches." Niemöller, Bonhoeffer, and other northern leaders demanded a hard line of complete noncooperation with the government. Bonhoeffer's famous pronouncement was: "He who knowingly separates himself from the Confessing Church in Germany, separates himself from salvation."[22] The Confessing Church among the disrupted churches organized with this in mind. Members of the Confessing Church received red membership cards. In 1935 there were some five hundred thousand cardholders in Westphalia and about three hundred thousand in the Rhineland. Martin Niemöller answered the question whether one could be a good Christian without possessing a membership card in this way: "It is my opinion that an evangelical Christian who does not have the red card will simply be lost in isolation in the future, or along with his family must fall prey to the anti-Christ."[23]

The self-understanding of the Confessing Church as the only legitimate German Evangelical church was tested by the relationships with the ecumenical movement. When invitations were issued for the Fanø (Denmark) conference of the Universal Council for Life and Work in August 1934, the Confessing Church was first asked to participate as a second church alongside the official church. Largely because of Bonhoeffer's efforts, the conference recognized the Confessing Church and virtually rejected the position of the *Reichskirche*.

PERSECUTION OF THE CONFESSING CHURCH

From 1933 on those pastors and church officials standing in opposition to the state's take-over of the church machinery were subjected to varying degrees of harassment and punishment. In the early years they sometimes found relief by appealing to the courts, for payment of salaries, for example, held back by the Nazi church authorities as retribution for "disloyal" statements or ac-

---

[22] Dietrich Bonhoeffer, "Zur Frage nach der Kirchengemeinschaft," *Evangelische Theologie*, III (1936), 214–233, reprinted in *Die mündige Welt*, I (1959), 123–144.
[23] Schmidt, *op. cit.*, p. 128.

tions. Paul Schneider (1897–1939), who died in Buchenwald, was once imprisoned for a week for his criticism of the singing of the Horst-Wessel song by SA troops at the funeral of a member of the Nazi party. Karl Barth was expelled from his chair of theology at Bonn in June 1935 for refusing to take an oath of allegiance to Hitler and for his political opposition. He continued to take an active part in the events in Germany from his new academic position in Switzerland.

Writing in Basel in the summer of 1935, Barth expressed his regret that the German church had restricted her resistance to concerns of her own and had not spoken out against actions of the Third Reich affecting others: "She has fought hard to a certain extent for the freedom and purity of her proclamation, but she has, for instance, remained silent on the action against the Jews, on the amazing treatment of political opponents, on the suppression of the freedom of the press in the new Germany, and so much else against which the Old Testament prophets would certainly have spoken out."[24] This witness was made the following year when Confessing Church leaders presented a memorial to the Führer's own office. A copy of their charges found its way into the foreign press. As reprisal an official of the "Provisional Church Office" was placed in a camp where he soon died.

Niemöller himself was arrested again on July 1, 1937. For years he had been completely fearless in defying the restrictions placed upon him. Crowds had flocked to hear his appeals to follow the "Jewish rabbi, Jesus Christ." His trial was delayed until February 1938, as the prosecutors gathered evidence to convict him of misuse of the pulpit and resistance to the authority of the state. News of his arrest had galvanized the international press, and hundreds of appeals from prominent non-Germans flooded the court, demanding his release. After a long trial, the judge pronounced an extremely mild sentence, virtually equivalent to a finding of innocence: a fine and a short prison term, already met by the months of pretrial imprisonment. Niemöller was happily preparing to rejoin his family when he was seized by Gestapo agents. They took him to the Sachsenhausen concentration camp near Berlin as the "personal prisoner" of Hitler, without a shred of legality whatsoever. There he became the symbol of the "other

[24] Barth, *op. cit.*, p. 45.

Germany" for the outside world, until he was released by the invading Allied armies in 1945. His aged father, on one of the last visits to his son's cell, told him that the Eskimos in North Canada were praying for him and that the Bataks on Sumatra sent him their greetings.[25]

According to the latest history of the German religious life of this period, the Confessing Church could be compared to "a small fishing boat, whose occupants were no tough, weather-hardened salts, but rather men in whose hearts hope and fear held sway, thankful for the dawn of the next day, but in whose existence a bit of church history was realized which was purer and more impressive than that of the church dignitaries in their conference rooms, whose lack of direction was later hidden under seemingly weighty apologetic documentation."[26]

THE CONFESSING CHURCH AFTER THE WAR

With the outbreak of World War II much of the organized activity of the Confessing Church came to a halt. Many pastors were drafted into the army; others continued their resistance in quiet ways. Some, above all Dietrich Bonhoeffer, conspired to overthrow Hitler. With the end of the war, the church officialdom, made up of the German Christians, disappeared overnight as rapidly as they had come into power originally. Men of the Confessing Church were the only ones able to make a new beginning. It was the leaders of the intact churches, Bishops Meiser and Wurm who grasped the initiative. In a meeting at Treysa in late summer of 1945, plans were laid for rebuilding the church. Although it took three years, a new overall organization did come into being— the Evangelical Church in Germany (EKiD)—with Bishop Wurm as chairman and Pastor Niemöller as the deputy chairman and head of the section on foreign affairs.

The most significant early action of the postwar German church was the Stuttgart Declaration of October 1945. Ten of the Confessing Church leaders who had led the resistance to Hitler, publicly confessed their guilt: "We accuse ourselves that we did not

[25] Helmut Gollwitzer, "Martin Niemöller: Protestant und Opponent aus Glauben," in Günter Gloede, ed., *Oekumenische Profile* (Stuttgart: Evang. Missionsverlag, 1963), II: 194–207; Schmidt, *op. cit.*, p. 154.
[26] Kupisch, *op. cit.*, pp. 172–173.

witness more courageously, pray more faithfully, believe more joyously, love more ardently." This act, though condemned and widely misunderstood by the German public at that time and since as an admission of collective guilt, cleared the air. Representatives of the ecumenical movement, in whose presence the declaration was made, immediately responded with a warm invitation for the Germans to enter into cooperative work in the World Council of Churches, then in process of formation. After World War I interchurch relations were poisoned for decades by the question of war guilt. The admission of complicity by precisely those Germans who came out of the war with the cleanest records made possible German rehabilitation in the eyes of the foreign churches.[27]

There were those in the Confessing Church who wished to take the opportunity of the postwar rebuilding as the chance for fundamental reform of the German church. Niemöller called for a church based on the congregations, not on bishops, on the Barmen basis: "I am absolutely sure that a completely independent church is, even for Germany, the church of the future, and what she will gain in vitality will compensate for whatever she may have to give up in 'influence.' . . . The Confessing Church was never a ministers' church; it was, from the very beginning, a Church of a brotherly organization and brotherly life." He noted with disappointment that the men of the "neutral party" were organizing themselves to restore the old pattern.[28]

In fact, those churchmen favoring restoration did win the day over the Niemöller party. They stressed the importance of a close link with the state, while wishing to retain independence in arranging their own internal affairs. Not only could the state help the church financially, but the relationship would allow the church to play a role in influencing the course of national affairs. An outward evidence of this position was the formation of the Christian Democratic Party with support from both the Catholic and Evangelical churches.

Niemöller's idea was that the Confessing Church could remain in existence to serve as a conscience for the general church, while

---

[27] Littell, *Phoenix*, pp. 189–190; R. Rouse and S. C. Neill, eds., *A History of the Ecumenical Movement* (London: S.P.C.K., 1954), pp. 364–366, 715.

[28] Martin Niemöller, *Of Guilt and Hope* (New York: Philosophical Library, [n.d.]), pp. 38–51.

giving up its claim to be the only legitimate church in favor of the EKiD. This concept took on form in the "brotherhoods" (*Brüderschaften*) who have challenged the establishment views on the remilitarization of Germany, the relationship with the eastern European states, and with the German Democratic Republic. They have, however, lost major positions of influence in the inner circle of the German church. This is symbolized by the maneuverings to remove Niemöller from influential positions in the church, first from the deputy chairmanship and later from the leadership of the bureau of foreign affairs. His outspoken statements on controversial political issues, his opposition to confessional partisanship, and his conversion to pacifism helped to provide the occasions for the ouster.

As one of the presidents of the World Council of Churches, (1961–1968) Niemöller retains a key role in the ecumenical church. A recent biographer characterized him as a true ecumenical man: "He is a man to whom the institutions and privileges which the church enjoyed in the 'Constantinian Era' seem already antiquated, partly in extreme dilapidation, and in any case untrustworthy. . . . [He] is one of the few men who already lives in the church's future, far in advance of the necessities of the present. For this reason he has understanding and interest in the form of existence of the free churches." In fact, some of his followers urged him in 1957–1958 to pull away from the EKiD and form an independent church, but he emphatically declined to do so.[29]

The question of the correct relationship of the church to the state is still a live issue for the German church. One of the foremost defenders of the restored structure, Bishop Otto Dibelius, in one of his last publications (an answer to criticism of the church by Rudolf Augstein, publisher of *Der Spiegel*, German newsmagazine) before his death in 1967, conceded that the topic was of greatest urgency: "It has long been quite clearly the consensus that the days of the people's church [*Volkskirche*] are numbered and that in the foreseeable future the Christian church in Germany will be the church of a minority. . . . [The] eyes of all are focused on the moment in which the oft-cited 'Constantinian Era' will come to an end." Dibelius concluded that this will provide the

---

[29] Gollwitzer, *loc. cit.*, pp. 203, 207; Schmidt, *op. cit.*, p. 250; "If the others wish to go, let them go—we are not going!"

opportunity for the church to become what she was originally intended to be.[30]

New Forms of the Church

Following World War II the churches in Europe and North America made great strides forward, as measured by external statistics. Millions of dollars were expended on buildings to house new congregations or to replace older edifices. Attendance and church membership soared. Some spoke of the century of the church. But beneath the outward prosperity was an underlying malaise which was soon laid bare by sociologically oriented journalists and scholars with rather cruel literary surgery. Soon the consensus emerged among the thoughtful religionists that the churches were in crisis. What had seemed success was revealed as soggy acculturation to the spirit of the times. To the key issues facing modern societies, Christians seemed to have no answers. Race, technology, urbanization, war, the generation gap—all found the churches either speechless or too quick with pious panaceas which no longer convinced. Intellectuals and the ever-increasing number of youth pursuing higher education lost respect for the institutional church.

In the face of growing secularization on the one hand and ecclesiastical incompetence on the other, there arose those movements which seemed to offer some answers. They were small, embarrassingly small, in number. The speed with which response to them came, however, was proof that their experiments were focusing on questions vital to dedicated Christians. There was a hunger for new ways, new forms which promised integrity, genuineness, and engagement. Much—probably too much—has been written about these movements, but rarely has attention been focused on their likeness to the Believers' Churches. Without conscious effort to model their activities after earlier historical expressions, there has been fashioned, out of the need of the moment, covenant communities with worship forms, disciplines, and styles of life such as have been met before in this study. It is too early to see how much long-range influence the renewal movements will have, but all indications are that it will be significant.

[30] Otto Dibelius, *Christus und die Christen* (Berlin: Christlicher Zeitschriftenverlag [1965], pp. 25–26.

CHURCH OF THE SAVIOUR

An army chaplain was talking about a soldier he had baptized to the commanding officer of the soldier's unit. "Tell me, how is Joe getting along?" "What do you mean?" asked the officer. "I mean as a Christian. What kind of life is he leading?" The other laughingly replied: "If Joe's a Christian, nobody in the company knows it." This was a moment of truth for the chaplain, who decided on the spot to reject henceforth any compromise with nominal Christianity. From that time on integrity of church membership became the guiding principle of his ministry.[31]

The chaplain was Gordon Cosby (b. 1917), a Baptist pastor from Lynchburg, Virginia. The place was Normandy during the struggle to liberate France in World War II. Cosby's decision developed into a postwar congregation in Washington, D.C., called the Church of the Saviour. Beginning in 1946 with a handful of interested participants and thirty dollars in the treasury, the fellowship quickly became the outstanding example of church renewal in North America by demonstrating the power of integral church membership. It has since inspired similar endeavors in the United States and abroad.[32]

Already during the remainder of his military service Cosby began putting his ideas into practice. He made membership in the regimental church something special, to be sought after rather than shamefacedly admitted. The chaplain selected a key man in each company ("sky pilot") who gathered a small nucleus around him. Together they were responsible for the spiritual welfare of their comrades, providing a group in which Christian experience, however faltering, could be shared, and perplexities, however great, could be aired. Attendance at Sunday services tripled. In the face of the wartime exigencies of the invasion of Germany and the Battle of the Bulge, Cosby (who was twice awarded the Bronze Star for battlefield valor) worked out the guidelines for the church

[31] Quoted in Elizabeth O'Connor, *Call to Commitment* (New York: Harper & Row, 1963), pp. 10–11. This book, written by an associate of Cosby, is the fullest treatment of the Church of the Saviour. Just published is a sequel by the same author, *Journey Inward, Journey Outward* (New York: Harper & Row, 1968).

[32] See Beverly Cosby, "A Covenant Community in Action," *Union Seminary Quarterly Review*, XVI (1960), 277–289, for the description of a congregation in Lynchburg, Virginia.

at home of which he dreamed. It would be ecumenical, interracial, and aimed at the unchurched. Specific disciplines of study, time, and resources would be demanded. Small groups could provide the vitality to keep the common life vibrant.

Cosby's war experience convinced him that the American churches were not doing their job. Many church members he met were not prepared to stand up to the tensions, temptations, and terror of military life and combat. "A fair percentage of those boys had received everything their churches at home had to offer," he explained later. "Yet the spiritual resources just weren't there when they needed them most. The religion they had thought was their own had really been only a kind of social veneer. When you took that away—well, awful things happened."[33]

Cosby poured out his hopes for a new kind of church in his letters home. His wife, the former Mary Campbell, and his sister-in-law, Elizabeth Anne Campbell, were caught up by the same vision. They communicated to friends their ideas about the new church and prepared a brochure outlining its basic features. After V-E day, demobilization, and Cosby's return, a group of twelve began meeting each Sunday afternoon. They formed a "School of Christian Experience" to provide a solid basis for the new church concept. When they failed in their attempt to attract subsidies from philanthropists for their plan, they ventured ahead with their own limited funds. On October 5, 1946, the first official meeting of the Church of the Saviour was held in Alexandria, Virginia. Within a year they had found and refurbished an old house to serve as a meeting place, with a chapel, offices, common room, classrooms, and dining room.

October 9, 1947, saw nine people ready to stand in a worship service to make this commitment of membership:

> I come today to join a local expression of the Church, which is the body of those on whom the call of God rests to witness to the grace and truth of God.—I recognize that the function of the Church is to glorify God in adoration and sacrificial service, and to be God's missionary to the world, bearing witness to God's redeeming grace in Jesus Christ.—I believe as did Peter that Jesus is the Christ, the

[33] Quoted in Catherine Marshall, "What I've learned at Gordon Cosby's Church," *Reader's Digest* (December 1953), 48–52; this article is condensed from "Human Nature Can Be Changed," *Christian Herald* (December 1953), 21, 62–67.

Son of the living God.—I unreservedly and with abandon commit my life and destiny to Christ, promising to give him a practical priority in all the affairs of life. I will seek first the Kingdom of God and His Righteousness.—I commit myself, regardless of the expenditure of time, energy, and money to becoming an informed, mature Christian.—I believe that God is the total owner of my life and resources. I give God the throne in relation to the material aspect of my life. God is the owner. I am the ower. Because God is a lavish giver I too shall be lavish and cheerful in my regular gifts.—I will seek to be Christian in all my relations with my fellow man, with other nations, groups, classes, and races.—I will seek to bring every phase of my life under the lordship of Christ.—When I move from this place I will join some other expression of the Christian Church.[34]

This was the base upon which they launched their attempt "to recover in one local expression of the Church universal something of the vitality and life, vigor and power of the early Christian community." The discipline of study took on more structured form, becoming the equivalent of one year's seminary work, in the estimation of one observer.[35] Candidates for church membership had to pass four courses on Christian doctrine, ethics, growth, and the Bible. Following the completion of the study course, an applicant was asked to prepare a paper which set forth his self-understanding of his relationship to Jesus Christ, his present spiritual discipline with specifics, areas of his life which needed improvement, and the tasks he was currently performing as a part of the Church. The council, a governing body of the congregation made up of two staff members and eight elected representatives, reviewed the paper. If it was found adequate, the council appointed a sponsor or spiritual guide to direct further study and self-examination. Specific reading assignments (in 1963, Bonhoeffer's *Life Together* and a book on the ecumenical movement) had to be carried out. An applicant was led to consider on the deepest levels his readiness to full involvement in the life of the Church which membership entailed. When the process was completed, the applicant-member then made his personal commitment before the assembled congregation. Each member reaffirms this commitment

[34] O'Connor, *op. cit.*, pp. 20–21.
[35] Stephen C. Rose, *The Grass Roots Church* (New York: Holt, Rinehart & Winston, 1966), p. 32.

annually, as did the early Quakers. Candidacy for church membership was sufficiently rigorous that by 1953 only sixty-seven members belonged, despite much larger numbers attending services and church activities.

Late that year, an article written by Catherine Marshall was given mass circulation by *Reader's Digest*.[36] This resulted in a flood of inquiries, visits, telephone calls, and requests for interviews and counsel. The small membership found themselves giving all of their time to the onslaught. Though they welcomed it, they found it detrimental to the spiritual health of their church. This motivated the first of many restructurings, this time into four fellowship groups. Later they organized separate mission groups or task forces to bring the witness of the congregation to the city. The forms this outreach took were sometimes unusual and often enlisted many nonmembers, but they all were built about a core of committed church members. The core is "comprised of those who have had conscious experience of Christ and have moved into discipleship. For some He has come in cataclysmic ways; for some in quiet ways; but He has come, and this is what makes the difference."[37]

Three young women, sent out to search on behalf of the church, found a 175-acre farm in Maryland ("Dayspring") which was bought and converted at great cost of funds and time by the membership into a retreat center. This was used by them and other religious groups on weekends and as a permanent "Renewal Center" for alcoholics with a professional staff. Hundreds of hours of voluntary secretarial work went into the Washington Church Federation. Employment services, tutoring, and rehabilitation training reached slum dwellers. The most publicized enterprise was the Potter's House (begun in 1960), a coffeehouse on a busy city street which soon became a center for artists, poets, folk singers, harried businessmen, students, and casual visitors. It was the prototype of many across the nation in setting forth a new style of evangelism.[38] The Potter's House spun off a craft shop and school, a press and, more recently, a congregation. Each Sun-

[36] Marshall, *loc. cit.*
[37] O'Connor, *op. cit.*, p. 126.
[38] John D. Perry, *The Coffee House Ministry* (Richmond, Va.: John Knox Press, 1966), p. 19, gives credit to the Church of the Saviour and the book by Elizabeth O'Connor for the beginning of the "coffeehouse epidemic."

day an informal service in the coffeehouse attracts some who would never visit a usual church. Leadership is emphatically by laymen, reflecting one of the emphases of Cosby. One of these leaders is James W. Rouse, building broker, who is the moving force behind the planned city of Columbia, Maryland. With the cooperation of the National Council of Churches, Columbia will be the site of "a pilot area for the exploration of the best new forms of ecumenical ministry that can be cooperatively planned" with shared building facilities ("church core") and a team ministry across denominational lines.

Despite the apparent success of the Church of the Saviour, Gordon Cosby has recently called for even more radical restructuring of church life. This derives from his conviction that church institutions as they are now known are incapable of thoroughgoing renewal. What forms the new church will take is not clear to him, but in any case they would have more likeness to the isolated pockets of early Christianity than to the proud establishments of Christendom.[39] Using an image popular among medieval dissenters and the Hutterites, Cosby had earlier portrayed the marks of the Christian whatever the institutional form of the church might be:

> These Christians are a people who will throw themselves into the breach between the peace and healing of God and the loneliness, anguish, and terror of the world's lost. They stand as a bridge between man and God, willing, even eager, to become ground grain, broken bread, crushed grapes, poured-out wine. They are willing to be fed upon by the earth's hungry until those hungry ones can feed directly upon Jesus. The world has always needed such people, and it has survived because, here and there, there have been a few such people.[40]

EAST HARLEM PROTESTANT PARISH

There are thousands of miles between the Italian Alps and the tenements of East Harlem in New York, but a curious link binds them. On 106th Street there is the Romanesque-style Church of the Ascension, originally built in the first years of this century to serve immigrant Waldensians, descendants of the persecuted

[39] Gordon Cosby, "Not Renewal, But Reformation," in Stephen C. Rose, ed., Who's Killing the Church? (Chicago: Renewal Magazine, 1966), pp. 53–58; these views are discussed in Rose, Grass Roots Church, pp. 17–28.
[40] O'Connor, op. cit., p. 158.

medieval sectarians who took refuge in the Italian Alps. Today the edifice is used by the East Harlem Protestant Parish, an inner-city ministry which has attracted the world's attention since its beginnings in 1948. The link is not merely accidental, for the style of life developed by the Parish is reminiscent of that of the ancient dissenters.[41]

The "point of primary enactment" of worship for the East Harlem parish is the agape or love feast held on Maundy Thursday preceding Easter. Pews at the front of the Church of the Ascension are removed and long tables set up. In the early evening hours the interracial congregation gathers for a meal of fellowship.[42] They partake of long loaves of Italian bread and fish. (The Waldenses observed a meal in much the same way, using the same kind of foods.)[43] As the Parish service proceeds, members of the congregation come in groups of eight to the front of the church, where the minister kneels and cleans their shoes with the ends of his stole in a symbolic re-enactment of Jesus' washing the feet of his disciples at the Last Supper. This foot-washing service, preserved by Roman Catholicism and Orthodoxy as a ceremonial act of bishops and hierarchs, remains part of the communion service for Mennonites and Brethren, and was formerly practiced by the Moravian Brethren.

A look at the way the East Harlem Protestant Parish began helps to explain the parallels. The initiator of the parish was Don Benedict (b. 1918).[44] As a college student Benedict had been

[41] The basic study of the East Harlem Protestant Parish is by Bruce Kenrick, *Come Out the Wilderness* (New York: Harper & Brothers, 1962). Two books by a co-founder are based on the parish experience: George W. Webber, *God's Colony in Man's World* (New York: Abingdon Press, 1960) and *The Congregation in Mission* (New York: Abingdon Press, 1964). Some of the most detailed reporting is found in the *Union Seminary Quarterly Review* from 1948 to date.

[42] This is described in detail by George W. Webber, "Worship in East Harlem," *Union Seminary Quarterly Review*, XVII (1961), 143–151 and in his *Congregation in Mission*, pp. 98–100.

[43] E. Lippelt, "Das Geheimnis des Naumburger Meisters," *Zeitschrift für deutsche Geistesgeschichte*, IV (1938), 23ff; K. Goldammer, "Der Naumburger Meister und die Häretiker," *Zeitschrift für Kirchengeschichte*, LXIV (1952/1953), 97–102.

[44] Donald L. Benedict, "Rebel With a Cause" (unpub. autobiography), quoted in Raymond L. Owens, "An Analytic History of the Sectarian Orientation of the Ministry of the West Side Christian Parish" (unpub. master's dissertation, University of Chicago, 1962), pp. 7–26. See also "Commandos in the City," *Time* (February 21, 1964), 56.

attracted to the Social Gospel, and immersed himself in the study of Marxism and pacifism. At Union Theological Seminary he joined a group concerned with relevant Christianity. Intense discussions led to the purchase of a house in a Newark, New Jersey, slum. There they began a cooperative and organized what they called the "First Century Church." They determined to pattern their lives upon the early Christians. When the United States entered the Second World War, Benedict and seven other Union students refused to register for the draft. For this act of civil disobedience they were sentenced to federal prison. Between prison terms, they created a "group ministry" in Detroit in connection with the Central Methodist Church pastored by Henry Hitt Crane, an outspoken pacifist churchman.

During Benedict's third prison term, the combination of a Trotskyite cellmate and Reinhold Niebuhr's writings convinced him that the liberal pacifism he had followed was untenable. War's end found him on Iwo Jima as a sergeant in the army. Upon returning to Union Seminary in 1947, he was even more convinced than he had once been, as he studied the city, that the organized church was failing to meet the needs of the workers, the disinherited of the city ghettos. When he engaged in detailed sociological survey, he discovered that the mainline Protestant churches were completely absent in the areas of high population density. Another Union student, George W. Webber, had the same concern. Together they worked out a proposal for an urban mission. This required, they said, careful study, a group ministry, store-front churches, and deep involvement in the social and intellectual life of the neighborhood. They pointed out that the only Protestant groups active in the inner city to meet with any response from the Negro and Puerto Rican populations were the sects in their store-fronts: "The success of the sects among these people only makes us feel more strongly the urgency of the need for a new approach. . . ." What was needed was "a church that will identify itself with these people and their frustrating problems of city slum living, that will be actively concerned with housing and playgrounds and conditions for work."[45]

In 1948 they received initial funds from several church agen-

[45] D. Benedict and G. W. Webber, "Proposal for a Store Front Larger Parish System," *Union Seminary Quarterly Review*, III (1948), 17–20; Owens, *op. cit.*, pp. 16–17.

cies; later the project was supported by eight denominations and other sources. Benedict and Webber with their wives were joined by Archie Hargraves (b. 1916), a Negro and former journalist and Union student, and his wife. They began the East Harlem Protestant Parish by setting up a card table on the sidewalk and enrolling ghetto children for summer Bible schools, which met in local store-front congregations. They found an empty store on East 100th Street, formerly a butcher shop, which they converted by their own labor into a small chapel. The first Sunday of announced services they were hard put to accommodate the children who packed the twenty-by-twenty room for Sunday school, but waited in vain for adults to come to the church service. The sole worshipper turned out to be an elderly Puerto Rican woman, who, however, brought them a crucifix which was immediately mounted on the brightly colored wall of the chapel.

To break down the suspicion of the neighborhood, the group ministry cleared vacant lots for playgrounds, sponsored outdoor movies, and worked to clean up the streets. Since the people still did not come to them, they went to the people. They systematically called on suspicious ghetto dwellers and told them of their work. If there was any interest, they organized small meetings in the apartments, beginning with light refreshments, scripture reading and prayer, and concluding by focusing on concrete problems —landlord trouble, lack of heating, loss of employment, illness. These meetings were called agape meals, and the food was considered to be a modern equivalent of communion elements.[46] The vigorous action taken by the parish ministry to alleviate individual problems slowly convinced some of the Harlem residents of the genuineness of their interest. Increasingly, some were willing to become involved in the church life. They were asked to accept the following disciplines for membership:

1. To accept Christ as Lord and Saviour;

[46] Owens credits Hargraves with this innovation; *ibid.*, p. 29. See also George E. Todd, "Worship in an Urban Parish," *Union Seminary Quarterly Review*, XIII (1958), 43–45: "Holy Communion was often celebrated at these meetings in the tenement apartments. Perhaps somewhat romantically we called these meetings Agape meal groups. They recalled to us, and we wanted them to recapture, something of the spirit of the *love feasts* described in the New Testament, at which Christians gathered for a common meal to remember their Lord and to pray for His return among them in power" (p. 45).

2. To meet regularly for counsel with a minister;
3. To be active in a non-church community organization;
4. To plan church action each month for community goals;
5. To pray and read the Bible daily;
6. To "walk together in love for God and for our neighbors."[47]

The group ministry, in a manner similar to the early Waldensian leadership, followed a more rigorous discipline in four areas of their life than the membership. First, they covenanted to maintain a devotional discipline of prayer, Bible reading, weekly communion, semiannual retreat, and visible worship centers in their homes. They undertook an economic discipline in which salaries were made dependent on need, according to size of families or special situation. The third discipline was the vocational commitment to the parish program. Work plans and projected activities were to be matters of group criticism and counsel. No one should take another position without the agreement of the group and a competent replacement. A final discipline was one which was harder for some of their sponsors to accept. This was a political discipline which pledged the ministers to engage in study of the governmental machinery that affected their district and to involvement in joint action in the political processes to improve the living conditions of their neighbors.

Both the church and secular press soon heard of the parish, particularly when the group ministry took to the streets to demonstrate against vindictive landlords or run for political office.[48] Street processionals celebrating the liturgical highpoints of the church year attracted further attention. Seminary students joined them to assist in the program. It soon became famous as the most effective effort of Protestantism to deal with the crisis of the inner cities. Appeals came to the parish to aid in developing similar projects elsewhere. The first "daughter" experiment was Oak Street in New Haven. Benedict left to organize church work in Cleveland, staying there for six years before going to Chicago as head of the Chicago City Missionary Society (recently renamed Community Renewal Society), a well-endowed agency of Congregationalist background.

Even earlier the Parish idea was introduced to Chicago in

[47] Kenrick, op. cit., p. 85.
[48] A typical report is William Harlan Hale, "Going Down This Street, Lord . . . ," Reporter (January 13, 1955), 15–18.

1951–1952, when Archie Hargraves developed a plan for a "West Side Christian Parish," modeled closely on the East Harlem pattern. In an early description of the program submitted to the Church Federation of Chicago, there is a significant comparison to primitive Christianity: "It is understood that the church or churches that are formed will not be of any denomination in creed or polity, and their nature may even be more like the churches of the first century, before there was Roman Catholicism or Protestantism. The essentials will be the people's knowledge of God and Christ and the Christian life of the people, and their Christian fellowship and work with one another."[49]

A tangible result of this expectation took form in the Church of Hope on Maxwell Street, in the slums of west-side Chicago.[50] The key figure in the small congregation was Julius Belser (b. 1929), of Church of the Brethren background. With others, he developed in 1959 a close-knit church with spiritual, economic, and political disciplines. Don Benedict called it the "closest thing to the first-century church I know."[51] College and seminary graduates lived voluntarily on the level of a welfare recipient and called alcoholics and addicts their brothers. One of their early statements said: "In this little church of eight Christians, the new life and hope in Jesus Christ becomes real. Three of our members cannot read and write but they are learning what it is. Their lives are increasingly open to one another. They speak words of admonition when they see a brother in sin. Their daily lives are involved together—this is not all confined to Sunday morning." In 1961 the Church of Hope united with the Reba Place Fellowship, an intentional community largely of Mennonite makeup, located in Evanston, Illinois.[52]

"The guiding principle behind this city slum church has been to demonstrate the meaning of Christianity in terms of people's everyday problems," announced an early release on the East Harlem work.[53] Despite changes in structure and program in both New York and Chicago, this basic orientation has persisted. The

[49] Quoted in Owens, *op. cit.*, p. 40.
[50] *Ibid.*, pp. 64–103.
[51] "Faith in the City," *Newsweek* (December 25, 1961), 69, quoted in Owens, *op. cit.*, p. 64.
[52] *Ibid.*, pp. 95–99.
[53] "East Harlem Revisited," *Union Seminary Quarterly Review*, V (May 1950), 25–29.

major difference between this movement and others existing prior to it which have also sought to make Christianity relevant is the surprising analogy in faith and practice with early forms of the Believers' Church, though independently developed in these parishes.

UNDERGROUND CHURCHES

Both the Church of the Saviour and the East Harlem Protestant Parish are expressions of renewal action within Protestantism. A kindred stirring of the waters is found within Roman Catholicism, as concentric waves of reform spread from the impact of Vatican Council II. Because some of these manifestations do not have hierarchical approval, the phrase "underground churches" has been coined for them by journalists. It is used to describe the informal gatherings of those for whom the traditional cultus is no longer fully satisfying and for whom the pace of *aggiornamento* is too slow. Daniel Callahan, a leading Catholic journalist, analyzes the movement as a sect tendency in the sense of Ernst Troeltsch's sociological typology, and foresees continuing polarization of viewpoints between conservatives and radicals. In Callahan's view, personalist theory, existential philosophy, and biblical theology all contribute to the trend:

> An outcome of this theological mix is the mushrooming of underground and extra-parochial communities, one of whose purposes is to provide models of what the whole church of the future might be. And they are providing some very exciting models, besides providing a large number of people an escape valve for their pent-up reform zeal. The vital thing to note, however, is that the model they tend to provide is closer to that of sect than of church. . . . They are, if you will, sects within the church, but intent on remaining in the Church in order to provide patterns for the future.[54]

This is precisely the hope of one of these groups, Emmaus House (founded in 1966), an experimental house-church along first-century lines. The House's coordinator, Father David Kirk, explains that "the church is moving toward a honeycomb of creative ecumenical communities. We're trying to be both a symbol of

[54] Daniel Callahan, "Church and Sect: Should the Church Be Inclusive or Exclusive?" *Commonweal* (November 3, 1967), 140–143.

what the church will be and a catalyst in making it happen."[55] Six are on the staff—three priests, two laywomen, and a Protestant layman—and currently twenty-five members meet regularly in the narrow brownstone on 116th Street in East Harlem. They plan to carry on cooperative work with the East Harlem Parish in an "Ecumenical Action Ministry." Their social action, tutoring, publishing, lectures, and job placement services are balanced by an intense liturgical life which includes contemporary songs at Sunday Mass and self-composed canons. More than fifteen hundred visitors, priests and nuns, black-power militants, and the curious, indicate the drawing power of Emmaus House despite its uncertain future because of official churchly displeasure.

In Atlanta, the Community of Christ our Brother has diocesan approval as a "parish without bounds." This venture, begun in February .1967, is evidence of another approach being tried in several cities. A group of forty (ten of whom are Protestant) meet twice a week. On Tuesday they gather in homes to "pray, study, plan, and enjoy the friendship of one another and guests." On Sunday evening they celebrate the Eucharist, although kept from intercommunion by canon law. They have decided against building their own meeting place, preferring to use their resources for meeting human needs directly. Important for them is their participation in the life of the city through voluntary help and investigation. Although the experiment is too new to be carefully evaluated, the administrator says: "I have been a priest for fourteen years, but never before have I personally experienced such a desire for Christian involvement with people; never before have I understood the meaning of the close bond between priests and laymen called for by Vatican II. Never before have I watched human potential budding and blossoming in people as I have in the gatherings of the Community of Christ our Brother."[56]

In Chicago a like group meets. It calls itself "Vatican $2\frac{1}{2}$" to express its disappointment with the slowness of ecclesiastical reform. New Jersey has its "Christian Layman's Experimental Organization," an interfaith community which comes together for prayer, study, and informal Eucharists despite church disap-

---

[55] "A Kind of Mecca," *Newsweek* (November 27, 1967), 92–93.
[56] Donald Foust, "Parish Without Bounds," *Commonweal* (August 25, 1967), 514–515.

proval.[57] Whatever the future of these groups may be, in many ways they are recapitulating the same concerns and practices which emerged in previous centuries as the Believers' Church.

Having concluded a survey of these manifestations of church renewal since the late twelfth century, it is possible to turn to a topical discussion of those beliefs which characterized these Christians.

[57] "The Underground Church," *Time* (September 29, 1967), 53.

PART THREE

The Character of Believers' Churches

AFTER completing an overview of representative Believers' Churches, it is necessary to turn to a discussion of their characteristics. In doing so, attention will be directed to those emphases which distinguish them from other Christian communions, rather than to those beliefs which they hold in common. With minor exceptions, these movements were not heretical in the technical sense of espousing doctrines formally condemned by Classical Protestantism nor did they denounce elements of the faith usually considered essential. They were generally noncreedal in posture, but they did not so much reject the teachings contained in the ancient creeds as resist the demand for rigid adherence to them. This was for two reasons: first, they believed that creedalism had become a substitute for living faith; and secondly, they wished to remain open for new insight from the scriptures.

The basic orthodoxy of these churches was sometimes conceded by their opponents. After a debate in 1532 between state-churchmen and Anabaptists at Zofingen near Zürich, the Reformed theologians reported: "We are of one mind in the leading articles of the faith." Zwingli had earlier agreed that there was consensus on all doctrines which affected the "inner man" while differences remained on such problems as whether a Christian could be a magistrate. Wolfgang Capito, the Strasbourg reformer, acknowledged that "as concerns the principal articles and vital points of faith" of the Anabaptists "they do not err at all."[1] Anabaptist writings often followed the form of the Apostolic Creed, as did Peter Riedemann's *Rechenschaft*. When the Baptists drafted their confessions of faith in the seventeenth century, they could use with no difficulty major portions of the Westminster

[1] Quoted in John C. Wenger, *Even Unto Death* (Richmond, Va.: John Knox Press, 1961), p. 57.

(Presbyterian) and the Savoy (Congregational) Confessions. Even the Quakers, according to modern research, were more evangelical than has often been held.[2] Members of the Church of the Brethren testified that they could conscientiously affirm all but three theses of the Heidelberg Catechism. Although labeled doctrinally deviant by the institutional churches, the Believers' Churches were at pains to distance themselves from those religious and philosophical tendencies which departed from the base of scriptural revelation.

The intent of this section, then, is to focus on those aspects of the life and thought of the Believers' Churches which were and are constitutive. These include both what the Quakers have called "concerns"—a locus of persistent and organized effort—and basic principles around which the movements formed. It is these aspects which allow them to be discerned as distinct in some way from other Christian bodies. While not every group will demonstrate every one of these characteristics, there is predominant congruence with this profile. Direct quotations coming from their several histories will help to sharpen the conceptual statements.

---

[2] See the discussion in D. Elton Trueblood, *The People Called Quakers* (New York: Harper & Row, 1966), pp. 63–84.

· VIII ·

Discipleship and Apostolicity

NOTHING has called attention recently to the demands of Christian obedience as has Dietrich Bonhoeffer's book *The Cost of Discipleship*, sealed as it was by his martyrdom in 1945 at the hands of the SS troopers. Sophisticated neo-orthodox ratiocinations about opting for lesser evils were abruptly shattered by this unequivocating call to discipleship. Perhaps the shift in the process of translation from the stark one-word *Nachfolge* of the German original to the calculation implicit in the four-word English title symbolizes contemporary reluctance to respond simply and directly to the call.

Bonhoeffer's forceful declarations allowed no misunderstanding: "Christianity without the living Christ is inevitably Christianity without discipleship, and Christianity without discipleship is always Christianity without Christ." "Cheap grace is grace without discipleship, grace without the cross, grace without Jesus Christ, living and incarnate." "Faith is only real when there is obedience, never without it, and faith only becomes faith in the act of obedience."[1] Seen in the setting from which they originated, the church struggle of the Confessing Church in the Third Reich, these strike home with almost physical impact, as did his insistence that any Christian in Germany remaining at that time outside of the Confessing Church was thereby placing himself outside the realm of salvation. These theses have been taken up, almost too glibly, by Anglo-Saxons, until discipleship, mission, and costly grace threaten to become jargon. Current ecumenical discussions

---

[1] See the discussions in John D. Godsey, *The Theology of Dietrich Bonhoeffer* (Philadelphia: Westminster Press, 1960), pp. 151–172, and John A. Phillips, *Christ for Us in the Theology of Dietrich Bonhoeffer* (New York: Harper & Row, 1967), pp. 95–105. The English edition of *Nachfolge* is R. H. Fuller, trans., *The Cost of Discipleship* (London: S.C.M. Press, 1948).

are clearly influenced in their posing of questions and vocabulary by Bonhoeffer's thinking.

These themes had of course been sounded before in Christian history. Augustine observed in his *Confessions* that "he is thy best servant who does not look to hear from thee what he himself wills, but who wills rather what he hears from thee." The late-medieval writer of the *Imitation of Christ* explained: "Whoever desires to understand and take delight in the words of Christ, must strive to conform his whole life to Him." A Catholic heritage of this type, however, was no recommendation for Bonhoeffer's Lutheran colleagues, who saw in his teachings an "enthusiastic" tendency. When he established his semimonastic *Brüderhaus* in the illegal Finkenwalde seminary, these fears seemed to be confirmed.[2]

Discipleship

A more helpful way to interpret Bonhoeffer's thought is to put it into the pattern of the Believers' Church. His was a reiteration of a central concern reaching from Peter Waldo's determination to "follow nakedly a naked Jesus" to the present day. It is not "Are You Running with Me, Jesus?" but "Am I Following You, Jesus?" Hans Denck, an influential if marginal Anabaptist, put it concisely in his pronouncement: "No one can truly know Jesus unless he follows Him in his life."

Major interpreters of the Anabaptists place discipleship at the very core. Harold S. Bender (1897–1962), dean both of Mennonite institutions and Anabaptist historiography, wrote the classic portrayal in his often reprinted article "The Anabaptist Vision." In it he emphasized that "first and fundamental . . . was the conception of the essence of Christianity as discipleship. It was a concept which meant the transformation of the entire way of life of the individual believer and of society so that it should be fashioned after the teaching and example of Christ." To buttress this judgment, Bender cited the work of three European scholars, Johannes Kühn, Alfred Hegler, and Paul Wernle.[3] Another au-

---

[2] Albert C. Outler, trans. and ed., *Augustine: Confessions and Enchiridion* (Philadelphia: Westminster, 1955), p. 224; Thomas à Kempis, *Imitation of Christ*, Book I, chapter 1; Eberhard Bethge, *Dietrich Bonhoeffer* (Munich: Chr. Kaiser Verlag, 1967), pp. 587–602.

[3] Harold S. Bender, "The Anabaptist Vision," *Church History*, XIII (1944), 3–24; *Mennonite Quarterly Review*, XVIII (1944), 67–88; Guy S.

thority, Robert Friedmann, places great weight on this interpretation, indicating that the main issue between Anabaptists and Classical Protestantism was whether such a life of discipleship could in fact be realized, or whether it was not rather an ideal set forth to demonstrate to man his human frailty by his very inability to attain it.[4] The latest study of Lutheran-Anabaptist relationships concluded that "if Lutheranism has as its heart the search for a merciful God in view of the overwhelming burden of human sin which alienated man from God, Anabaptism developed around the central idea of a righteous walk with the Lord after the experience of repentance and rebirth."[5]

The same orientation is evident in other expressions of the Believers' Churches. When the Schwarzenau Brethren issued their appeal to the Palatine Pietists to join them in baptism they exclaimed: "Dear brethren! What is then better than being obedient and not despising the commandments of the Lord Jesus Christ, the King of all Glory!"[6] John Wesley said of the conditions of membership he required: " 'Is a man a believer in Jesus Christ, and is his life suitable to his profession?' are not only the *main* but the *sole* inquiries I make in order to his admission into our Society."[7] Kierkegaard (called by Forsyth "the melancholy Dane in whom Hamlet was mastered by Christ") made the same point in a different way: "For long the tactics have been: use every means to move as many as you can—to move everybody if possible—to enter Christianity. My tactics have been with God's help to use every means to keep it clear what the demand of Christianity really is—if not one entered it." A recent study makes the case that the Dane can best be understood by placing him within the context of Protestant radicalism.[8]

Hershberger, ed., *Recovery of the Anabaptist Vision* (Scottdale, Pa.: Herald Press, 1957), pp. 29–54, slightly revised version; J. C. Wenger, *The Mennonite Church in America* (Scottdale, Pa.: Herald Press, 1966), pp. 315–331.

[4] Robert Friedmann, "Recent Interpretations of Anabaptism," *Church History*, XXIV (1955), 132–151.

[5] John S. Oyer, *Lutheran Reformers Against the Anabaptists* (The Hague: Martinus Nijhoff, 1964), p. 212.

[6] Donald F. Durnbaugh, ed., *European Origins of the Brethren* (Elgin, Ill.: Brethren Press, 1958), p. 117.

[7] Albert C. Outler, ed., *John Wesley* (New York: Oxford University Press, 1964), p. 78.

[8] Quoted in Peter Taylor Forsyth, *The Work of Christ* (London: Independent Press, 1910), p. xxxii. See Vernard Eller, *Kierkegaard and Radical*

The Quaker leader T. Canby Jones confirms the centrality of discipleship in his definition: "A believing people hears the voice of its living Lord, obeys him in all things and witnesses unapologetically to his power in every phase of the life of the world." Discipleship comes, he states, as the human response to God's gracious covenant: "I will walk among you, and will be your God, and you shall be my people . . . I have broken the bars of your yoke and made you walk erect" (Leviticus 26: 11–13). For Jones, the "only conceivable response to such love is obedience, total obedience, holy obedience, grateful obedience. Out of gratitude arises the will to obey and keep his statutes, commandments, and ordinances."[9]

The Fall of The Church

Corollary to the insistence on the fundamental nature of discipleship for the Believers' Churches is their conviction that this quality was lacking within Christendom. Lip-service to the faith rather than life-service to Jesus Christ seemed common. The very preoccupation with the call to discipleship is evidence that many of their fellows preferred a different walk. Therefore, they often made the assessment that Christianity had lost the "first love," the first zeal of the apostles. The church, especially as it took papal form, became for some the Anti-Christ. Puritans used the imagery of the book of Revelation to tell of the fate of the true church, tying this in with the view that it was the Waldenses in their mountain valleys who preserved the connection with the early Christians: "This is the Desert [sic] whither the Woman fled when she was persecuted by the Dragon with seven heads and ten horns. . . . That here it was that the Church fled, and where she made her Flocks to rest at noon, those hot and scorching seasons of the ninth and tenth centuries."[10]

Discipleship: a New Perspective (Princeton, N.J.: Princeton University Press, 1968).

[9] T. Canby Jones, "A Believing People: Contemporary Relevance" (unpub. typescript, Conference on the Concept of the Believers' Church, 1967), pp. 7, 11; a shortened version of the paper is "A Believing People Today," *Mennonite Life*, XXII (October 1967), 177, 188–193.

[10] Samuel Moreland, *History of the Evangelical Churches of the Valleys of Piedmont* (London, 1658), quoted in George H. Williams, *Wilderness and Paradise in Christian Thought* (New York: Harper & Row, 1962), p. 63.

Luther, Zwingli, and Calvin also maintained that a fall had occurred about this time. When Gregory VII and, later, Boniface
VIII made their sweeping claims to temporal power, thus dragging
the church into the political arena, the fall took place. This enabled them to consider themselves the continuators of the true
church and the papal church an innovator. This point of view
found its massive documentation in the so-called Magdeburg Centuries, written by Matthias Flacius Illyricus (1520–1575). The
multivolumed ecclesiastical history was designed to prove that
Lutheranism was directly connected with the first Christians.
Protestant reformers saw themselves as proponents of true Christianity over against the "papists" on the one side and the "sectarians" on the other.[11]

To illustrate the issue, the Christian church in the sixteenth
century may be compared to a tree. There were several opinions
as to what should be done with it. The Romanists advocated
keeping·the tree just as it had grown, even though some of the
branches were withered and some rotten. The tree was sacred
and should not be touched. Reform-minded Catholic humanists,
of whom Erasmus would be the best example, wanted the tree
pruned of dead wood, so that it might bear better fruit. Major tree
surgery was called for, said the Protestant Reformers. The only
way to save the tree was to cut off whole limbs in order to get
back to the healthy trunk. Finally, there were the Radical Reformers who contended that the entire plant above ground was sick.
The only solution was to cut back to the healthy roots and let new
life spring up from them.

There is a growing consensus that the term Radical Reformation is the most appropriate designation for the dissenters of the
Reformation period, following the suggestion of George H. Williams. The common desire of these men was to go back to the
beginning. They were "agreed in cutting back to that root and in
freeing church and creed of what they regarded as the suffocating
growth of ecclesiastical tradition and magisterial prerogative."[12]
It is an oversimplification, but tends toward the truth to say that

[11] The best discussion on the fall of the church is Franklin H. Littell, *The
Anabaptist View of the Church*, second rev. ed. (Boston: Starr King, 1958),
pp. 46–78. On Flacius, see Walter Nigg, *Die Kirchengeschichtsschreibung*
(Munich: C. H. Beck, 1934), pp. 48–65.

[12] George H. Williams, ed., *Spiritual and Anabaptist Writers* (Philadelphia:
Westminster Press, 1957), p. 22.

whereas the "mainline" Protestants were preoccupied by the fall of man and remained hopeful for a purified church, the Radical Reformers had hope even for fallen man and were convinced of the fall of the institutional church. Where the latter differed among themselves concerned the possibility of restoring a true church. The Spiritualists said that it was impossible; the evangelical Anabaptists said that it not only was possible, but was imperative if they were to be faithful to Christ.

It may be that the Radical Reformers were influenced by humanism in speaking of the church's fall. Renaissance men were fond of speaking of the golden period of Greece and Rome, followed by the dank, dark, and dismal Middle Ages. Enlightenment could come, they believed, by recovering the virtue of the past. The equivalent in the religious sphere was to look to the early church as normative. Whereas the secular humanists worked to recover and publish classical literature, Christian humanists like Erasmus sought to make the sources of the faith—the scriptures and the writings of the fathers—available in undistorted format. Zwingli was an ardent friend and follower of Erasmus, and the Swiss Brethren were Zwingli's followers. However, those who have studied the relationship of Anabaptism and humanism are cautious about drawing the lines of influence too directly. "While doubtless the Zürich Anabaptists such as Grebel were familiar with the classical ideal, the prevalence of religious primitivism in Anabaptism is due more to the fact that Christianity is a historical religion with a sacred book in which all reforms seek their inspiration and confirmation" (Littell).[18]

For most of the Radical Reformers, the fall in the church came in the fourth century when Christianity became first one of the tolerated faiths and later the only tolerated faith. To their way of thinking, when Emperor Constantine began to favor Christianity, and was himself baptized shortly before his death, the church started on a downward path. Unlike the traditional Christian view which has, since Eusebius, seen Constantine's conversion as the beginning of the glorious period of Christian influence and dominance, the Anabaptists saw this as a tragedy. They have not been alone in this judgment. Gottfried Arnold's important church history took this line of interpretation. The "Gloomy Dean" Inge is

---

[18] Littell, *op. cit.*, pp. 54–55.

quoted as saying that after Constantine there was little in church history which was not dark. The writer of a book on the English Free Churches made the point very clearly: "When the Church was persecuted by the Empire she was pure in motive and morals: but under the patronage of Constantine it became the fashion for the Roman nobility and obsequious pagans to enter the Church: and pagans they remained within her membership."[14]

John Wesley felt very strongly that the fall occurred with Constantine, although signs of decay had become known previously. In his sermon "The Mastery of Iniquity," he wrote:

> . . . the grand blow which was struck at the very root of that humble, gentle, patient love . . . was struck in the fourth century by Constantine the Great, when he called himself a Christian, and poured in a flood of riches, honours, and power, upon the Christians; more especially upon the clergy. . . . Just so, when the fear of persecution was removed, and wealth and honour attended the Christian profession, the Christians did not gradually sink, but rushed headlong into all manner of vices. . . . Then not the golden, but the iron age of the church commenced. . . . And this is the event which most Christian expositors mention with such triumph! . . . Rather say it was the Coming of Satan, and all his legions from the bottomless pit; seeing from that very time he hath set up his throne over the face of the whole earth, and reigned over the Christian, as well as the pagan world, with hardly any control!

To Wesley's way of thinking, the same sway of iniquity held forth in the supposedly reformed Christian countries of his own day, in England, Germany, Sweden, and the rest.[15]

Quakers were just as outspoken in condemning Christianity as fallen and corrupt. To George Fox, since the days of the apostles "false churches appeared as papists and protestants, [with] no difference in nature."[16] The Plymouth Brethren and the Disciples were agreed that a decline in the health of the church had taken place, and they were active in diagnosing both the causes of the ailment and the needed cures. Alexander Campbell was notorious for his attacks upon organized religion, and also upon the clergy:

[14] Henry Townsend, *The Claims of the Free Churches* (London, 1949), p. 45, quoted in Littell, *op. cit.*, p. 56.

[15] John Emory, ed., *The Works of the Rev. John Wesley* (New York: Carlton Lanahan, [n.d.]), II: 63–64.

[16] Quoted in Lewis Benson, *Catholic Quakerism* (Gloucester, U.K.: the author, 1966), p. 11.

"Money, I think, may be considered not merely as the bond of union of popular establishments, but it is really the rock on which the popular churches are built."[17] An influential book among the peace churches in recent times was that of the Dutch pacifist C. J. Heering called *The Fall of Christianity*, which related the loss of the peace witness of the early church to the Constantinian alliance of church and state.

In post-World War II Germany, the theme of "Constantinianism" has been hotly debated, since the East German churchman Günter Jacob, general superintendent of Cottbus, announced at a synod of the Evangelical Church:

> Aware spirits characterize the situation of Christianity in contemporary Europe by the fact that the end of the Constantinian epoch has arrived. The Constantinian fusion marked the departure from this genuine way of the Church of Jesus Christ, a way in the world which according to the view of the New Testament will be a way of suffering before the hostility and opposition of the world. With the end of illusions about the Constantinian epoch and a return to the early Christian witness we no longer have the right to claim privileges and a monopoly for support of the Gospel from the State.[18]

It is hardly necessary to make the point that most of the flood of books on renewal in North America and western Europe in the past ten years have begun by describing the "fall" that has taken place within the institutional church (with some never getting past their devastating sociological analyses). To be true, many of these writers would not accept the same periodization of the fall as the Believers' Churches, but the effect of their critique is similar and some specifically contrast the present situation with the early church.

Restitution

In 1832 Pope Gregory XVI issued an encyclical condemning the French leader Lamennais who was calling for the Roman Catholic Church to drop its dependence upon the state and to chart a new course. At the heart of the papal decree was this statement:

[17] David E. Harrell, Jr., *Quest For a Christian America* (Nashville, Tenn.: Disciples of Christ Historical Society, 1966), p. 66.
[18] Quoted in Littell, *op. cit.*, pp. 56–57.

As it is invariable, to use the words of the Fathers of Trent, that the Church "has been instructed by Jesus Christ and his apostles and that it is informed by the Holy Spirit which constantly instills every truth" it is completely absurd and eminently insulting for anyone to hold that a "restoration" or "regeneration" is necessary to preserve and increase the Church; as if it could be judged open to failure or to ignorance or to other drawbacks of this nature.[19]

While not always phrased in so blunt a manner, here is displayed the essential posture of the church type. Security for mankind is considered to be bound up with an infallible institution resting on the unbroken succession of authority. The symbol for this view is the doctrine of apostolic succession.

Standing in opposition to this is the Protestant principle of perpetual reformation. The church is human as well as divine, and therefore needs constant renewal. It not only can err, but often has. In the place of apostolic succession is the concept of apostolicity—living in the manner and the virtue of the first followers of Jesus Christ. In some ways the difference reflects the long-standing controversy over authority for the church—should it be scripture or tradition?

John Henry Cardinal Newman put the Catholic position in these words: "It is sometime said that the stream is clearest near the spring. Whatever use may be fairly made of this image, it does not apply to the history of a philosophy or a belief, which, on the contrary, is more equable, and purer, and stronger when its bed has become deeper, and broad, and full." The Quaker Rufus Jones phrased the other view this way: "Fortunately we can make our way back even yet to the Headquarters of the mighty stream and feel, if only dimly, the purity, the splendour, the beauty, the mystery and the power of the River of Life as it bursts forth from the eternal depths. But when we come down to the lowlands, where it now runs in its wide, though shallower bed, we find merged in one stream the indivisible waters from almost every land and people of the earth."[20]

It is clear that for the Believers' Churches it is the latter expression which is true. Though holding fast to both the Word and the

---

[19] Peter N. Stearns, *Priest and Revolutionary* (New York: Harper & Row, 1967), p. 189.

[20] Quoted in Franklin H. Littell, "The Anabaptist Concept of the Church," in Hershberger, *op. cit.*, p. 127; Rufus Jones, *The Church's Debt to Heretics* (London: J. Clarke, 1925), pp. 22–23.

Spirit, they were quite prepared to jettison tradition. As wayfaring pilgrims and citizens of heaven, they wished to cast off the impeding baggage of custom and cultus. A leading interpreter of the free churches, Franklin H. Littell, makes restitution of the beliefs and practices of the early church *the* key to the "Anabaptist View of the Church." He notes approvingly the characterization of the Anabaptists by the noted Heidelberg church historian, Walther Köhler, who wrote: "They wished to restore the Early Church at Jerusalem as a community of saints sharply separated from the world."[21] Even before the sixteenth century, the medieval dissenters appealed to the age of the apostles and the martyrs as the basis for their reform activity. The Unity of Czech Brethren, in its early period under the guidance of Peter Chelčický, followed a philosophy of a "return to the spirit of primitive Christianity."[22]

In the Radical Reformation all branches were united in believing in the fall of the Church but were of different minds on the desirability of the restoration or restitution of the apostolic church. Sebastian Franck was eloquent on the fall, but opposed any new forms as equally corrupt. Spiritualists like Franck shared the view of Luther and Zwingli that the true church was invisible. They differed on the conclusions to be drawn from it. The Reformers decided that since form and polity were inconsequential, the state might as well be allowed to exert its authority, at least in the emergency situation. The Spiritualists opposed organization per se. Anabaptists were in opposition to both, telling the Reformers that the state should not meddle with the church, and telling the Spiritualists that there must be a visible church. Their view found expression in the formative period (1524) in a letter from the Swiss Brethren to Thomas Müntzer: "Go forward with the Word and establish a Christian church with the help of Christ and his rule. . . . Use determination and common prayer and decision according to faith and love, without command or compulsion. Thy God will help thee and thy little sheep to all sincerity. . . ."[23]

Quakers quite explicitly saw themselves as the heirs of the early church. "Primitive Christianity Revived" was the phrase used by William Penn. Isaac Penington asserted that "Quakers are not

---

[21] Littell, "Concept," p. 120.
[22] Otokar Odlozilik, "Two Reformation Leaders of the Unitas Fratrum," *Church History*, IX (1940), 255.
[23] Williams, *Writers*, p. 79.

persons who have shot up out of the old root into another appearance, as one sect hath done out of another . . . but the ground hath been shaken . . . in us; and the old root of Jesse hath been made manifest in us."[24] Quakerism was but a "New Nickname for old Christianity." There was common agreement in Puritan England that appeal to the first Christians was appropriate. Richard Hooker, the influential Anglican theologian, granted the truth of this attitude "for it is out of doubt that the first state of things was best, that in the prime of Christian Religion Faith was soundest, the Scriptures of God were then best understood by all men, all parts of godliness did then most abound." However, the reasonable divine could not bring himself to believe that this correct principle should be taken too strictly:

> It is not, I am right sure, their meaning that we should now assemble our people to serve God in close and secret meetings; or that common brooks or rivers should be used for places of Baptism; or that the Eucharist should be ministered after meat; or that all kind of standing provision for the Ministry should be utterly taken away, and their estate made again dependent upon the voluntary devotion of men. In these things they easily perceive how unfit that were for the present, which was for the first age convenient enough.[25]

What Hooker was not able to conceive was in fact the platform of many of the Believers' Churches, "convenient" or not. Baptists, Brethren, and Disciples proceeded to arrange their church life on just this basis.

It has recently been demonstrated that a powerful motivation for John Wesley's labors was the desire to restore the forms and power of early Christianity. His university training came at the time of a patristic revival. Oxford tutors and professors were eager to go beyond protestantism and catholicism, back to the beginnings of the church. In Wesley's reading, there is abundant evidence of his acquaintance with the work of men such as William Cave whose studies on the early church were used by Gottfried Arnold. Wesley took a copy of the latter's book, the *True Portrayal of the First Christians* (1696), along to Georgia. Another important influence upon him was Anthony Horneck, the founder

[24] Benson, *op. cit.*, p. 9.
[25] Richard Hooker, *The Laws of Ecclesiastical Polity* (1594–1597), quoted in H. E. Fosdick, *Great Voices of the Reformation* (New York: Modern Library, 1954), pp. 348, 350.

of the English society idea. Horneck's book *The Happy Ascetic* held up as a model the life of the early Christians.[26]

The Church of the Brethren clearly had the belief that the early church was normative. In an early account of their formation, the writer described how "they felt powerfully drawn to seek again the footsteps of the first Christians." The group asked their leader, Mack, to baptize them "upon their faith after the example of the first and best Christians."[27] The foundation of the Plymouth Brethren and the Campbell movement upon the principle of restitution has already been described. Thomas Campbell called for his followers to "conform to the model and adopt the practice of the primitive church, expressly exhibited in the New Testament."[28] More recently, books on church renewal show the same tendency, as witnessed by such a title as *A Tent-Making Ministry* by a World Council of Churches agency, suggesting St. Paul as a pattern. Don Benedict's "First-Century Church" in New Jersey set out to live as nearly as possible according to the manner of the church portrayed in the fourth chapter of Acts, and provided a partial model for the East Harlem Protestant Parish.

Church Discipline

To speak of the restoration of a New Testament Church was tantamount to speaking of a disciplined community. Discipleship itself, by definition, called for discipline. Members of the Believers' Churches would have had no understanding for a recent statement on church membership issued by the United Church of Christ of Canada. Here is reference to two concepts of churches, one "broad and inclusive" such as the churches of Europe where citizenship and church membership are virtually synonymous, the other "narrow and exclusive" which demands a personal decision to accept Christ as Lord as a prerequisite for belonging. The statement sets forth the position of the United Church; it "stands at neither of these extremes but like most of the larger Protestant

[26] Martin Schmidt, *John Wesley: a Theological Biography* (London: Epworth, 1962), I: 132, 211, 222; John Van Kirk, "Re-Thinking John Wesley's Contribution: the Early Phase of His Churchmanship" (unpub. B.D. dissertation, Chicago Theological Seminary, 1964).
[27] Durnbaugh, *op. cit.*, pp. 120–122.
[28] "Declaration and Address," in H. S. Smith, *et al.*, *American Christianity* (New York: Charles Scribner's Sons, 1960), I: 580.

Churches it follows a middle way in this manner. . . . It makes little attempt to lay down minimum standards of religious attainment, or to discriminate between 'true believer and nominal Christian.' . . . The Church, like the children of Israel, is a 'mixed multitude' (Exodus 12:38). . . ."[29]

Quakers spoke of the necessity to come "out of the mixture" and enter the straight and narrow path of Christian life. Indeed this emphasis is found in all of the Believers' Churches. The Unity of Brethren made persistent effort to practice discipline of membership, as demonstrated in their history. Significantly, in their relationship with Lutherans and the Reformed, this matter was of the first importance. "Tell the Brethren," Luther said at one point, "that they shall hold fast that which God has given them, and not relinquish their constitution and discipline." He regretted that he was not able to institute the same. Comenius later made the assessment that the Unity possessed a remedy for any possible evil: "This remedy is her discipline, by which simony, avarice, pride, contentions, false doctrines are suppressed, and godliness is furthered. She [the Unity] is an example of Christian simplicity, in that she avoids doctrinal disputes, and controversies of every kind, works for peace, and labors for a reformation of the Church universal."[30]

It is known that the Reformed tradition added to the marks of the church maintained by the Lutherans—the word truly proclaimed and the sacraments truly administered—the mark of discipline. John Knox in his *Order of Excommunication* likened the exercise of church discipline to the quarantine of disease: ". . . it would be a work both uncharitable and cruel to join together in one bed persons infected with pestilent and other contagious and infectious sores. . . ."[31] A somewhat different attitude was expressed by the Anabaptists, who saw the practice of discipline as a means of restoration of the wayward brother. Menno Simons in a list of signs by which the church may be distinguished does not list church discipline, but that this was necessary is repeatedly

[29] J. K. Zeman, "A Believing People: Theological Interpretation (Critique)" (unpub. typescript, Conference on the Concept of the Believers' Church, 1967), p. 2.

[30] Edmund de Schweinitz, *The History of the Church Known as the Unitas Fratrum* (Bethlehem: Moravian Publication Office, 1885), pp. 249, 602.

[31] Quoted in James L. Adams, "The Place of Discipline in Christian Ethics," *Crane Review*, IX (1967), 140.

affirmed in his writings. His position was that the brotherhood was only confirming a rupture which had already taken place when they announced a ban.[32]

The spirit and manner of Anabaptist discipline is seen in their earliest rule (*Ordnung*), developed in the Austrian Tyrol about 1527. It is given here in condensed form, also omitting the extensive biblical citation which accompanied every point. The title is "Discipline of the Believers: How a Christian is to Live":

> Since the almighty God and heavenly Father . . . has called us at this time out of pure grace into His marvelous light to one body, one spirit, and one faith, united in the bonds of love . . . we have all in one another's presence openly agreed to regulate everything in the best possible way. For the improvement of our brotherhood, for the praise and honor of the Lord, and for the service of all the needs, we have unanimously agreed that this rule shall be kept among us by all the brethren and sisters. When, however, a brother or sister is able to produce a better rule it shall be accepted from him at any time.
>
> 1. When the brethren are together they shall sincerely ask God for grace that He might reveal His divine will and help [them] to note it and when the brethren part they shall thank God and pray for all the brethren and sisters of the entire brotherhood.
>
> 2. We shall sincerely and in a Christian spirit admonish one another in the Lord to remain constant, to meet often . . . even at midweek.
>
> 3. When a brother or a sister leads a disorderly life it shall be punished: if he does so publicly, [he] shall be kindly admonished before all the brethren; if it is secret it shall be punished in secret, according to the command of Christ.
>
> 4. Every brother and sister shall yield himself in God to the brotherhood completely with body and life, and hold in common all gifts received of God, [and] contribute to the common need so that brethren and sisters will always be helped; needy members shall receive from the brotherhood as among the Christians at the time of the apostles.
>
> 5. The elders and preachers chosen from the brotherhood shall with zeal look after the needs of the poor, and . . . extend what is needed for the sake of and in the stead of the brotherhood.
>
> 6. A decent conduct shall be kept among them before everyone,

[32] See the discussion in Franklin H. Littell, A *Tribute to Menno Simons* (Scottdale, Pa.: Herald Press, 1961), pp. 23–36.

and no one shall carelessly conduct himself before the brotherhood with words or deeds, nor before those who are "outside."

7. In the meeting one is to speak and the others listen and judge what is spoken, and not two or three stand together. No one shall curse or swear, nor shall idle gossip be carried on, so that the meek may be spared.

8. When the brethren assemble they shall not fill up with eating and drinking but reduce expenses to the least [eating] soup and vegetables or whatever God gives; when they have eaten, all the food and drink shall again be removed, for one should use with thanksgiving and moderation the creatures which God has created, pure and good for our subsistence.

9. What is officially done [in disciplining] among the brethren and sisters in the brotherhood shall not be made public before the world. The good-hearted interested but not yet converted person, before he comes to the brethren in the brotherhood shall be taught. When he has learned and bears a sincere desire for it, and if he agrees to the content of the Gospel, he shall be received by the Christian brotherhood as a brother or a sister, that is, as a fellow member of Christ.

10. All the brethren and sisters after they have committed themselves, shall accept and bear with patience all that He sends us, and shall not let themselves be easily frightened by every wind and cry.

11. When brethren and sisters are together, being one body and one bread in the Lord and of one mind, then they shall keep the Lord's Supper as a memorial to the Lord's death, whereby each one shall be admonished to become conformed to the Lord in the obedience of the Father.

12. As we have taught and admonished the brethren and sisters we shall always watch and wait for the Lord that we may be worthy to enter [the kingdom] with Him when He comes, and to escape or flee from the evil that will come to the world.[33]

Baptists were always known for conscientiousness in practicing church discipline, as can be seen in the records gathered by William Warren Sweet, for example, of frontier congregations in America. This began early, for Thomas Helwys' original congregation had the practice of proceeding to the "censures" every Sunday afternoon after they had completed the service of worship.

[33] Robert Friedmann, "The Oldest Church Discipline of the Anabaptists," *Mennonite Quarterly Review*, XXIX (1955), 162–168.

Quakers used various forms of discipline, one of the most effective being the yearly list of queries which each member was expected to answer in painstaking self-judgment. The Church of the Brethren practice was to have church officials, often the deacons, visit each home before the annual communion or love feast, to see if there was harmony within the individual family and the church family. Reconciliation of differences, if there were such, had to be worked out before the communion could be celebrated.

With the Wesleyans, discipline played a large role. The intensity of John Wesley's devotion to the examining of the lives and beliefs of his followers was thought to verge on the tyrannical by the Roman Catholic scholar Ronald Knox, but Wesley himself thought it essential.[34] In 1742 he spent a week examining the London members "that I might know the state of their souls to Godward." The system of bands and classes allowed for strict supervision. In a visit to the society at Newcastle in 1743, Wesley read the rules to the members, and then excluded sixty-four for various offenses, ranging from Sabbath-breaking to wife-beating. At the class meetings where attendance was demanded, such questions were used: "Do you desire to be told of all your faults? . . . Do you desire we should tell you whatsoever we think, whatsoever we fear, whatsoever we hear concerning you? What known sin have you committed since our last meeting? What temptations have you met with? . . . What have you thought, said, or done, of which you doubt whether it be sin or not?"[35] Given the evident demoralization of English life of his day, the procedure was not only needed but essential for wholesome religion.

Some of this quality, though perhaps not in the same intensity, has been picked up by the renewal movements. The Church of the Saviour has spiritual counselors for applicant-members, to help in the examination of conscience. Their membership pledge is repeated each year. The Group Ministry of the East Harlem Protestant Parish and the Church of Hope of the West Side Christian Parish developed systems of mutual criticism and admonition, in an attempt to achieve disciplined action.

Discipline can easily slide into unlovely legalism, and it would not be difficult to find many examples in the histories of the Be-

---

[34] Ronald A. Knox, *Enthusiasm* (Oxford: Clarendon Press, 1950), pp. 426–430.
[35] Quoted in Adams, *loc. cit.*, pp. 140–141.

lievers' Churches. The temptation of the "church type" in trying to penetrate the world is acculturation; the temptation of the "sect type" is moralism. At its best, though, discipline expressed the loving concern for the brother which informs this excerpt from a letter of Quaker leaders at Balby in 1656 to their brethren in North England: "Dearly Beloved Friends, these things we do not lay upon you as a rule or form to walk by, but that all, with the measure of light which is pure and holy may be guided; and so in the light walking and abiding, these things may be fulfilled in the Spirit, not from the letter, for the letter killeth, but the Spirit giveth life."[36]

It is clear to contemporary observers of church life in the western world that excessive discipline is not a problem. Rather, it is the almost universal absence of meaningful requirements for church membership that threatens church life. Restoring integrity of membership is high on the list of priorities of the church renewal advocates. Experts in pastoral psychology and mental health are appealing to churches to practice the kind of caring guidance which many people desperately seek in secular agencies and clubs. Biblical scholars are demonstrating the crucial role that discipline played in early Christian life. In a well-meaning but exaggerated reaction against the narrowness of petit-bourgeois standards considered to be Christian virtues, Christians have swung to the equally dangerous pole of antinomianism. A return to a considered measure of discipline is imperative and inevitable if the church is to survive.[37]

It was among Congregationalists that the phrase "the gathered church" was developed. The two or three gathered in the name of the Lord as "visible saints," were seen as the basic unit of the church. But, it was quickly made clear that the gathering was not for the selfish enjoyment of the few. Rather, it was to provide the basis for the service and witness to the many. The church gathered must also be the church dispersed. To this second phase we now turn.

---

[36] D. Elton Townsend, *The People Called Quakers* (New York: Harper & Row, 1966), pp. 266–267.
[37] See the excellent discussion in William Klassen, *The Forgiving Community* (Philadelphia: Westminster Press, 1966), pp. 175ff.

· IX ·

Mission and Evangelism

Two Quakers were conversing, as the story goes, about life after death. "Dost thee think," said one, "that only those of us belonging to the Society of Friends will be permitted to enter heaven?" The other replied: "Hardly; for so small a number it would scarcely be worth the upkeep." Many of the Believers' Churches have, indeed, modest numbers on their rolls. The Quakers and the Church of the Brethren with about two hundred thousand members, the Plymouth Brethren and Mennonites with about four hundred and fifty thousand—these are not overly impressive figures after several centuries of existence. The much publicized renewal movements of this century have infinitesimal memberships. On the other end of the scale, of course, are the Baptists and Methodists with their twenty-plus millions. But even these do not bulk large against the totals reported for Lutheranism, Eastern Orthodoxy, and Roman Catholicism.

Anyone who has worked more than casually with church statistics will agree that this kind of comparison is misleading. The ratios take on a different significance when one remembers that some communions list each infant that has ever been baptized, regardless of later activity or inactivity, whereas others list only active adult members. Still others which are considered national churches count every citizen as a member. In Sweden, for example, the Lutheran Church claims ninety-eight percent of the Swedish population, whereas her own census shows less than five percent in any effective relationship. Easter communicants of the Church of England—claiming two-thirds allegiance of the population—number about 4.6 percent. Only eleven percent of Italian men observe the minimal requirements of the Roman Catholic faith—one confession and one communion per year. Estimates of the number of Russian Orthodox faithful vary—between fifteen and fifty million. When statistics are this blurred, any meaningful comparison is impossible. There is reason for thinking that if church membership could be calculated upon the basis of certain agreed-upon outward indices—attendance at services, financial support, participation in the sacramental life—there would be no great difference between the Believers' Churches and the others. There is, however, no agreement on what constitutes membership, and therefore a basis for effective judgment is lacking.[1]

Apologists for the smaller churches have sometimes said that the reason for their lack of numbers has been the heightened standards for church membership. The Historic Peace Churches, for example, would be limited to those willing to take the stand of conscientious objection to war. Aside from the fact that today the pacifist position is not mandatory for membership in these groups (except for some Mennonite bodies), it is clear that other factors were also involved. Ethnic ingrowth, complacency, and loss of the early vision can also be identified. It can further be pointed out that among the fastest growing religious groups today, the Pentecostalists, there are the greatest demands in terms of time, resources, and personal discipline made upon members.

"Sect" and "church" types together are currently faced with a crisis in their understandings of mission, evangelism, and conversion. Up to eighty percent of Anglican young people who ratify at confirmation "with their own mouth and consent" the vows made on their behalf when they were baptized as infants, lapse in later years, reports the bishop suffragan of Middleton, England. This loss, he states, is causing the clergy of established churches to look at the problem of conversion, with which they are not "at ease," in a new way. With undertones of nostalgia, the bishop writes of the ages of faith in Christendom, when "virtually everybody grew up within the Church, generation after generation" for this was "naturally and inevitably dictated by the Christian culture pattern within which men lived out their lives." After rejecting the approach to conversion of the sect groups, which is found narrow and too individualistic, he concludes: "We should pray and work

[1] Franklin H. Littell, "A Common Language," *Journal of Ecumenical Studies*, III (1966), 362–365; Paul Zieger, "Religionsstatistik," *Weltkirchenlexikon* (Stuttgart: Kreuz Verlag, 1960), 1249–1252; Frank W. Price, "World Christian Statistics," in H. W. Coxill and K. Grubb, eds., *World Christian Handbook 1968* (Nashville and New York: Abingdon Press, 1967), pp. 48–52.

that the Church should have so clear an understanding of relevant conversion, of relevant spirituality, of relevant understanding of what constitutes Christian faith in a secular society, and so clear an understanding of the action of God's grace in secular men, that paradoxically, it can sustain and hold men within its body, who are less than saints."[2]

The Territorial Church and Missions

This comment introduces a consideration of the connection between the church and the area in which it lives. Recent anthropological popularizations have tried to show the link between the "territorial imperative" observable in animal life and the pugnacious character of man. They might have found some further evidence for their claims by looking at the history of modern Europe between 1500 and 1648. Roman Catholicism and Magisterial Protestantism (using G. H. Williams' phrase) both claimed universal dominion in western Europe as the true church, and therefore locked in mortal combat. The bloody battles of the religious wars (in which, it may be admitted, religion was sometimes the pretext for other aims by the rulers) were only stopped by the compromise of territorialism. "As the prince, so the religion" (*cuius regio, eius religio*) was the solution negotiated by weary plenipotentiaries at the conference tables of Münster and Osnabrück which treaties jointly made up the Peace of Westphalia. Even before this, Protestantism showed signs of contenting itself with the role of particularist churches in the areas where it had become the dominant faith. The peace treaty of Augsburg (1555) had followed the same principle, but without using this specific phrase.

This provides one explanation of the "mystery" expressed by some: "The paradox of the Protestantism of the Reformation era is that while it called the church back to its apostolic faith, it was largely content to leave the fulfilment of the apostolic mission to the church of Rome."[3] For some years continental scholars have been hard put to answer the charge of the absence of missionary

[2] E. R. Wickham, "Conversion in a Secular Age," *Ecumenical Review*, XIX (1967), 291–296.
[3] Charles W. Ranson, *That the World May Know* (New York: Friendship Press, 1953), pp. 62, 65.

motivation on the part of the Reformers. They gleaned the writings of Luther and Calvin to find what little evidence was available to document such a concern. Detailed descriptions of the efforts at mission in southeastern Europe among the Slavs and the politico-religious campaigns among the Lapps by Scandinavian Lutheranism or the abortive Brazilian adventure by Calvinists still looked pathetic when matched with the world-wide labors of Jesuits and Franciscans. Roman Catholic controversialists used the absence of mission effort in their attempts to demonstrate Protestant heresy. Robert Bellarmine wrote at the end of the sixteenth century: "Heretics are never said to have converted either pagans or Jews to the faith, but only to have perverted Christians. But in this one century the Catholics have converted many thousands of heathens in the new world. . . . The Lutherans compare themselves to the apostles and the evangelists; yet though they have among them a very large number of Jews, and in Poland and Hungary have the Turks as their near neighbors, they have hardly converted even so much as a handful."[4] Some Lutherans answered by stating that Lutheranism was the true Catholic church, and therefore any activity anywhere that met their standards was rightly to be reckoned as their own doing![5]

Luther's answer to such a charge would have been to point out that the salvation of mankind was in God's hand. The true gospel would eventually find its way into all corners of the earth, without man's doing. What was necessary was to preach the Word faithfully in the place in which God had placed one. "It is with this mission of preaching just as when a stone is thrown into the water, it makes wavelets and circles and streaks round itself, and the wavelets move always farther and farther away, one chasing the other till they come to the bank. So with the preaching of the Gospel."[6] A reading of Luther's life, however, will show how tirelessly he corresponded to those in many parts of Europe, how many students came to Wittenberg to sit at his feet in the classroom (or at his table!) and then took his teachings to their homes, thereby introducing the Reformation. Luther's pamphleteering

[4] Quoted in Stephen Neill, *Christian Missions* (Baltimore, Md.: Penguin Books, 1964), p. 221.

[5] Hans-Werner Gensichen, *Missionsgeschichte der neueren Zeit* (Göttingen: Vandenhoeck & Ruprecht, 1961), p. 12.

[6] Quoted in Gustav Warneck, *Outline of a History of Protestant Missions,* trans. G. Robinson (New York: Fleming H. Revell, 1906), p. 14.

proved to be the most effective vehicle of reform. Calvinism was even more aggressive in systematic attempts to spread the Reformed faith. Geneva became both a model for imitation and a staging ground for raids into Catholic areas. Still, the judgment stands: "When everything favorable has been said that can be said, and when all possible evidences from the writings of the Reformers have been collected [on the subject of mission], it all amounts to exceedingly little" (Neill).[7]

Protestant orthodoxy of the later sixteenth and seventeenth centuries developed great ingenuity in explaining why the missionary imperative was no longer operative. First, the Great Commission of Matthew 28 had literally been carried out by the apostles by their going to "all nations" and therefore was fulfilled. Ingenious erudition was employed to demonstrate this. A picture of three heads found in China was evidence of knowledge of the Trinity. Mexicans had received Christianity from the Ethiopians because they were said to connect baptism and circumcision as did the Africans.[8] Justus Menius, a Lutheran theologian, stated firmly that "God sent only the apostles into all the world"; all others were to follow the parish system. "The servant of the Gospel does not travel here and there about the land—in one church today, another tomorrow. . . . But one servant steadily watches over his assigned church with true industry and remains with it, leaving other churches untroubled and in peace."[9] Second, the heathen were considered to have forfeited their right to receive the gospel because of their barbarity. "The holy things of God are not to be cast before such dogs and swine," announced Ursinus. In the third place, if God wished for the heathen to be converted, He would see to it by Himself. "If the matter is of God, God will Himself further His cause and show ways and means so that the heathen shall 'fly as doves to the windows.' "[10]

When the mission impulse did come to Classical Protestantism, it came through the Pietism of Halle and Herrnhut. So reluctant was the church to undertake mission, that it had to be implemented by private societies and interested individuals. This point

[7] Neill, *op. cit.*, p. 222.
[8] Warneck, *op. cit.*, pp. 29–30.
[9] Quoted in Franklin H. Littell, *The Anabaptist View of the Church*, second rev. ed. (Boston: Starr King Press, 1958), p. 114.
[10] Warneck, *op. cit.*, pp. 38–39.

is made in an unintended way in the apologetic of a leading Lutheran mission historian writing on the topic "Were the Reformers Indifferent to Missions?" He states: "As long as foreign missions were nothing more than the hobby of a few pietistic outsiders, the church and their theologians had little interest in investigating the motives of so absurd an enterprise. But when it appeared that mission had come to stay, and the spread of the gospel in unevangelized areas of the world was occupying the attention of the ever growing number of Christians, scholars began to concern themselves with the origin and justification of the movement." The historian then goes on to try to show that the Reformers in fact were not indifferent, at least to the theology of missions, although practical exigencies of establishing their own reforms prevented them from doing much about it.[11]

Ernst Benz approached the same theme by asking why it was that in Europe no church history had been written from a world viewpoint, to complete the classic history of the early church written by Harnack. How was it that it remained for a historian of an American free church (Latourette) to undertake the task? His answer was that the confessional and particularist orientation of European scholars had kept them from even seeing the topic from an international, ecumenical vantage point. "In America there is quite a different relationship of church and mission, than we are accustomed to from our German situation. Most of the large Free Churches have their own missions and own mission fields, most with important overseas mission schools and mission universities. Whereas in Germany the mission societies, not the *Landeskirchen*, are the sponsors of missions, in the United States missions are considered to be a natural function of individual churches and congregations, and are carried on with much greater dynamic."[12]

The Believers' Church and Missions

In the duchy of Württemberg in the sixteenth century, all of the Anabaptist men were expelled or executed. The government allowed only women with small children to remain at home. These

[11] Hans-Werner Gensichen, "Were the Reformers Indifferent to Missions?" *Student World*, LIII (1960), 119–127.
[12] Ernst Benz, *Kirchengeschichte in ökumenischer Sicht* (Leiden: E. J. Brill, 1961), pp. 13–18.

they chained, however, to keep them from going to their relatives
and their neighbors to witness to their faith, as the government
had learned by experience was their custom. The Anabaptist
women were considered to be as dangerous in spreading the illicit
faith as their menfolk. The author of the most comprehensive
study of the missionary activity of the Anabaptists has likened
them to primitive Christianity in which the bearers of the gospel
were largely the common members. "The Reformation churches
have scarcely anything like it to set over against the Anabaptist
phenomenon." To him the "astonishing thing about Anabaptism is
not so much the activity of ordained leaders . . . as the missionary
commitment of the ordinary members."[13]

In this they were following the pattern of the medieval
Waldenses. The reason the medieval church took such draconian
action to stamp out these "heretics" was the extent to which they
were reaching the people. Pope Innocent IV complained in 1245
that the heresy was so firmly and widely planted that it was including princes and magnates as well as simple peasants. In the early
fifteenth century a French prelate estimated that one-third of
Christendom, if not more, had attended illicit Waldensian conventicles or was at heart a Waldensian. They have been called the
"first missionaries to disseminate a considerable knowledge of the
Bible among the people. . . . Once the Waldenses had re-estab-
lished direct contact with the Law of Christ, the Bible proved to
be once more that live volcano whose repeated eruptions forever
shake Christianity."[14]

The Unity of Brethren had a deep sense of mission. In Chelčický's Net of Faith a great deal of attention is paid to the missionary urgency displayed by the early Church. There is no limit,
said Chelčický, to the saving grace of Jesus Christ; it is sufficient
to save several worlds at one time! This would only be possible,
however, if his followers were willing to use the methods which
He used. They must drop their alliance with the state, and then
once again the church will recover its ability to reach the masses.

[13] Wolfgang Schäufele, "The Missionary Vision and Activity of the Anabaptist Laity," Mennonite Quarterly Review, XXXVI (1962), 99–115.
[14] Henry C. Lea, History of the Inquisition of the Middle Ages (New York:
The Macmillan Co., 1906), II: 427; Leonard Verduin, The Reformers and
Their Stepchildren (Grand Rapids, Mich.: Eerdmans Publishing Co., 1964),
p. 173; the quotation is from Walter Nigg, The Heretics, trans. R. and C.
Winston (New York: Alfred A. Knopf, 1962), p. 201.

In the several decades between the time of its founding and the end of the fifteenth century, the Unity had sent representatives to Austria, Brandenburg, Poland, Russia, Moldavia, Greece, Palestine, Egypt, and Turkey. Luke of Prague maintained in the sixteenth century that before Christians could be effective in converting the Turks to the gospel, they would have to live up to their own teachings at least as well as the Turks did to theirs. Mission, for him, presupposed a radical reform within the church.[15]

Franklin H. Littell has documented the thesis that the Anabaptists were the first to make the Great Commission the responsibility of every church member. There is indeed impressive evidence that most members felt the call to convince and convert others, relatives, neighbors, strangers. The rapid spread of the movement is otherwise inexplicable. The well-known Martyrs' Synod of 1527 staked out separate areas of mission responsibility in a "grand map of evangelical enterprise." The Hutterites later organized systematic missions throughout Europe from their communitarian bases in Moravia.[16]

Published source collections contain the records of numerous hearings of simple people who were arrested for holding illicit gatherings. The view of the Reformers was that no preaching could be done unless it was performed by a pastor duly ordained by the state. They called Anabaptists "hedge preachers" (*Winkelprediger*). Among the errors listed of the Anabaptists was that "anyone who has a true faith may preach, even if no one has commissioned him: for Christ has empowered any and every man to preach when He said 'Go, teach all nations'" (Matt. 28). Although Luther had earlier suggested in his preface to the German mass that earnest Christians could meet privately, he later became very defensive on unregulated meetings. "Therefore let everyone ponder this, that if he wants to preach or teach let him exhibit the call or the commission that drives him to it or else let him keep his mouth shut. If he refuses this then let the magistrate consign the scamp into the hands of his proper master—whose name is Meister Hans [the hangman]."[17]

[15] Amadeo Molnar, "The Czech Reformation and Missions," *Student World*, LIII (1960), 128–136.

[16] Littell, *Anabaptist View of the Church*, pp. 109–137; see also his "Protestantism and the Great Commission," *Southwestern Journal of Theology*, New Series II (October 1959), 26–42.

[17] The quotations are from Verduin, *op. cit.*, pp. 182, 184–185.

Early Anabaptism had a vision of responsibility for all the world. "They believed that the Church of the Restitution, the True Church with its disciplined laymen, carried history."[18] But faced with massive repression, another belief became prominent. This was the idea of the Church of the Remnant. God would have a small flock to bear witness to Him even in the midst of a cruel and corrosive world. The faithful must withdraw to sheltered areas and perpetuate themselves, but not try to storm heaven. It is in this guise, until recently, that the world has seen the descendants of the Anabaptists, the Mennonites, and the Brethren. Small enclaves of good if backward folk, they seemed content with their clan and culture. Both groups broke out of this shell in the late nineteenth century with extensive programs of foreign missions.

The Quakers clearly had a world vision at the beginning of their life. "Quakerism was a missionary movement before it was an organized religious society."[19] They were set on taking the message of the Light that was Christ to all the world with a "fine carelessness about geography or about language difficulties."[20] Fox wrote: "Answer the witness of God in every man, whether they are the heathen that do not profess Christ, or whether they are such as do profess Christ that have the form of godliness and be out of the power."[21] Wesley's broad horizon of churchmanship is well known. A favorite saying of his was: "Go not to those who want you, but to those who want [i.e., need] you most."[22] The circuit plan was his answer to the question of how to reach the unchurched in England and America. His deputy Thomas Coke was the leading figure in early Methodist world missions. "Brother," said Wesley to him, "go out and preach the Gospel to all the world." Following Coke's assignment as superintendent in North America, he developed an active program in the West Indies. In 1784 he published his "Plan of the Society for the Establishment of Missions among the Heathen," but there was no re-

---

[18] Littell, *Anabaptist View of the Church*, p. 109.

[19] D. Elton Trueblood, *The People Called Quakers* (New York: Harper & Row, 1966), p. 247.

[20] Hugh Barbour, *The Quakers in Puritan England* (New Haven: Yale University Press, 1964), p. 67.

[21] Quoted in Harold Loukes, *The Quaker Contribution* (New York: The Macmillan Co., 1965), p. 33.

[22] Quoted in Rupert E. Davies, *Methodism* (Penguin Books, 1963), p. 67.

sponse to the call. Coke died in 1814 on his way to Ceylon with six other Methodists.[23]

Before this the Pietists in Germany had opened a new era in missions. It began at the court of the King of Denmark in the early eighteenth century. Influenced by a Pietist chaplain, the king became concerned about the spiritual life of his subjects in the Danish colonial possessions in India and Greenland. Two young men, recent students at Halle under August Hermann Francke, came to his attention as desiring employment in missions. Their names were Bartholomew Ziegenbalg and Henry Plütschau. The men reached Tranquebar south of Madras in East India in 1705 and began there a mission which for nearly one hundred years was the only Protestant outpost on the subcontinent. The most famous of their successors (who came from Halle as replacements) was Christian Frederick Schwartz who labored without a break from 1750 to 1798 to such advantage that he became known as the "priest-king of Tanjore" and won widespread admiration from the indigenous people of all classes. It was said of him: "The knowledge and integrity of this irreproachable missionary have retrieved the character of Europeans from imputations of general depravity." It was the work of these Danish-Halle missionaries which had inspired Susanna Wesley to instill a love of missions in her children in the Epworth rectory.[24]

The Renewed Moravian Church under the leadership of Count Zinzendorf, himself a student at Halle, was responsible for the most extensive missionary activity of the eighteenth century. "Here was a new phenomenon in the expansion of Christianity, an entire community, of families as well as of the unmarried, devoted to the propagation of the faith."[25] Their first outreach was to Greenland and to the West Indies, where they were prepared to become slaves, if need be, in order to minister to the Negroes. Great loss of life attended their mission efforts, but by 1800 they had fifteen fields of service from Russia to North America among the American Indians. A striking painting illustrating the first

[23] Ernest A. Payne, *The Growth of the World Church* (London: Edinburgh House Press, 1955), pp. 40–43.

[24] The quotation is from Neill, *op. cit.*, p. 233.

[25] Kenneth S. Latourette, *A History of the Expansion of Christianity* (New York: Harper & Brothers, 1939), III: 47.

fruits of the mission endeavor was executed in 1747 for a hall in Herrnhut. "In two decades the little church of the [Moravian] Brethren called more missions to life than did the whole of Protestantism in two centuries."[26]

The Great Century of Missions

"Sit down, young man; when it pleaseth the Lord to convert the heathen, he will do it without your help or mine." The speaker was Dr. John Ryland, respected leader of the British Baptists, and he reflected the thinking of most contemporary theologians. The one addressed was young William Carey, sometime cobbler, schoolteacher, and preacher. Carey was not to be squelched. He persisted in preparing and publishing his *Enquiry into the Obligations of Christians to Use Means for the Conversion of the Heathens* (1792), called the single most influential missionary treatise in the English language, to prove his point. The first section is aimed at disproving the contention that the Great Commission was directed only to the apostles. The explorations of Cook and others, of which Carey was an avid student, showed that there were portions of the globe completely unknown during biblical times. The Commission, therefore, could not possibly have been confined to the apostles. "Have not the missionaries of the *Unitas Fratrum* encountered the scorching heat of Abyssinia and the frozen climes of Greenland and Labrador, in their difficult languages and savage manners?" he asked in replying to those who said that Europeans could not possibly survive in many lands. In a sober style likened to that of a Blue Paper for the British Parliament, Carey built his case, buttressing it with careful statistical tables showing that, by his calculation, seven out of nine of the world's population were ignorant of Christianity.

Even then he barely gained his point. A meeting of the Midland Baptist ministers was about to be dismissed, when Carey cried: "Is there nothing again going to be done, sirs?" Grudgingly, a minute was recorded approving the preparation of a plan for missions to be presented at the next meeting. From this halting beginning was born the Particular Baptist Society for Propagation of the Gospel Amongst the Heathen (1792). The first monies raised,

[26] Warneck, *op. cit.*, p. 63.

after Carey's proposal for regular, if small, contributions by individuals and congregations, were sent to the Moravian missionaries whom Carey so admired. Then in 1793 he went himself to India, taking with him a reluctant wife and three children. The East India Company presented him with great difficulties when he arrived. Finally he found a foothold in the Danish territory of Serampore above Calcutta. There he built a mission enterprise which in its comprehensiveness became a classic. His letters back to England, when circulated, provided the stimulus for the organization of many other societies.[27] Although Carey believed in cooperative mission activity in theory, he judged that "given the divided state of Christendom, it would be more likely for good to be done by each denomination engaging separately in the work, than if they were to embark on it conjointly."[28]

It was the Baptist historian, Kenneth Scott Latourette, who gave the nineteenth century the name "Great Century" of missions. He found that he needed three of the seven volumes of his comprehensive history on the expansion of Christianity to tell the story of that period. Latourette based his assessment on the fact that the nineteenth century saw the most extensive geographic spread of Christianity, both by increased outreach in those areas previously opened, and also by the entrance of Christianity into the "large majority of such countries, islands, peoples, and tribes" heretofore untouched. In the United States, which grew more rapidly than any other nation, the percentage of church membership rose dramatically in the 1800s. Even in Asia, where numerically the increase was small, "Christianity was effecting mass permeation of culture and was shaping ideas, customs, and institutions as in no other previous period." The upsurge of mission vigor was the result, Latourette found, of a revival in Christianity, following her successful resistance to the challenge of eighteenth-century revolution and rationalism. Many new movements arose which provided the vitality and drive to carry out the task. The century was climaxed by the call for the "evangelization of the world in our generation," the slogan of the Student Volunteer Movement, led by the Methodist John R. Mott. A contemporary

[27] Payne, *op. cit.*, pp. 44–52.
[28] Ernest A. Payne, "Carey's 'Enquiry,' " *International Review of Missions*, XXXI (1942), 180–186.

asserted: "Our field is the world. Our object is to effect an entire moral revolution in the whole human race."[29]

The Plymouth Brethren, without overhead organization, sent many of their number across the world under the theme "Christian Missions in Many Lands." One of their men, F. S. Arnot, played a major role in opening up Africa for missions. The Mennonites and Brethren became active late in the nineteenth century, as did Quakers from America and England who began foreign missions once more. According to Latourette's careful studies, the groups sending out the missionaries were primarily those in the traditions of Pietism, Wesleyanism, and revivalism of the eighteenth and nineteenth centuries.[30] Today more than three-fourths of the Protestant missionary staff and resources stem from churches of free church parentage.[31]

Evangelism: Social or Individual?

Since World War II there is agreement that it is wrong to speak of foreign missions. All countries are, in fact, mission fields, western nations included. One of the most needy areas is within the church membership itself, which despite formal affiliation has but minimal biblical and doctrinal knowledge and insufficient dedication to the task of the church. It is called our "greatest unevangelized field."

Where outspoken disagreement comes is on the focus of evangelism.[32] Should it follow the pattern of the waves of revivals which have repeatedly swept and formed the Anglo-Saxon church world, and the entire western world to a degree? This emphasis would concentrate the church's energies in effecting individual conversion by personal evangelism. The crusades of Billy Graham are a convenient symbol of this approach. Or should it be, as a whole school of modern writers are proclaiming, that evangelism today must be located in the secular world? The programs of the

[29] Latourette, op. cit., IV: 2–3, 18–19.

[30] Ibid., p. 65.

[31] Franklin H. Littell, "The Concerns of the Believers' Church," Chicago Theological Seminary Register, LVIII (December 1967), 17.

[32] The question was formulated in this way by John Howard Yoder, "The Believers' Church in Mission" (unpub. typescript, Conference on the Concept of the Believers' Church, 1967), pp. 30–32.

evangelism department of the National Council of Churches of Christ in the U.S.A. and the materials of the World Council of Churches' study on the mission structure of the church symbolize the second approach. Is it to be the thrust of the World Conference of Evangelism of Berlin of October 1966 or the World Conference on Church and Society of July 1966 at Geneva? The former element charges the latter with abandonment of the basic work of the church by humanitarian dabbling in areas of social change which should be left to the experts. The latter charge the former with privatism, with lack of responsibility for the social structures which need changing. Is it Jesus as "personal saviour" or the Lord over the "power structures"?

Advocates of personal evangelism deny that they are devoid of social concern. Change the man, they say, and he will bring his changed personality to his secular occupation in a redemptive fashion. Save enough men, and you will change the world. Billy Graham is quoted as exclaiming on the eve of his 1966 mission to England: "If a crusade is blessed in London, it can influence the continent of Europe and the whole British Commonwealth and can have an effect in the United States. It can touch the world!"[33] A favorite story, which epitomizes this position, tells of a man who had to take care of his small boy. The father, eager to read his newspaper, wanted to distract his son. He therefore took from a magazine a page upon which was a map of the world. Cutting each country of the world from the map, he gave the pieces to the boy to put together as a puzzle, certain that this would take considerable time. He was hardly settled again in his chair when the boy returned with the assembled map. When asked how he could have completed the project so fast, the boy replied: "It was simple. On the other side of the page there was a picture of a man. I just put the man together, and then the world fit into place."

The program of the other school has taken form around Harvey Cox's *Secular City*, Colin Williams' study books, and the writings of Gibson Winter, to name some of the best known. "The church is God's avantgarde, and its function is to be where the action is,

[33] Quoted by Cecil Northcott, "The Graham Crusade: Abdication of Evangelism," *Christian Century* (May 25, 1966), 674. See also William G. McLoughlin, Jr. *Modern Revivalism* (New York: Ronald Press Co., 1959), pp. 503–505.

out in the world," says Archie Hargraves of the Chicago Urban Training Center.[34] Some of this camp deny that they have lost an interest in personal evangelism. "Evangelism must include both the pointing to the presence of Christ as Lord in the affairs of the world and the pointing to the call of Christ as Saviour of each of us," says Colin Williams.[35] But the primary emphasis is clearly on the church ascertaining where God is acting in the world and moving its resources into the struggle, be it for civil rights, against South African apartheid, or contending for better conditions in the urban slums. "Our present reformation is primarily concerned with the church's relationship to the secular order and only secondarily with the church's internal life" (Cox). Don Benedict of the Community Renewal Society predicts: "We will get real schisms over the church-in-the-world issue. Some congregations are going to be split right up the middle in the next ten years."[36]

John Howard Yoder, a Mennonite scholar, asserts that the stance of the Believers' Churches cuts across the debate to form a new configuration:

> The error of individualism is not adequately tempered by insisting that saved individuals will get together sometimes or that saved individuals will be socially effective. But neither is it to be corrected by replacing personal change and commitment with the remodeling of the total society. The complement to personal decision is the "new humanity" of covenant community. Preoccupation with making world history come out right or making the secular city be the city of God is not adequately tempered by saying that even the best technopolis would still be imperfect or that there will still need to be voluntary associations within the coming great society. But neither must concern for the social dimension of the kingdom be replaced by a mere call to a new attitude. The political novelty which God brings into the world is a community of those who serve instead of ruling, who suffer instead of inflicting suffering, whose fellowship crosses social lines instead of reinforcing them. This new Christian community in which the walls are broken down not by human idealism or democratic legalism but by the work of Christ, is not only a vehicle of the gospel or fruit of the gospel; it is the good

[34] Quoted in "U.S. Protestantism: Time for a Second Reformation," *Newsweek* (January 3, 1966), 33–37.
[35] Quoted in Howard E. Royer, "A World-Oriented Evangelism," *Messenger* (March 16, 1967), 15.
[36] "U.S. Protestantism," p. 35.

news. It is not merely the agent of mission or the constituency of a mission agency. This is the mission.[37]

A review of the history of the Believers' Church shows that this position is close to the truth. The Anabaptists did not have the cause of religious liberty in the commonwealth in mind when they demanded freedom from the state to worship, but their suffering witness helped to establish it. The Quakers' testimony against slavery proved to be a major factor in its abolition. John Wesley's determination to have a well-ordered church was not designed to stabilize the English proletariat, but it is assessed to have done just that. The Confessing Church did not set out to protest the political evils of the Third Reich, but ended up as the most effective example of the "good Germany" and as the agent for restoring Germany, in the first instance, into the family nations.

The discussion of social evangelism involves the definition of the appropriate relationship of church and state. As indicated earlier, there are those who would place the weight of identifying free churches on this aspect alone. The next topic, therefore, needs to take up the often critical issues of the interrelation of religion and government.

[37] Yoder, *op. cit.*, p. 32.

· X ·

Church and State

THE acid-tongued traveler Mrs. Frances Trollope delivered herself of this assessment of the American religious scene vintage 1830:

> The whole people appear to be divided into an almost endless variety of religious factions. . . . Besides the broad and well-known distinctions of Episcopalian, Roman Catholic, Presbyterian, Calvinist, Baptist, Quaker, Swedenborgian, Universalist, Dunker, etc. etc. etc., there are innumerable others springing out of these, each of which assumes a church government of its own; of this, the most intriguing and factious individual is invariably the head. . . . It is impossible, in witnessing all these unseemingly vagaries, not to recognize the advantages of an established church as a sort of headquarters for quiet unpresuming Christians, who are contented to serve faithfully, without insisting upon having each a little separate banner, embroidered with a device of their own imagining. . . . I believe I am sufficiently tolerant; but this does not prevent my seeing that the object of all religious observances is better obtained when the government of the church is confided to the wisdom and experience of the most venerated among the people than when it is placed in the hands of every tinker and tailor who chooses to claim a share in it.[1]

She reflected in her attitude not only English prejudice but also the accepted view on the correct relationship of church and state. In all but two of the original American colonies there had been church establishments. The Congregational Church of Massachusetts still retained officially sponsored privileged status at the time

---

[1] Frances Trollope, *The Domestic Manners of the Americans* (New York: Dodd, Mead and Co.), quoted in Milton B. Powell, ed., *The Voluntary Church* (New York: The Macmillan Co., 1967), pp. 69–70. The same passage is used in Daniel Boorstin, *The Genius of American Politics* (Chicago: University of Chicago Press, 1953), p. 145.

of her writing, despite the general process of disestablishment which began at the onset of the American Revolution. In 1774 John Adams remarked to the Baptist Isaac Backus, who was agitating for the demise of state churches, about the Bay State worthies that "we might as soon expect a change in the solar system as to expect that they would give up their establishment."[2] When the Standing Order of Connecticut was under final siege in 1818, its champion Lyman Beecher was found by his son in a disconsolate mood: "I remember seeing father, the day after the election, sitting on one of the old-fashioned, rush-bottomed kitchen chairs, his head drooping on his breast and his arms hanging down. 'Father,' said I, 'what are you thinking of?' He answered solemnly: 'The Church of God.'"

Beecher was later to admit that the introduction of the voluntary system he had fought so bitterly turned out to be the "best thing that ever happened in the State of Connecticut." Cut off from all dependence upon governmental support, churchmen were forced to develop their own resources, and gained by it.[3]

Separation of Church and State

The sacral view of spiritual and temporal power united to uphold society has venerable ancestry. It appears in some form in every culture. For many it has seemed an impossibility for morality and piety to exist, to say nothing of the security dependent upon them, in a country where the religious life of the populace was uncontrolled from above. This was certainly the common opinion in the sixteenth century. A Dutch Reformed pastor exclaimed: "How can there be a quiet and peaceful life and how can a country flourish if its citizenry is divided by diverse conceptions of religion? There is nothing so baneful for the community as disunity, diversity, and contention in matters religious." A necessary conclusion, then, is that "unity achieved by the sword of the magistrate is the one and only beginning, the middle, and the end, of peace and prosperity in the land."[4] This was precisely the view of

---

[2] Quoted in William G. McLoughlin, *Isaac Backus and the American Pietistic Tradition* (Boston: Little, Brown & Co., 1967), p. 132.

[3] Quoted and discussed in Winthrop S. Hudson, *The Great Tradition of the American Churches* (New York: Harper & Brothers, 1953), pp. 64–65.

[4] Quoted in Leonard Verduin, *The Reformers and Their Stepchildren* (Grand Rapids, Mich.: Eerdmans Publishing Co., 1964), p. 90.

the Congregationalist pastor of Chelsea, Massachusetts, who told the assembled legislature in 1778 "the fear and reverence of God, and the terrors of eternity are the most powerful restraints upon the minds of men. . . . Established modes and usages in religion, more especially the stated public worship of God, so generally form the principles and manners of a people that changes . . . may well be esteemed very dangerous experiments in governments." He cautioned: "Let the restraint of religion once be broken down, as they infallibly would be by leaving the subject of public worship to the humors of the multitude, and we might well defy all human wisdom and power to support and preserve order and government in the state."[5]

In the absence of a national religion, some hold, people seek a substitute by making a religion of the nation. The phenomenon of nationalism as a modern religion has often been noted. More recently, there are those applying this analysis to the United States.[6] From the beginning, it is argued, Americans have considered themselves to be under God's special providence; He set up the American Israel as a vehicle for His mighty purpose. When in the nineteenth century the practice of denominationalism became widespread (which by definition disclaims ambition to universal dominance) the shift was made to allegiance to the nation as the fulfiller of certain church functions. First, the nation was considered to be the "primary agent of God's meaningful activity in history." It assumed another function of the church, secondly, by becoming the primary society "in terms of which individuals, Christian and non-Christian alike, found identity." Finally, the nation became the primary community in which "historic purpose and identity were defined." This approach helps to explain those American characteristics most foreigners find perplexing—the crusade mentality against the enemy (whether Kaiser Bill, Hitler, or Communism), the rancor against well-meaning critics of the system, the sancrosanct quality attributed to such defenders of the federal dream as J. Edgar Hoover or General Lewis Hershey. It is the unquestioned identification of the national interest with the

---

[5] Quoted in McLoughlin, *op. cit.*, pp. 139–140.
[6] John E. Smylie, "The Christian Church and National Ethos," in P. Peachey, ed., *Biblical Realism Confronts the Nation* (Lebanon, Pa.: Fellowship Publications, 1963), pp. 33–44; Robert N. Bellah, "Civil Religion in America," *Daedalus*, XCVI, No. 1 (Winter 1967), 1–21.

cause of light and truth that led the Roman Catholic lay theologian Michael Novak in October 1967 to call for a new reformation: "It is very difficult for many American Christians even to conceive the possibility that American civilization is profoundly anti-Christian, *precisely in those very places where it is most pious, patriotic, and full of noble sentiment.* The awareness of the sovereignty of God has been lost."[7]

The persistence of the sacral mentality is obvious in the much publicized collaboration of the Roman Catholic Church and conservative regimes in the Iberian peninsula and in Latin America. It is also quite evident in some Protestant countries, especially in Scandinavia. To this day all citizens of Sweden are considered to be members of the Lutheran state church if they *or their parents* were baptized. It has only been since 1951 that a person could petition the Swedish government to withdraw from church membership without joining a free church, and but few have taken advantage of this even though Swedes are notoriously indifferent to organized religion. In Norway the national church alone receives benefits from church taxes levied by the state upon all citizens, although there are Roman Catholic, Methodist, Baptist, and Pentecostalist minorities. In a recent case the Lutheran officialdom attacked a bill proposing that teachers of religion in the public schools might also be selected from the ranks of dissenters "who are members of a denomination which on the major points has the same doctrines as the national church." Their argument was that this training constitutes the Lutheran catechetical instruction and therefore they must control it. For the Scandinavian nations, it is still largely true that the church is deemed to be the state in its religious aspect.[8]

Thus it has been against a very deep and powerfully flowing tide of custom that the Believers' Churches swam when they advocated a clean separation of church and state. Peter Chelčický was one of the first to make the point: "Civil authority is as far removed from Christ's truth inscribed in His gospel as is Christ's faith from the necessity of using such authority. Those in power are not led by

[7] Michael Novak, "We Need a New Reformation . . . HERE!" *Together*, XI (October 1967), 15–19, an Interchurch Feature printed also by eight other denominational periodicals.

[8] *Christian Century* (August 24 and September 21, 1966), 1025–1026, 1142–1146.

faith nor does faith need them." Even when the nobility were allowed to join the Unity of Brethren, they were not permitted to practice the otherwise customary patronage of pastoral appointment. According to the American historian De Schweinitz: "It constituted the first exemplification of that polity [of separation] which has been crowned with the greatest success in our own country."[9]

The Anabaptists came into existence, as has been seen, because of this very question. As followers of Zwingli, they were ready to proceed with the full reformation of the church upon biblical principles, whereas he decided that the city fathers must set the pace. The Swiss scholar Fritz Blanke concluded that "the Grebel circle had the courage to withdraw from the Reformed folk church in Zürich and set out to establish a church to correspond to the pattern of primitive Christianity, namely a church of the few who have come to personal faith in Christ and have been baptized on the basis of their faith." In so doing, they founded a free church, that is, a "Christian fellowship based on voluntary membership and independence of the state."[10] That this was the common stance of the Radical Reformers could easily be documented. A typical statement is that found in the Hutterite *Great Chronicle*: "In 1519 Martin Luther began to write against the frightful abominations of the Babylonian Harlot, and to disclose all her wickedness . . . yes, as with thunderclaps to bring it all down. . . . But as soon as he joined himself to the secular rule, seeking protection there against the cross . . . then it went with him as with a man who in mending an old kettle only makes the hole bigger, and he raised up a people altogether callous in sin."[11]

For many years it was customary to look to Luther and Calvin as the founts of modern religious freedom. It is quite true that the long-range implications of their doctrines have contributed immeasurably to the growth of modern democracies. But, more precise investigation has clearly indicated the extent to which both were still steeped in medieval thought, especially as it related to

[9] Quoted in Peter Brock, *The Political and Social Doctrines of the Unity of Czech Brethren* (The Hague: Mouton and Co., 1957), p. 46; Edmund de Schweinitz, *The History of the Church Known as The Unitas Fratrum* (Bethlehem, Pa.: Moravian Publication Office, 1885), p. 362.
[10] Fritz Blanke, *Brothers in Christ* (Scottdale, Pa.: Herald Press, 1961), p. 15.
[11] Quoted in Verduin, *op. cit.*, p. 37.

the church-state connection. As the ideas of voluntaryism and religious liberty spread more widely, scholars took another look for their antecedents and found them in the ranks of the Radical Reformation rather than among the Magisterial Reformation. "Free-churchmen and state-churchmen, both in lands where a single confession has been established and in lands where the church has been disestablished, are increasingly interested in the experience and principles of the Radical Reformers who were martyrs to a way and organization of Christian life which, in mitigated circumstances, is or will be the way for almost all Christian bodies almost everywhere in the world today or tomorrow" (Williams).[12]

The very name of the left-wing of Puritanism—Separatists—draws attention to the programmatic principle of rejection of the state church, and inevitably, therefore, of the tie to the state (although the second step was often long in being realized). When the Separatists raised the question in pointed fashion whether the Church of England could claim to be a true church at all, Anglicans reacted with shock and dismay. Such criticism was thought not only deleterious to sound religion but seditious as well. Said one: "Does not this open a door to all confusion, in Church and State, and give every man (all as well as any) liberty, if they judge anything amiss in Church or State, to turn Reformers, if Superiours cannot or will not Reform it? . . . I think I may safely say, this is an Anabaptisticall Munster principle, at the bottome: and say no more."[13]

For the Baptists arising from within Separatist Puritanism, the tenet of separation of church and state has been a key in self-understanding from the beginning and its contribution toward that end has been that denomination's proudest claim. Their early (1612) confession made the point that "the Church of Christ is a company of faithful people, separated from the world by the word and Spirit of God, being knit unto the Lord, and one unto the other, by baptism, upon their own confession of the faith and sins."[14] There was no room for state interference in this eccle-

---

[12] George H. Williams, "Studies in the Radical Reformation (1517–1618)," *Church History*, XXVII (1958), 49.

[13] Quoted in Geoffrey F. Nuttall, *Visible Saints* (Oxford: Basil Blackwell, 1957), p. 63.

[14] Ernest A. Payne, *The Fellowship of Believers*, revised ed. (London: Carey Kingsgate Press, 1954), p. 25.

siology. In New England, the Middle Colonies, Virginia, and North Carolina, Baptists agitated long and successfully for the cause of separation, making common cause with otherwise disliked deists and rationalists to effect their goal. Isaac Backus was the most prominent figure in this long campaign. This same value is at the top of the list of priorities for the Baptist Joint Committee on Public Affairs, nationally, and the Baptist World Alliance, internationally, as an issue such as a proposed United States ambassador to the Vatican has demonstrated.

This did not mean that the Baptists taught that their members could not accept government office, for many did when conditions allowed it. They were closer in this to the viewpoint of the Quakers, who have held a much more positive attitude on the possibilities of Christian influence within government than have the Anabaptist-Mennonites. The Methodists were less vociferous in their separatist stance. They were skeptical, at least after the death of their founder, of the virtues of establishment, and even Wesley coolly elaborated a definition of the true church of God which disqualified most Anglican parishes. Indicative of the Methodist position on establishment is their statement in the book of discipline published in 1787: "We are not ignorant of the Spirit and Designs it has ever discovered in Europe, of rising to Preeminence and Worldly Dignities by Virtue of a national Establishment, and by the most servile Devotion to the will of temporal Governors; and we fear, the same Spirit will lead the same Church in these United States (tho' altered in its Name) to similar Designs and Attempts, if the Number and Strength of its Members will ever afford a Probability of Success; and particularly, to obtain a national Establishment which we cordially abhor as the Great Bane of Truth and Holiness, the greatest impediment in the World to the Progress of vital Christianity."[15]

A Methodist bishop teamed with a Disciples of Christ editor and others to begin the agency most active in guarding the "wall of separation" in latter-day American life. This is the controversial Protestants and Other Americans United for Separation of Church and State (now Americans United), which is said to have extensive Baptist support as well.

Before and since Mrs. Trollope foreign observers have reported

[15] Quoted in Franklin H. Littell, "The Importance of Anabaptist Studies," *Archiv für Reformationsgeschichte*, LVIII (1967), 15–28.

that the great experiment of free churches is the most remarkable characteristic of American religious life and for that matter of national life. "The glory of America is a free Christianity, independent of secular government, and supported by the voluntary contributions of a free people," said Philip Schaff. "This is one of the greatest facts in modern history."[16]

Religious Liberty

The clarion call for separation of church and state sounded primarily a negative note. The positive side of the same concern is the appeal for religious liberty. What is now taken for granted in much of the world as an elementary right was quite literally a revolutionary doctrine when first proclaimed as truth by the Radical Reformers. As Rufus Jones reminded his readers: "These free privileges were purchased at great cost . . . and they are now enjoyed by multitudes who have no consciousness that those who first proclaimed the ideals died for them."[17] Central in this affirmation was the concept that true faith must come from the uncoerced conscience. In Chelčický's language: "Whoever is not sincerely brought to the Christian faith through preaching of the gospel shall never be brought by force. . . ."[18] It has never been phrased better than by the Anabaptist Claus Felbinger, writing from his prison cell in 1560: "God wants no compulsory service. On the contrary he loves a free, willing heart that serves him with a joyful soul and does what is right joyfully."[19]

Very early after the Constantinian sea-change in the church's fortunes, there were voices raised to describe the paradoxical shift of Christianity from the status of a persecuted sect to that of a persecuting institutional church. Hilary of Poitiers charged in A.D. 365 that the faith which once was threatened by exile and dungeon and despite this still claimed men's allegiance, now used compulsion upon others. Once propagated by hunted priests, it now hunted priests itself. There is more than merely a difference

---

[16] Philip Schaff, *Germany: Its Universities, Theology and Religion* (Philadelphia: Lindsay & Blakiston, 1857), p. 105.

[17] Rufus Jones, *The Church's Debt to Heretics* (London: J. Clarke, 1925), p. 237.

[18] Brock, *op. cit.*, p. 49.

[19] Quoted in William R. Estep, *The Anabaptist Story* (Nashville: Broadman Press, 1963), p. 143.

in centuries between the Christianity of the martyrs Polycarp and Cyprian and the Christianity of Innocent III, who rejoiced on hearing the news of the indiscriminate slaughter of the Cathari and Catholics alike in southern France in the early thirteenth century at the hands of Simon de Montfort's army. "Wherefore we give praise and thanks to God Almighty, because, in one and the same cause of His mercy, He hath deigned to work two works of justice, by bringing upon these faithless folk their merited destruction in such a fashion that as many as possible of the faithful should gain their well-earned reward by the extermination of the flock."[20] The French prince's lust for plunder thus received papal approval in one of many crusades increasingly launched not against the moslem infidel but against political and religious rivals within Christendom. Before the twelfth century, the church fathers had taught that the heretics' blood should not be shed, but after a rationale was provided by Thomas Aquinas and others these hesitations were quickly forgotten.[21]

Something of the dissenters' determined spirit in the face of persecution is found in the case of a Waldensian captured in Caignan, France, in 1560. This man named Mathurin was thrown into a cell and given three days to reconsider, failing in which he would be burned at the stake. His wife feared that the hard usage might cause him to weaken in his faith, so she sought permission to speak to him. The authorities granted the request, thinking that a wife's pleas might cause a change of heart. When they heard her exhort the husband to maintain his belief, they were furious and threatened to burn her as well. She answered that there was no need to wait for three days on her account, because she was ready to endure death rather than recant. She did ask them to permit her to accompany her husband in death, which took place the next day.[22]

The Anabaptists maintained that infant baptism should be rejected, not alone because they found no biblical warrant for it and because it made impossible the requisite repentance and conver-

[20] Quoted in G. G. Coulton, *Inquisition and Liberty* (London: William Heinemann, 1938), republished (Boston: Beacon Press, 1959), pp. 103–104.

[21] Joseph Lecler, *Toleration and the Reformation*, trans. T. L. Westow (New York: Association Press, 1960), I: 79–89.

[22] Hanspeter Zürcher, "*Nehmen sie den Leib . . . !*" *Märtyrerschicksale* (Zürich: Zwingli-Verlag, 1943), pp. 171–172.

sion, but also because it represented a coercion of belief. Pilgram Marpeck complained that infant baptism forced people to enter the kingdom of God, whereas exactly there compulsion was out of place. "All they have eternal punishment awaiting them who seek to sustain the Kingdom of God with recourse to the civil power." Imprisoned Anabaptists languishing at Trieste in the sixteenth century while the galleys to which they were condemned were awaited, drew up a statement of faith. One item read: "Where has God commanded His child, saying 'Child, go into the whole world, . . . teach all nations, him however who refuses to accept or to believe your teaching you are to catch, torture, yes, strangle until he believes'?" When a clergyman sent to convert them countered with Augustine's "compel them to come in," they responded: "It is by His word and His judgment that Christ constrains men!"[23]

Leaders of the Magisterial Reformation were well aware of this position, and rejected it out of hand. Ulrich Zwingli's successor at Zürich, Henry Bullinger, cited this conviction in building an argument against them:

> They say that one cannot and may not use force to compel anyone to accept the faith seeing that faith is a free gift from God. It is wrong, say they, to compel anyone by force or coercion to embrace the faith, or, to put anyone to death because of erring faith. It is an error, they assert, that in the Church any other sword is used than that of the Divine Word. The secular kingdom, they hold, should be separate from the church and no civil ruler ought to exercise his authority there. The Lord has commanded, they hold, simply to preach the Gospel, and not to compel any one by force to accept it. The true Church of Christ, according to them, has this characteristic that it suffers and endures persecution but does not inflict it upon any.[24]

Menno Simons appealed to the authorities in his book *Christian Baptism* (1539) to respect the conscience of the Anabaptists: "Therefore we pray you . . . by the mercy of God, to consider and realize if there be reasonableness in you, in what great anxiety and anguish we poor, miserable people are placed." For, said Menno,

[23] Both quotations are found in Verduin, *op. cit.*, pp. 74–75.
[24] John Horsch, *Mennonites in Europe* (Scottdale, Pa.: Mennonite Publishing House, 1950), p. 325.

"if we abandon Jesus Christ and His holy Word, we fall into the wrath of God." On the other hand, "if we remain firm in His holy Word, we are put to your cruel sword."[25]

Some of the classic and influential statements advocating religious liberty were made by Puritans. Robert Browne, who wrote that "the Lord's people is of the willing sorte," laid out the bases for the covenanting community of voluntary members. "The Spirit of Christ is in himself too free, great, and generous a Spirit, to suffer himself to be used by any human arm, to whip man into belief; he drives not, but gently leads into all truth, and persuades men to dwell in the tents of like precious faith; which would lose of its preciousness and value if that sparkle of freedom shone not in it," announced the Savoy Confession. Baptists were zealous in pleading for religious liberty from John Smyth on. He is credited with the first appeal in English on its behalf, in which he set forth the position that the magistrate is not to meddle with religion nor compel adherence to any form or tenet, but rather must allow the free choice of each man's conscience. His successor Thomas Helwys died in captivity for his own testimony to the same freedom, and for his daring in reminding the king of it.[26] Baptists stemmed from the Separatist congregation in Gainsborough of whom it was said that as the "Lord's free people" they formed a "church estate in the fellowship of the Gospel, to walk in all His ways, made known to them or to be made known unto them, according to their best endeavor, whatsoever it should cost them."[27]

Basic to this stance is the contention that all men are equal before the Lord. Roger Williams found out that New England was not ready for this claim, when he broke a lance on behalf of the local Indians. While it is not strictly true that the first English colonists first "fell upon their knees, and then upon the aborigines," early efforts at bringing Christianity to the Indians were soon superseded by warfare. Theologians were not lacking who could justify the forcible dispossession of the natives. To them Williams addressed his quatrain:

[25] Quoted in John C. Wenger, *Even Unto Death* (Richmond, Va.: John Knox Press, 1961), p. 71.
[26] Discussed in Estep, *op. cit.*, pp. 216–218.
[27] Payne, *op. cit.*, p. 18.

Boast not, proud English, of thy birth and blood,
  Thy brother Indian is by birth as good,
Of one blood God made him and thee and all,
  As wise, as fair, as strong, as personal.[28]

The idea of equality found its most persistent advocates among the Quakers, whose belief in the light of God in each man provided theological grounding, as against the double predestination of some of their Calvinist contemporaries. This teaching was put to the practical test as Friends found opportunity in the New World to apply it to the problems of governing colonies. Methodists also went on record favoring this general outlook. Wesley insisted that no man can choose or prescribe for another's faith. Rather, every man must follow the dictates of his own conscience in simplicity and sincerity. "He must be fully persuaded in his own mind, and then act according to the best light he has." The Arminian-inclined revivalist repeated in different contexts his motto taken from II Kings 10:15, that if his acquaintance's heart were right as was his, then he would ask no further questions. "Dost thou love and serve God? It is enough."[29]

Voluntary associations sprang from this principle, and have shaped the course of western culture. The French scholar Élie Halévy observed that the Wesleyan revival created the foundation of the nineteenth-century English social order. Lacking the intent and power to secure authority by fiat, the free churches developed a moral authority which was even more pervasive.[30] This "nonconformist conscience," as it was later called, had far-reaching ramifications for English political, economic, and social life, as has its counterpart in America. The emphasis placed upon freedom of religious choice by the restitution groups—Disciples and Plymouth Brethren—is amply illustrated by their histories. The Disciples have taken the principle perhaps as far as it can go, in theology as well as polity. Liberty went so far that until recently any one present at one of their conferences, member or not, could speak and vote on issues up for debate. The Confessing Church

---

[28] Roger Williams, *A Key into the Languages of America*, quoted in Christopher Hill, *Puritanism and Revolution* (New York: Schocken Books, 1964), p. 123.

[29] Albert C. Outler, ed., *John Wesley* (New York: Oxford University Press, 1964), pp. 96–97; Harry E. Fosdick, ed., *Great Voices of the Reformation* (New York: Modern Library, 1952), p. 513.

[30] Hudson, *op. cit.*, pp. 101–102.

had surprising success in Nazi Germany in upholding the right of the church to run its own affairs. Yet more recently, those Christians searching for new forms within the Church are demonstrating their insistence upon greater freedom, in this case not from governmental pressure but from ecclesiastical jurisdiction.

Peace Witness

As challenging to the authorities as the rejection of the church-state union has been the refusal by many of those in the Believers' Churches to perform military service. Few were pacifist in the modern sense, but many were nonresistant or "defenseless" Christians.[31] That is, they acknowledged the responsibility of the "powers that be" to use force as a last resort in maintaining order, but were not prepared to commit violence themselves. The justification for this was a dualism between church and world which demanded a high ethic of Christians not expected in the secular realm. Medieval Catholicism developed the teaching of the two ethical levels of the counsels and the precepts—the former would only be followed by monks, the latter with its lesser requirements would be observed by all others. Luther shifted the dualism within each person by his doctrine of the two kingdoms. The Anabaptists placed the line between the covenant community and the world, believing that the Sermon on the Mount was not addressed solely to those with monastic vocations.

By no means all of the Believers' Churches followed the Anabaptists in this. Baptists have had a long history of patriotic support of governments since their hearty participation in Cromwell's Ironside regiments. Today, for example, they have more than fulfilled their quota of chaplains to the American military services. On the other hand, they produced Martin Luther King. Methodists have also usually supported military obligations, although many outstanding peace workers have come from among them, and strong antiwar pronouncements have been issued by their assemblies. In World War II, they ranked just below the Friends in number of objectors to military service. Most Plymouth Brethren have found that their fundamentalistic theology fits well

[31] For a discussion of the distinctions between the two, see Guy F. Hershberger, War, Peace, and Nonresistance (Scottdale, Pa.: Herald Press, 1953), pp. 170–206.

with military service but some are pacifists; a surprisingly high number of them are found in the British officer corps. Even within the so-called Historic Peace Churches—the Mennonites, Brethren, and Quakers, who have kept as denominations official peace testimonies—there have been members in the twentieth century who have not upheld the conscientious-objector position. These churches, however, have provided the majority of objectors in World Wars I and II. In the Civil War the Disciples of Christ are estimated to have had the largest proportion of pacifists of any southern denomination excluding the peace churches. *The Christian Century,* founded by one of their ministers, has often pursued a pacifist line.[32]

The reason for the peace position for some of the Believers' Churches is not hard to find. Given the orientation of discipleship to the Prince of Peace and devotion to the early church as norm for conduct, nonresistance follows quite logically.[33] Scholars are agreed that the early church did not engage in military service until the end of the second century. Patristic writers who then accepted the validity of military duty were stern in condemning bloodshed, which is not paradoxical because of the police function of the soldiery at that time. By the fifth century things had changed to the extent that only Christians were allowed to be soldiers. The earlier peace ethic was continued within the church by the monastics, who were not only permitted to follow the New Testament but obliged to do so. When the Reformers disposed of monasticism, they left no place for those called to the more rigorous standard.

Both the Waldenses and the Unity of Brethren were known for their nonresistant positions. Their refusal to carry weapons was in fact one method of detecting them used by their enemies. The Waldenses condemned any shedding of blood, whether in war or by capital punishment. Members of the Unity, especially in the early period when under the influence of Chelčický's teachings, were outspoken opponents of war. He had satirized those who balked at eating pork on Friday but who saw nothing wrong with

[32] Walter B. Posey, *Frontier Mission* (Lexington, Ky.: University of Kentucky Press, 1966), p. 401.

[33] For a brief discussion, see Geoffrey F. Nuttall, *Christian Pacifism in History* (Oxford: Basil Blackwell, 1958). A fuller statement is given by Roland H. Bainton, *Christian Attitudes Toward War and Peace* (New York and Nashville: Abingdon Press, 1960).

human slaughter any day of the week. Chelčický urged his followers to bear injustice humbly and patiently, and not to avenge themselves but to imitate Christ who was led as a lamb to the butcher and opened not his mouth.

Anabaptists used the same imagery. Conrad Grebel said in 1524 that followers of Christ "must reach the fatherland of eternal rest, not by overcoming bodily enemies with the sword, but by overcoming spiritual foes." Christians "use neither the worldly sword nor engage in wars, since among them taking human life has ceased entirely."[34] Andrew Castleberger, in whose house in Zürich the Bible circle met after 1522, taught that a soldier who received money for killing was the same as a murderer, a strong statement in a land which was famed for its mercenaries. Their standpoint was made perfectly clear in the letter sent to Thomas Müntzer in 1524. The German leader (who never received the letter) was to die within the year after the battle of Frankenhausen at which he had urged on the peasants in their uprising against the lords. The Swiss Brethren had heard something of his leanings to violence, for they admonished him:

> The gospel and its adherents are not to be protected by the sword, nor are they thus to protect themselves, which as we learn from our brother is thy opinion and practice. True Christian believers are sheep among wolves, sheep for the slaughter; they must be baptized in anguish and affliction, tribulation, persecution, suffering and death; they must be tried with fire, and must reach the fatherland of eternal rest, not by killing their bodily, but by mortifying their spiritual enemies. Neither do they use worldly sword or war, since all killing has ceased with them.[35]

The Society of Friends has been the most articulate of all these groups in protesting warfare and killing, and suggesting alternative courses of conduct for governments. In the popular mind Quakers are completely identified with pacifism. Actually, at their inception, there is evidence that they were not unwilling for the sword to be used in a good cause. George Fox several times urged the Puritan army to take warfare into the camp of the papal enemy, as

---

[34] Quoted in Hershberger, *op. cit.*, p. 82.
[35] George H. Williams, ed., *Spiritual and Anabaptist Writers* (Philadelphia: Westminster Press, 1957), p. 80. In a postscript (or second letter) they criticized again what they had heard about Müntzer's preaching that the princes "are to be attacked with the fist" (p. 84).

retribution for the Inquisition. But very soon, Quakers saw that this was inconsistent with their other beliefs.[36] Fox wrote Cromwell in 1654 that he had been sent by God "to stand a witness against all violence and against all the works of darkness, and to turn people from the darkness to the light, and to bring them from the occasion of the war and from the occasion of the magistrate's sword."[37] Seven years later the assembled Friends made a declaration which has stood firm since then: "All bloody principles and practices as we to our own particular do utterly deny, with all outward wars and strife and fightings with outward weapons for any end or under any pretense whatsoever." Isaac Penington drafted a careful statement which reveals the positive attitude of the Quakers to the state and its possibilities: "I speak not this against any magistrate's or people's defending themselves against foreign invasions, or making use of the sword to suppress the violent and evil doers within their borders (for this the present estate of things may and doth require . . .); but yet there is a better estate which the Lord hath already brought some into, and which nations are to expect to travel towards."[38] For their part Quakers had decided to live already in the manner in which in some enlightened time all men would live. This was exemplified by the Quaker speaking publicly on peace to whom a listener said: "Well, stranger, if all the world was of your mind I would turn and follow after." He replied: "So then thou hast a mind to be the last man to be good. I have a mind to be one of the first and set the rest an example."[39]

Mennonites and Brethren joined at the start of the Revolutionary War in a petition to the assembly of Pennsylvania to be excused from military service. "We have dedicated ourselves to serve men in every thing that can be helpful to the preservation of men's lives, but we find no freedom in giving or doing, or assisting in any thing by which men's lives are destroyed and hurt." They announced willingness to pay taxes, but war taxes would need to

[36] Hill, *op. cit.*, p. 145; Thomas G. Sanders, *Protestant Concepts of Church and State* (Garden City, N.Y.: Anchor Books, 1965), pp. 136–143.

[37] Quoted in Frederick B. Tolles, *Quakers and the Atlantic Culture* (New York: The Macmillan Co., 1960), p. 38.

[38] Sanders, *op. cit.*, pp. 139, 143.

[39] Related in Howard Brinton, *Friends for 300 Years* (New York: Harper & Brothers, 1952), p. 162.

be taken from them by force, as they were.[40] They held to the same position during the Civil War, having more difficulty securing exemption in the South than in the North, because of the greater shortage of manpower in the Confederation. General Stonewall Jackson said of them: "There live a people in the valley of Virginia, that are not hard to bring to the army. While there they are obedient to their officers. Nor is it difficult to have them take aim, but it is impossible to get them to take correct aim. I, therefore, think it better to leave them at their homes that they may produce supplies for the army."[41] During World War I great pressure was put on pacifists in local communities to back the war. The experience of the Mennonite John Schrag in Kansas is typical. A prosperous farmer, born in Russia of German ethnic stock, he was seized by a mob in an attempt to make him consent to buy war bonds. When he refused, they smeared his hair and beard with yellow paint and displayed him to mocking passers-by. He would have been lynched if local police had not removed him to a nearby city, where he was tried and eventually absolved of a charge of insulting the flag and sedition.[42]

Representatives of the three peace churches agreed in the 1930s to take joint action in the event of another war. This enabled them to help shape legislation when conscription was reimposed at the outset of World War II. The result was the creation of Civilian Public Service as an alternative to military duty. The three churches continued common efforts after the war, helping to organize the Church Peace Mission in the United States. In Europe they organized a series of theological conferences under the title "The Lordship of Christ Over Church and State," commonly referred to as the Puidoux Conferences, after the small Swiss village where the first meeting was held in 1955. These meetings have been called the first serious conversations between the Radical Reformers and the *Volkskirchen* since the sixteenth century.[43]

[40] *A Short and Sincere Declaration* (1775), republished in Donald F. Durnbaugh, ed., *The Brethren in Colonial America* (Elgin, Ill.: Brethren Press, 1967), pp. 363–365.
[41] Quoted in Hershberger, *op. cit.*, p. 107.
[42] James C. Juhnke, "John Schrag Espionage Case," *Mennonite Life* (July 1967), 121–122.
[43] Dale Aukerman and Harold W. Row, "Talks Resumed After 360 Years," *Brethren Life and Thought*, VI (Winter 1961), 29–32; Donald F. Durnbaugh, "The Puidoux Conferences," *Brethren Life and Thought*, XIII (Winter 1968), 30–40.

The International Fellowship of Reconciliation also sponsored these meetings. The I.F.O.R. was founded in 1914. The outbreak of World War I forced an international peace conference of churchmen to disband in Constance. Two of the delegates, the German Frederick Siegmund-Schultze and the English Quaker Henry Hodgkin, pledged themselves as they parted in the train station at Cologne that they would keep the spirit of peace intact whatever came. The Fellowship of Reconciliation was the result. Organized first in Britain in December 1914, it was made international in October 1919, and soon had branches in twenty countries. Active in the German branch after World War II was Martin Niemöller, the former submarine commander and Confessing Church leader. The threat of nuclear warfare and the plight of the divided Germany were precipitating factors in his controversial decision to become a pacifist.

Among the *Brüderschaften,* who see themselves as the continuation of the Confessing Church, the peace issue has taken front rank. In 1961 the Church Brotherhood of Northwest Germany declared: "The mass weapons of destruction have made it clear: war is murder." Some prominent German theologians have come close to the absolutist pacifist position. Hellmut Gollwitzer, another Confessing Church leader, wrote in 1957: "It seems that now with the advent of the new war weapons, which cannot be overlooked, the true nature of war has now become evident, which was previously latent, tamed, and limited but always the same. . . . It could be, therefore, that the qualitative dividing line, which may be observed between the previous and present weapons of destruction, already exists between the activity of a policeman and a soldier, which Christian pacifism has maintained for a long time."[44] A similar development is also discernible within the contemporary church renewal movement, where revulsion against specific wars in Asia has broadened in some cases to opposition to wars in toto.

Involvement in the State

A new book on Protestant concepts of church and state uses Mennonites, Quakers, and Baptists to typify several recurrent pos-

[44] H. Treblin and H. Weitbrecht, *Christusbekenntnis - Friedenszeugnis* (Hamburg-Bergstedt: Herbert Reich, 1963), p. 14ff.

tures. In addition it speaks of the Lutheran two-kingdom position and the "transformationist" position of realism and responsibility as seen by the author. Mennonites represent "Christian life without political compromise," and are portrayed in much the same way the Niebuhr brothers did earlier. Acknowledgment is made that here is a consistent position which is good to have around, although it is held at the price of irrelevancy. The Quakers are said to have shifted from "theocracy to pacifism." Their course has been from the "Holy Experiment" of attempting to run a Christian commonwealth in Penn's Woods and New Jersey to their present activity in "speaking truth to power." Baptists are used as exemplars of the strict separationist stance with primary concern to guard the wall dividing church and state. This characterization has been hotly denied by a respected Baptist historian as inaccurate and misleading.[45]

In fact the involvement with the state has been a very complex situation, even with those groups which have fitted Troeltsch's sect pattern the most closely. The Unity of Brethren soon found itself faced with taking in lords into its membership and made the necessary adjustments. The Anabaptists, though clearly rejecting participation as magistrates in the sixteenth century, ran virtual theocracies in Russia and South America later on. In the Netherlands where they were first tolerated and accepted, the Mennonite Church became fully a part of the Dutch life to the extent that a deacon of the Hague congregation was the minister of the Dutch Navy! The Church of the Brethren long discouraged activity in politics, as inappropriate for Christian conduct, but produced the governor of Pennsylvania during World War I in Martin G. Brumbaugh. Alexander Campbell was a delegate to a constitutional convention in Virginia, and spoke on political issues in his periodicals. John Wesley had a simple rule, "No Politics!"—but his spiritual descendants are often found in the political arena. In the ninetieth congress they were second only to the Roman Catholics in number of congressmen and led in the number of state governors.[46]

One point that must be made is that the effect of the life and

---

[45] Sanders, *op. cit.*; see the review by Winthrop S. Hudson in *Church History*, XXXV (June 1966), 227–234.
[46] "The Ninetieth Congress: a Religious Census," *Christianity Today* (December 9, 1966), 36–37.

witnesses of the Believers' Churches helped create modern western democracy. It can even be said that these groups have made their most effective contributions to politics by their faithful, even stubborn, adherence to their religious views. The influence in developing the style of voluntary associations has already been mentioned. Another example may clarify. The Historic Peace Churches following World War II were eager to find a method of alternative service to military participation more satisfactory than the C.P.S. camps, which often involved make-work with no social benefit and sometimes unsatisfactory arrangements with governmental agencies. They developed a plan of voluntary service overseas in a variety of social work projects. Some built homes for displaced persons. Others introduced improved agricultural methods to villagers in Greece and North Africa. Still others worked in refugee camps, teaching English and organizing recreation. They served without pay (receiving basic subsistence and medical care) for an equivalent time to that spent by draftees. Government recognition was secured for this plan of conscientious objectors working in these ways for the agencies of the peace churches in lieu of military service. The idea proved successful, and it was picked up by the Kennedy administration as the basis for the (greatly expanded) Peace Corps. This has been called the most creative venture of Kennedy's thousand days.

Another consideration is that the times have changed radically from a situation when a prince or a self-perpetuating oligarchy ran the state to the western scene where democracy is haltingly but nevertheless effectively present. Quite a different posture might be expected of Believers' Churches in such a changed context. The fact that the Quakers developed at the point in history when they did (when the Commonwealth period allowed an involvement in public affairs not possible before) certainly had an effect on their attitude to the state. Littell has described the difference that was made in local governments when free-churchmen began to participate.[47] The same principle of respect for each other's thinking, which they practiced in the religious setting to aid the pursuit of truth, when applied to civic problems was found to have favorable results. Rufus Jones was perhaps too optimistic but was making the correct approach when he stated that Continental Anabaptism

[47] Franklin H. Littell, "The Historic Free Church Defined," *Brethren Life and Thought*, IX (Autumn 1964), 78–90.

was the "first plain announcement in modern history of a program for a new type of Christian society in the modern world, especially in America and England . . . an absolutely free and independent religious society, and a State in which every man counts as a man, and has his share in shaping both church and state."[48] Even the Quaker usage of the "sense of the meeting" in lieu of voting has been introduced in some public settings as an effective administrative technique.

Another aspect is the shift in the function of governments themselves. Many of the areas of government responsibility today—education, welfare, health, recreation—were previously totally in private hands. This means that even those churches which have staunchly upheld a separation of church and state have found it both possible and helpful to cooperate with government on programs of social value. An example is the post-1945 aid to rehabilitate and reconstruct peoples and countries ravaged by the war. Shipping of goods and livestock contributed by church people was taken care of by governments in ways which served the best interests of all parties. The East Harlem Protestant Parish, to take another example, works closely with government programs benefiting the people of the inner city, and have adjusted their former program to do so.

The thinking of the Believers' Churches has not fully responded to the changed political situation, but it is shaping around the following assumptions.[49] The church seeks to be true to its own genius, and practices discipleship in its present setting. At the same time it helps the state to live up to its own best self-understanding of its responsibilities. Negatively put, the church resists attempts to sacralize the state or to allow the state to take to itself religious prerogatives. The church also guards against entrapment by the culture-religion. It does not expect the state to operate upon the ethic of the New Testament, but it does call upon it to deal justly. Totalitarian claims must be rejected, but the church can work with the state in many areas of life. The church will not try to duplicate institutions in those areas in which the state is

---

[48] Rufus Jones, *Studies in Mystical Religion* (1909), quoted in Harold S. Bender, "The Anabaptist Vision," *Church History*, XIII (1944), 3.

[49] See Franklin H. Littell, "The Churches and the Body Politic," *Daedalus*, XCVI, No. 1 (Winter 1967), 22–42; John Howard Yoder, *The Christian Witness to the State* (Newton, Kansas: Faith and Life Press, 1964).

acting competently, but should seek new areas of need and develop models which, if proved successful, can be taken over by the state. "For us who enjoy the blessings of religious liberty, the double task is to enrich the quality of the community of faithful people and—in the secular order—to learn to live with all men of good will without suspicion and without anxiety" (Littell).[50] This leads directly into the next topic, that is, mutual aid and service.

[50] Franklin H. Littell, "The Concerns of the Believers' Church," Chicago Theological Seminary *Register*, LVIII (December 1967), 18.

· XI ·

Mutual Aid and Service

It was the winter of 1569. A Dutch Anabaptist named Dirk Willems fled from his home by the back door as officials come to seize him entered by the front. When he came to a dike and canal, in his desperation he risked crossing on the thin ice and reached the other side safely. The leading pursuer was not so fortunate and broke through into the frigid water. Dirk Willems turned back and saved the official from certain death. Despite his selfless action he was taken, tried as a heretic, and burned slowly at the stake. He was heard to cry more than seventy times: "Oh my Lord! Oh my God!" A bailiff, who could not bear to look on any longer, finally ordered that the Anabaptist be put out of his agony.[1]

Was Dirk Willems foolish in choosing to save his pursuer instead of escaping, thereby making his capture and punishment possible? The question is academic, because in this action he was only following his faith, which expected acts of love for one's fellow man before thinking of self. So has it been for most of the time for most of the members of the Believers' Churches, although performance has certainly not always measured up to the ideal. But the ideal was always present. Probably no characteristic has been so often noted and so appreciated by society at large as the penchant of Believers' Churchmen in practicing mutual aid and service. No adequate book can be written on humanitarianism— be it abolition of slavery, aid to refugees, care of minorities, amelioration of working conditions, improvement of prisons, defense of civil rights—without taking into account the contribution of these groups.

The Quakers tell the story of a stranger who happened to enter a Friends' meetinghouse, expecting the usual Protestant Sunday

[1] John C. Wenger, *Even Unto Death* (Richmond, Va.: John Knox Press, 1961), p. 101.

worship. After sitting in the general silence for ten minutes, the puzzled visitor whispered to the soberly clad person seated next to him: "Excuse me, but when does the service begin?" The answer came back crisply: "Friend, the service begins right after the meeting is over!" This identification of the whole of life with consistent regard for the welfare of other people has been a hallmark of the Friends and other Believers' Churches. At times the emphasis on the gathered group has limited the scope of benefaction to the household of faith, but this has usually been broken through in time by individuals responsive to the broader vision. Dietrich Bonhoeffer's depiction of Christ as the man for others fits with the attitude of these people who, historically, have often in their following of Jesus attempted to be men for others.

Some have seen a link between the evidence of concern for mankind and the practice of foot washing observed by several of these movements. Kneeling in imitation of Christ to wash the feet of the brother in lowly service seems to condition men to be ready to serve the needs of the world in the same prosaic and practical fashion. Even some Quakers who on principle reject churchly sacraments have found meaning in this practice as they have participated in it with those for whom it is a natural part of church membership.[2] It is significant to note that the British Methodists use the story of the *pedilavum* (John 13) in the service of ordination for their deaconesses. Part of the charge to them states: "It may fall to you to preach the Gospel, to lead the worship of a congregation, to teach both young and old; you may be required to feed the flock of Christ, to nurse the sick, to care for the poor, to rescue the fallen, to succour the hopeless, to offer friendship, even at cost, to many, who but for you may never know a Christian friend."[3] The father of the extensive deaconess system of the German churches, Theodore Fliedner, was stimulated to introduce the order into Germany in the 1830s after a trip to the Netherlands where he saw the work of Mennonite deaconesses.[4]

In the following, the discussion has been divided into four sec-

[2] See D. Elton Trueblood, *The People Called Quakers* (New York: Harper & Row, 1966), p. 137.
[3] Gordon S. Wakefield, "Diakonia in the Methodist Church Today," in J. I. McCord and T. H. L. Parker, eds., *Service in Christ* (London: Epworth Press, 1966), p. 185.
[4] Frederick Herzog, "Diakonia in Modern Times: Eighteenth–Twentieth Centuries," *ibid.*, p. 142.

tions for convenience's sake, to deal with the individual, communal, social, and international dimensions. However, they are all of a piece, and historically have been thought of together.

The Individual Dimension

The concept of the priesthood of all believers was taken seriously by those of the Believers' Churches, and that quite in the sense that Luther had intended and not in the distorted later use of the phrase. It was not the modern version that each person is his own priest. They had no appreciation for Coleridge's claim that he was a member of the one true church, in fact the only member. Rather, they understood it in the sense that each man is a minister for every other person. Luther put it more boldly: each man is a Christ for his brother. It is for this reason that it is wrong to say of these groups, as sometimes happens, that they abolished the ministry. It would be fairer to say that they abolished the laity. All men were to be ministers. Baptism for them was ordination for ministry, as well as a sign and witness of their conversion. This meant that there was no possibility of salvation apart from others. Not for them Frederick the Great's cynical, if tolerant, decree that each man should be saved after his own fashion. Representative for them would be Count Zinzendorf's "I concede no Christianity without brotherhood."

In practice, this meant that a member of a Believers' Church would not be left alone to his own devices. On the side usually referred to as church discipline, this meant that he expected his brother to admonish him for shortcomings and failures, following the pattern established in the eighteenth chapter of Matthew's gospel. His brethren would also expect him to inform them if he noticed errors in their faith or Christian walk. This was clearly evidenced during the days of the Confessing Church when the weakness of one had immediate negative repercussions for the others. Martin Niemöller's correspondence was full of cautions and reprimands as well as encouragement. The former customary salutation among German pastors or colleagues had been replaced by "brother." If one of Niemöller's correspondents received a letter addressed "Very esteemed Mr. Brother" (*Sehr geehrter Herr Bruder!*) he could expect the contents to contain fraternal criticism.[5] The other side of the not being left alone was the certainty that any ill fortune, hardship, illness, or persecution would not be suffered alone but rather as part of the larger community. On the economic level, from the time of the Waldenses on, it has been observed that no beggars were to be found among their members. They took care of their own. Material matters were just as much a point of interest as were spiritual. Indeed that distinction between the two would not be congenial to them.

This meant that the financial affairs of members were very much felt to be part of the concern of the covenant community. If members were helped during economic disaster, they were also liable to discipline for irregularities in dealing with money. Careless assumption of debts, for example, was forbidden. The Elkhorn (Kentucky) Disciples of Christ congregation in 1860 "cut off Richard Allen upon the ground of his reckless manner of doing business[,] that is in purchasing property whenever he could get credit when he must have known he could not meet his promise which he failed to do[;] by doing [so] he had brought reproach upon the Church of Christ."[6] In 1758 two members of the Germantown congregation of the Church of the Brethren were set back from the breaking of bread (communion) until they could settle their differences over a land contract.

Max Weber noted the strictness of monetary probity among the Baptists in the South when he traveled in the United States in 1904. Acceptance into membership was only possible after a probationary period and minute inquiry into the applicant's conduct and previous life. "Admission to the congregation is recognized as an absolute guarantee of the moral qualities of a gentleman, especially of those qualities required in business matters. . . . If he got economic straits through no fault of his own, the sect arranged his affairs, gave guarantees to the creditors, and helped him in every way. . . ." He told of the puzzlement of a newly arrived German physician whose first patient emphasized before the examination began that he was a member of the Baptist Church. The specialist could not see why Baptist membership was

[5] Dietmar Schmidt, *Martin Niemöller* (Hamburg: Rowohlt Verlag, 1959), p. 125.
[6] Quoted in David E. Harrell, Jr., *Quest for a Christian America* (Nashville, Tenn.: Disciples of Christ Historical Society, 1966), p. 71.

germane to nose-and-throat checkup. An American colleague informed him that the reason for the announcement of the church affiliation was to put the physician at ease about the patient's readiness to pay the professional fees.[7]

Integral to the insistence upon financial stability was the corresponding expectation of simplicity in attire and standard of living. William Penn commented that "the very trimming of the vain world would clothe all the naked one."[8] The early Methodists had very strong feelings in this regard. "Do not waste any part of so precious a talent [saving money] merely in gratifying the desire of the eye by superfluous or expensive apparel, or by needless ornaments. Waste no part of it in curiously adorning your houses, in superfluous or expensive furniture, in costly pictures, painting, gilding, books, in elegant (rather than useful) gardens. Let your neighbors who know nothing better do this. . . . Lay out nothing to gratify the pride of life, to gain the admiration or praise of men." This is from John Wesley's sermon on "The Use of Money."[9] It must be said that the praiseworthy search for simplicity could be corrupted on the one hand by the developing of exquisite taste in simple furniture and expensive but plainly cut clothes, and on the other hand by preoccupation with legalistic attention to outward appearance to the neglect of weightier matters. The histories of Believers' Churches show sufficient evidences of these pitfalls.

Something of the same spirit of attention to individuals and the individual's responsibility is found in contemporary expressions such as the Church of the Saviour and other new forms of the church. The demands of time and resources made upon members preclude any form of conspicuous consumption.

The Communal Dimension

Balthasar Hubmaier answered the charge that he favored a com-

[7] Max Weber, "The Protestant Sects and the Spirit of Capitalism," in H. H. Gerth and C. Wright Mills, eds., *From Max Weber: Essays in Sociology* (New York: Oxford University Press, 1958), pp. 304–305.

[8] Quoted in Howard Brinton, *Friends for 300 Years* (New York: Harper & Brothers, 1952), p. 135.

[9] Albert C. Outler, ed., *John Wesley* (New York: Oxford University Press, 1964), pp. 245–246.

munal ownership of property (which seemed to bother the authorities even more than the parallel contention that Anabaptists practiced community of wives) by stating: "Concerning community of
goods, I have always said that everyone should be concerned
about the needs of others, so that the hungry might be fed, the
thirsty given to drink, and the naked clothed. For we are not lords
of our possessions, but stewards and distributors. There is certainly no one who says that another's goods may be seized and
made in common; rather, he would gladly give the coat in addition
to the shirt."[10] In this, he was denying the charge that the
Anabaptists plotted to seize all possessions and parcel them out to
the poor. Even the Hutterites, who did practice a community of
goods, were far from teaching that they could appropriate from
others. What they did, of course, was to pool their own resources.

The idea that material goods were only held provisionally in
stewardship was pervasive in the Believers' Churches. In 1557 a
Strasbourg Protestant reported that all candidates for baptism into
a local Swiss Brethren congregation were first asked whether "if
necessity required it, they would devote all their possessions to the
service of the brotherhood and would not fail any member that is
in need, if they were able to render aid."[11] A Church of the
Brethren doctrinal treatise written in colonial America phrased it:
"To this extent 'mine' and 'yours' may be spoken on this basis,
that this is mine and that is yours to administer and keep until a
time of need for the poor and suffering in and outside of the
congregation. To love one's neighbor as one's self shows clearly
what communion is. Thus it behooves him who has two coats to
give to him who has none, and he who has food, let him do the
same (Luke 3)." The treatise suggested on the amount of sharing
necessary: "Love has no aim or measure as to how much one
should give. Rather, it helps and gives gladly of its own volition as
long as it has something and is able to help."[12] It was not ex-

---

[10] Quoted in Peter J. Klassen, *The Economics of Anabaptism, 1525–1560*
(The Hague: Mouton and Co., 1964), p. 32. The second chapter, "The Eco-
nomics of Mutual Aid," has a good discussion of this whole topic.
[11] Quoted in J. Winfield Fretz and Harold S. Bender, "Mutual Aid,"
Mennonite Encyclopedia (1957), III: 796–801.
[12] Michael Frantz, "Simple Doctrinal Considerations . . . ," in Donald F.
Durnbaugh, ed., *The Brethren in Colonial America* (Elgin, Ill.: Brethren
Press, 1967), p. 453.

pected that a person would give so much that he would himself need to be cared for, as there was not the idea of gaining merits in heaven by almsgiving as held by medieval Catholicism.

One of the reasons that the Hutterites left Nikolsburg in Moravia in 1528 was that they believed the other Anabaptist faction was not showing sufficient care for the many refugees who sought asylum there. After setting up their communitarian colonies, they devoted much attention to the biblical and theological bases for their sharing. They could and did point to the early Christians, naturally, and found also many other parts of the New Testament which alluded to the care which Christians should have for their brethren. A favorite motto was "Communal living would not be hard if there were not such self-regard" (*Die Gemeinschaft wär nit schwer / Wenn nur der Eigennutz nit wär*). They also emphasized the importance of *Gelassenheit*, an untranslatable term much used by late-medieval mystics which connotes a complete yielding to God's will by the radical elimination of self-will. "To have all things in common, a free, untrammeled, yielding, willing heart in Christ is needed," wrote Ulrich Stadler about 1536.[13] A modern expression of the Hutterite spirit explains:

> The life of a member of a Hutterite community cannot be compared with the life of an ordinary citizen of the country who carries the whole responsibility of his affairs himself. Since the community is an assembly of many, the burdens are also put on the shoulders of many, as both abilities and needs are shared. . . . The commune is a single organism, consisting of one body and having one spirit and one heart. The spirit that rules is common to all. It cannot show a lack of concern under any circumstances. . . . Brotherly love and the uniting spirit of working together help to make the commune function.[14]

Mennonites today have probably organized mutual aid more completely than any other noncommunitarian group. Most common among their sixty-nine different mutual aid societies operating in the United States and Canada in 1956 were those providing for orphans and dependent children, for the aged, and fire and

---

[13] Robert Friedmann, "The Christian Communism of the Hutterian Brethren," in H. S. Bender, ed., *Hutterite Studies* (Goshen, Ind.: Mennonite Historical Society, 1961), pp. 76–85.
[14] Paul S. Gross, *The Hutterite Way* (Saskatoon, Can.: Freeman Publishing Co., 1965), p. 171.

storm insurance societies. They have also established mutual funds to lend money to conscientious objectors and to settlers in South America, and for new church buildings. The Disciples of Christ have developed a complex system of boards and agencies, some of which meet similar needs. Earlier, these could be handled on a local basis. In 1834 Alexander Campbell announced that among the five primary services demanded of Christians in local congregations were "direct contributions . . . for the poor saints, for widows and other objects of sympathy." By the 1840s they had developed a regular plan of giving each week for this purpose "as the Lord has prospered." The Nashville, Tennessee, church reported in 1847 that it had organized the whole city into wards, with a brother and sister responsible to visit each member in each ward each week, so that a report on their temporal and spiritual condition could be made each Sunday. Walnut Grove, Illinois, had two houses for the poor within the bounds of the congregation. An admiring visitor commented: "This looks like old-fashioned Christianity," a compliment coming from a restorationist Disciple![15]

In Germany in the 1930s the Confessing Church had to see to it that aid was forthcoming to the families of pastors who took exposed positions. When salaries were cut off, heavy fines imposed, or prison terms levied, common support was crucial to keep the movement going. The unsung heroes of the struggle were the financial secretaries who saw to the distribution of the funds. Dietrich Bonhoeffer in his *Life Together* gave a theological foundation to the practical situation. This type of sharing was rather novel in Germany where a rigid class system had kept individuals apart.

The Social Dimension

Danilo Dolci, the gifted Italian journalist, has informed the world about the cruel conditions under which life goes on in Mafiaridden Sicily. One of the poorest towns in the isolated center of the island (far from tourist attractions) is Riesi, notorious even on Sicily for its apathy, squalor, and hopelessness. In its small area, twenty-eight thousand people exist, most living in window-

[15] Harrell, *op. cit.*, pp. 72–74.

less one-room houses with six to twelve inhabitants (not counting the livestock) or in caves in the rocky hillsides. Into this case study in misery in 1962 moved a Waldensian pastor named Tullio Vinay. During World War II as pastor of the Waldensian church in Florence, he risked his neck sheltering Jews. Later he became widely known as the founder and builder of the Agape Youth Village in the Italian Alps. Now, in an extension of the Agape Community, he heads an international team in the *Servizio Cristiano* in Riesi. Vinay says of the project that it is an "attack on the whole town to transform it by giving it a new sense of life." The approach is multilevel—educational, financial, political, agricultural, sociological. Ecumenical aid made possible the construction of a social service center on the "Hill of Olives," housing a kindergarten, clinic, vocational school, counseling center for mothers and babies, and an experimental poultry farm. The theological base was articulated by Vinay in another context: "For us believers the 'new world,' the one of the search of the neighbor, of service and gift is not a utopia because Christ is risen and is already at work. And if He is risen, it is His world that is true, not the one of violence, and His truth cannot be buried." This venture, in a way, is not a new venture for Waldenses, for they had organized educational work in southern Italy and on Sicily in the late nineteenth century after the unification of Italy. Hospitals, orphanages, schools, and hostels were established in many cities and towns.[16]

Anabaptists also had a broader scope for charity than their own circle. Just before Christmas Day in 1553 a shipload of Reformed refugees from England, forced to leave their Strangers' Congregation in London when Queen Mary took the throne, were icebound in the harbor of Wismar after being rejected by Lutheran Denmark. The Wismar town council was also Lutheran, and refused to have anything to do with these "Sacramentarians," as the Reformed were called in consequence of the dispute between Luther and Zwingli over the Eucharist. Near Wismar were Mennonites, who, however, as heretics were forced to live in hiding. They heard of the plight of the travelers, raised money for them, sought out temporary jobs, and offered to give shelter to the children. This opened the way to long doctrinal discussions between the two

---

[16] Ray Davey, "The Two Faces of Sicily," *Frontier*, I, vol. 8 (Spring 1965), 45–48; *Agape Servizio Informazioni* (May 1967), [6].

groups which proved to be fruitless. Later the Reformed revealed the names and hiding places of their benefactors to the Lutheran town council. These Mennonites were living up to the principle expressed by one of their Swiss martyrs, Hans Leopold, who said of them: "If they know of any one who is in need, whether or not he is a member of their church, they believe it is their duty out of love to God to render help and aid."[17]

Dutch Mennonites were particularly faithful in aiding others. They enjoyed a tolerated position earlier than their co-religionists, which enabled them to gain the wherewithal to help others. In the early eighteenth century they provided funds for oppressed Anabaptists to leave the Bernese canton of Switzerland. They have a long record of helping persecuted dissenters to resettle in other countries. In the United States currently, the Mennonite Disaster Service is probably the best known example of Mennonite social service. When catastrophe strikes, a flood or tornado, teams of self-supporting skilled workers move into the stricken area to provide quiet and effective help. National publicity has been given to their quickly responding voluntary labor.

The Society of Friends has probably done more in the field of general humanitarian effort proportionately than any other religious body. This persistent effort has flowed naturally from their basic conviction that each man is a child of God and has within him that which can respond to truth and love. The unity of their devotional life with social action has captured the admiration of many. A professor at the University of Hull explained why he became a "convinced" Friend. "What particularly appealed to me . . . was the direct way in which the insistence on the quiet inward life became inevitably associated with its active outward expression in the world of affairs. In Quakerism I found the Christian and the social to be effortlessly intertwined."[18] Knowing firsthand the despicable conditions of prisons in England and America, the Quakers agitated for reform. Elizabeth Fry, a quiet and refined lady, braved the incredible clamor and degradation of the women's section of the Newgate Prison in London in 1813 in repeated visits and succeeded in changing for the better the life of the "idle, savage, drunken, unruly women." Quakers in Pennsylvania first developed the concept that prison life should be designed as

---

[17] Fretz and Bender, *op. cit.*, p. 797.
[18] Quoted in Trueblood, *op. cit.*, p. 256.

remedial rather than punitive. They planned therefore a "penitentiary" where prisoners could be isolated, the better for remorse and change (penitence) to take place. Although isolation proved to be too severe for most prisoners, other Quaker reforms were so successful that penal theory was revolutionized. The famous French visitor Alexis de Tocqueville came to America to investigate these prisons in order to make recommendations for improving French jails to his own government.[19]

Also remarkable was their attitude toward the insane. Instead of treating them as animals, as was customary, Quakers said that they were mentally ill. In 1796 William Tukes established "The Retreat" in York, England, where patients were treated as guests and physical restraints abolished. Therapy was provided by way of handicrafts. A Friends' asylum at Frankford, Pennsylvania, announced that it "is intended to furnish, besides the requisite medical aid, such tender sympathetic attention and religious oversight as may sooth agitated minds." This work was forwarded during and after World War II, as Quaker and other conscientious objectors were assigned to work as attendants in large state mental institutions. Their deep dismay over the outrageous conditions in some of the hospitals led to exposés and, more importantly, to many of them devoting their lives to the cause of mental health. A similar story can be told of the Mennonites, who also set up a string of clinics across the country, some of them pioneering in outpatient treatment.

Quaker opposition to slavery is proverbial. John Woolman and Anthony Benezet in this country were outspoken in bringing to the attention of their brethren first of all, and society in general, the evils of slaveholding and trading. Woolman would often decline to accept hospitality in a home where slaves were kept or would insist upon reimbursing slaves for work done for him personally. The tender way in which he explained his actions often won him the respect and agreement of the slaveowner. The German sectarian groups in America such as the Mennonites, Brethren, and Moravians had frowned on slavery from the time of their first landing. A Mennonite, Peter C. Plockhoy, issued the first public statement in North America against slavery in connection with regulations for a colony on the Delaware: "No lordships or servile

[19] Brinton, *op. cit.*, pp. 151–153.

slavery shall burden our company."[20] In 1688 the Mennonite-Quakers at Germantown, Pennsylvania, wrote up a trenchant critique of the practice which they passed on to the monthly meeting. It was not taken further, as too controversial, but the witness had been made. "There is liberty of conscience here which is right and reasonable, and there ought to be likewise liberty of the body," they said.[21] Quakers were active before the Civil War in running the "underground railway" of assistance to Negroes escaping to Canada, at considerable risk to themselves.

Methodism also had an early interest in society, particularly in the plight of the working people. The field preaching itself developed as a technique to reach those not touched by the antiquated parish system of the Anglican Church. John Wesley was always concerned with the unemployed. At the age of eighty-two he spent whole days walking about to collect money for the poor. George Whitefield's orphanage in Georgia was internationally known, although it did not have a long life of service. The English historian J. R. Green remarked that one of the outstanding results of the Evangelical Revival was the spirit of social service. William Booth was formed by Methodism, but finally had to break out to form his Salvation Army to take care of the need of the slums, which he depicted in shocking detail in his *In Darkest England* (1890).

Rising industrialism created many problems, and there were attempts made to meet them. Among the more successful were the model towns of the English Quaker chocolate makers, the Frys, Cadburys, and the Rowntrees. By each creating "a factory in a garden" they sought to improve the working conditions of their workers, for whom they built excellent housing and provided health services, pension plans, profit-sharing, and other now commonly accepted benefits. In America, the outstanding prophet for better conditions not only for labor but for the whole society was the Baptist Walter Rauschenbusch. After leaving seminary to take a pastorate in "Hell's Kitchen" on the West Side of New York, Rauschenbusch fought for playgrounds, housing, jobs, and better health conditions. As a seminary professor he became a

---

[20] Leland Harder, "Plockhoy and Slavery in America," *Mennonite Life*, VII (October 1952), 187–189.

[21] John C. Wenger, *History of the Mennonites of the Franconia Conference* (Scottdale, Pa.: Mennonite Publishing House, 1938), p. 413. (Spelling modernized.)

national figure with his books and lectures. In answer to his
critics, he prayed, "Thy kingdom come, thy will be done on
earth," and called for "Christian Socialism."

The International Dimension

On December 10, 1947, two representatives of the American
Friends Service Committee and the (British) Friends Service
Council were in Oslo to accept the Nobel Peace Prize on behalf of
their agencies. As this was a most formal occasion, they were
expected to appear appropriately dressed. Henry Cadbury, Harvard biblical scholar, was representing the A.F.S.C. in his capacity
as chairman of the Committee. Formal dress with tail coat was
not part of his wardrobe. The resourceful Friends were up to the
occasion, and produced the required tails from their Philadelphia
warehouse of clothes donated for the relief of foreign refugees.
After the awards were made, Cadbury reflected: "I doubt whether
either of the notables' wives who sat beside me at dinner knew
that I was wearing garments that had been destined to cross the
ocean a little later and more slowly among the tons of bales of
used and new clothing." Shortly before this, he had served on the
team of scholars which produced the Revised Standard Version of
the New Testament (published in 1945). During the years of
arduous labor in determining an accurate English text he had also
carried the heavy load of administrative work as chairman of the
relief committee. He was once asked whether the transition from
the scholarly world of biblical study to the tension and complexity
of the A.F.S.C. was not too abrupt. He replied that in both cases
he was "trying to translate the New Testament."[22]

The two anecdotes catch rather well the spirit in which the
Believers' Churches over the years have sought to transmute their
understanding of biblical teachings into concrete service, regardless of boundaries of nations or ethnic groups. This is one with
their concept of mission discussed previously. As far back as the
fifteenth century, Peter Chelčický enunciated the teaching: "If
anyone, a Jew or a heathen or a heretic or an enemy, is ever in
need, then according to the principles of love it is our duty to see

[22] Related in Mary Hoxie Jones, "Henry Joel Cadbury: a Biographical
Sketch," in Anna Brinton, ed., *Then and Now* (Philadelphia: University of
Pennsylvania Press, 1960), pp. 52–54.

that he does not die from hunger or cold or any other calamity."[23] From the beginning, then, there has been concerted effort to ease the burdens of those in need in other countries.

In the nineteenth century this took on more organized forms. The Disciples of Christ called for a collection of money to be distributed in the United Kingdom in 1847 when Alexander Campbell visited there. Most of the thirteen hundred dollars collected was given to industrial laborers in Scotland. At the time of the Franco-Prussian war in 1870–1871, British Quakers organized a Friends War Victims Fund and sent volunteers to care for the wounded and homeless on both sides of the lines. This set the immediate precedent for their Friends Ambulance Unit and the War Victims Relief Committee of World War I. When the fighting began in 1914 several Quakers visited the front on their own initiative and then took their findings to the home society. This resulted in the extensively circulated appeal to the whole British Empire: "We find ourselves today in the midst of what may prove to be the fiercest conflict in the history of the human race. Whatever may be our view of the processes which have led to its inception, we have now to face the fact that war is proceeding on a terrific scale and that our own country is involved in it. . . . Our duty is clear: to be courageous in the cause of love and in the hate of hate." A leader in the overnight organization of the ambulance unit was Philip Noël-Baker, to be given the Nobel Prize himself in 1959 for his endeavors in halting international war.

By early November 1914, the first unit of trained medical attendants was in action on the Continent under the sponsorship of the Red Cross. Immediately after their landing in Dunkirk they found three thousand Allied soldiers in railway sheds waiting— some for as long as three days—for transportation to hospitals, with only a handful of men to look after them. By the end of the war more than six hundred were working in the units, each volunteer paying for his own training and maintenance. When the United States was swept into the war in 1917, the American Friends Service Committee was born. It also trained and sent six hundred Quakers and non-Quakers to France in medical and reconstruction work. Other groups gave money to support the program. During the years from 1917 until 1919 Quakers worked in

[23] Peter Brock, *The Political and Social Doctrines of the Unity of Czech Brethren* (The Hague: Mouton and Co., 1957), p. 62.

Russia and Serbia, and then in Austria and Germany, both suffering direly from the effects of the long war and the naval blockades. Herbert Hoover, himself a Quaker, was in charge of the relief of Europe; he asked the Friends to administer a large-scale feeding operation in Germany, much of the funds for which came from German-Americans in the United States. The outbreak of further wars, such as the Spanish Civil War in the thirties, and the impact of the depression created such need that it was decided to keep the agency functioning.[24]

In 1920 the suffering of thousands of Russians, including many Mennonite settlers there, caused the several Mennonite bodies in the United States and Canada to form the Mennonite Central Committee. In the year preceding, a delegation of Russian Mennonites had toured North America reporting on the mass starvation in their country. Several hundred thousand dollars were raised for immediate relief and three men were sent to help in the operation, one of whom lost his life in the chaos of the civil war between the White and Red armies. The next big push was the effort to relocate Russian Mennonites in other countries, when the forced Soviet collectivization of agriculture hit the Mennonite farming districts. The M.C.C., working with brethren in Germany and the Netherlands, managed to resettle two thousand in the Chaco of Paraguay and others in Canada despite fantastically complicated red tape in the negotiations between the governments involved, shipping companies, and the people themselves.

Post-World War II brought even larger resettlement problems. Some thirteen thousand were placed in the United States, Canada, Paraguay, and Uruguay between 1945 and 1951. One of the most dramatic incidents involved a group of a thousand Russian Mennonites who had made their way to Berlin, then under four-power occupation. The Soviet government demanded their return as Soviet citizens, but the refugees feared a harsh fate awaited them if they were repatriated. M.C.C. worked out the details in 1947 for their transportation across the Russian-occupied zone of Germany to Bremerhaven, where a chartered ship waited to take them and some two thousand five hundred other refugees from Holland and West Germany to Paraguay. Less than twenty-four hours before their scheduled departure from Berlin, the American mili-

[24] Janet Whitney, "Quakers and the Nobel Prize," in A. Brinton, *op. cit.*, pp. 253–269.

tary government told the M.C.C. representative, Peter Dyck, that the Russians were prepared to resist by force the departure of the refugee train. Flying them out of the city was contemplated, but this was given up because of the probability that the planes would be shot down. Washington gave orders that force should not be used to move the refugees because of the possibility of triggering a war. They were caught in Berlin. The chartered ship went ahead with loading the other refugees, and then was kept waiting past sailing time, with costly penalties accruing for each extra day in port. Finally, a few hours before the delayed time of sailing was reached, word came from Berlin that the Russians had relented. The Mennonites were given ninety minutes to be ready to leave their camp in West Berlin, and the American army took them by truck to a train of forty freight cars which brought them safely to the ship thirty-six hours later. The work of the M.C.C. expanded to many other countries after World War II, so that by 1965 there had been or were presently projects in fifty-four countries. Three hundred volunteer staff served overseas in 1964.[25]

The Church of the Brethren contributed personnel and funds, first to the A.F.S.C. and then to the M.C.C. programs, but sentiment grew that they should have their own service agency. In 1941 the Brethren Service Committee was instituted. Its first major job was the organization and administration of Civilian Public Service Camps, along with the other peace churches, as its part of the agreement with Selective Service. To do this it raised and spent nearly two million dollars. One of the more significant projects of the C.P.S. years was the "starvation unit" at the University of Minnesota in which Brethren conscientious objectors voluntarily went on scientifically controlled minimum-calorie diets. The purpose was to study the effects of starvation on humans and learn the best ways to restore them to health, looking forward to the extensive tasks of human rehabilitation at the end of the second world war. More than three thousand men were in B.S.C.-administered camps and units, of whom thirteen hundred were members of the Church of the Brethren.[26]

[25] John D. Unruh, *In the Name of Christ* (Scottdale, Pa.: Herald Press, 1952), *passim;* "MCC Born in 1920 Amid Revolutionary Crisis," *Mennonite Weekly Review* (September 23, 1965), 1, 6–7.
[26] Leslie Eisan, *Pathways of Peace* (Elgin, Ill.: Brethren Publishing House, 1948); Lorell Weiss, *Ten Years of Brethren Service* (Elgin, Ill.: Brethren Service Commission, [1952]).

The most popular Brethren-sponsored relief program was the unique "heifer project." This was conceived by Dan West as he distributed reconstituted milk to children during the Spanish civil war. Coming from a farm background, West had the idea that it would be better to bring cows to Spain to provide long-term nourishment. Moreover, as the first heifer calf of the donated cow was to be given away to another needy person, this would start what later was called a "chain reaction of love." On his return to the United States he spoke of the idea and in 1944 it was put into action. A heifer named "Faith" was sent from northern Indiana to Puerto Rico, where the three Historic Peace Churches had established community reconstruction and medical projects. (They had been eager to work overseas during the war but had been prevented, despite careful preparation, by an unfriendly Congress.) Government planners liked West's idea, for replacement of depleted livestock herds in Europe was one of the main objectives of postwar recovery. When the United Nations Relief and Rehabilitation Administration was formed, it called on the Brethren to supply one thousand livestock attendants for ocean shipments to Europe. In return free shipping overseas was assured for the Heifer Project. The rural constituencies of other denominations were attracted by the down-to-earth practicality of the scheme, and the agency soon became interdenominational. Some countries could not support cows, so goats and poultry were sent. By 1966 more than eighty-four nations had received shipments of more than one million animals. The Brethren were also influential in creating the Christian Rural Overseas Program (C.R.O.P.), which has provided tons of food to be channeled through the relief agencies of Church World Service and the World Council of Churches.[27]

Another Brethren initiative which received ecumenical support was the aid to Greek villagers begun in 1950. Volunteer workers moved into the mountains near the Albanian border to help the poverty-stricken local people and the refugees. By concentration on one area, they succeeded in improving the entire economy and future prospects of the villages. Agriculturalists developed demonstration farms and hybrid seeds. Cotton was introduced as a

[27] Kermit Eby, The God in You (Chicago: University of Chicago Press, 1954), pp. 43–54; "Fences and a Warm Nose," Church of the Brethren Messenger (July 21, 1966), 13; Harold E. Fey, Cooperation in Compassion (New York: Friendship Press, 1966).

staple crop and poultry-raising and beekeeping begun. Girls were trained in domestic arts, including canning to provide nourishment during the long months after the growing season was over. Youth clubs were organized, houses and a new church were built. All this was done in close cooperation with the Orthodox church, which had originally been skeptical of allowing Protestants to enter for fear of proselyting. The team became fully ecumenical and international by sponsorship through the World Council of Churches.[28]

Baptists began their modern program of international relief in 1920 with a conference in London. They made three major decisions at that time. They decided on a three-year program of relief; the American Baptists committed themselves to raise one million dollars; and a commissioner for Europe was appointed. Aid from the program went to fifteen countries. One whole ship was filled with food and clothing in 1921 for distribution in Europe. At the close of World War II a "crusade" began which raised sixteen million dollars by 1947. Some of this went to help rebuild the many destroyed Baptist church buildings across Europe and to resettle refugees. The American Baptist World Relief Committee, organized in 1940, raised and allocated more than thirteen million dollars, working primarily through other agencies such as Church World Service. The Baptist World Alliance Relief Committee in its enlarged form after 1947 cooperated with several Baptist bodies in meeting needs not covered otherwise. Between 1947 and 1950 the equivalent of ten million dollars of relief goods and medical supplies was given away.[29]

The small Waldensian church in Italy also was sensitive to needs beyond its immediate vicinity. An offshoot of the Agape community chose work in Kriftel, Germany, near Frankfurt/Main, among the foreign laborers. In 1965 eight persons were in the international team helping the *Gastarbeiter* to adjust to a different and sometimes hostile culture. They characterized their work as a "presence" in practicing availability for whatever needed to be done (*disponibilità*). Back in the Waldensian valleys the church founded the Uliveto community, a farm colony for so-

[28] Edgar H. S. Chandler, *The High Tower of Refuge* (New York: Frederick A. Praeger, 1959), pp. 79–83.
[29] Dana M. Albaugh, *Who Shall Separate Us?* (Chicago: Judson Press, 1962).

called "hard-core" Russian displaced persons, too old or too ill to be accepted for resettlement overseas. The elderly guests help to support themselves (and achieve self-esteem) by tending rabbits, poultry, and bees. According to Edgar H. S. Chandler, W.C.C. refugee director, "I suppose that if one could magnify Uliveto many millions of times, to global proportions, there would be a happy world. As that cannot be, we can only take this refugee haven in the Italian Alps as an indication of a new horizon, of a way of finding peace at last for people spurned by the rest of the world."[30]

[30] "An Ecumenical Team Serving Foreign Workers," News From Agape (November 1965), 25–32; Chandler, op. cit., pp. 237–238.

· XII ·

Sectarian and Ecumenical

DURING World War I a delegation of leaders of the Church of the Brethren went to Washington, D.C. Their mission was to ascertain the government's regulations on noncombatant service, and to do this they interviewed the Provost Marshal. During the discussion the general asked one of the group how many different branches of the Brethren there were. On hearing the reply he smiled and said: "You are pretty good scrappers for a peace people after all."[1]

The same judgment could be leveled at the Believers' Churches generally. Their histories are checkered with division. The latest edition of a handbook of denominations in the United States, for example, lists twenty-seven Baptist, four Brethren, three Disciples, eight Plymouth Brethren, nine Quaker, fifteen Mennonite, and twenty-two Methodist bodies. It can, of course, be pointed out that other communions are also divided. In the same reference work there are thirteen Presbyterian denominations listed and six Reformed. In 1900 there were twenty-four Lutheran groups in the United States, divided along doctrinal and ethnic lines. A major effort has been made in the past years to bring the Lutheran family together, but their listing still occupies half a page in the handbook.[2]

There are two contrasting ways to view the phenomenon of church division. The current method of ecumenism sees it as a scandal. This pattern was set as early as 1929 by H. Richard Niebuhr's influential book *The Social Sources of Denominationalism* which denied that the diversity of denominations was based, as apologists claimed, on fundamental disagreement on belief and

---

[1] J. E. Miller, *Stories from Brethren Life* (Elgin, Ill.: Brethren Publishing House, 1942), pp. 136–137.
[2] Frank S. Mead, *Handbook of Denominations in the United States*, fourth ed. (New York: Abingdon Press, 1965), pp. 233–240.

tradition. Rather, the differences were found to be related to social class, nationality, sectionalism, and economic factors. Denominations, for Niebuhr, represented "the moral failure of Christianity." The history of the church has been a history of schism, and "the history of schism has been a history of Christianity's defeat."[3]

The lack of unity among Christians, many now contend, has robbed the church's testimony of its credibility. How can the churches tell the nations to live together in peace when they cannot even live together as followers of the same Lord? Continued separation is a demonstration of the churches' unfaithfulness to God's call to be one body in Christ. Mission is hampered by divisiveness. The "Open Letter to the Churches," which introduced the church-unity principles worked out by the Consultation on Church Union (1966), sets forth this view: "The Church is one, made so by the act of God in Christ. Its life is the one Holy Spirit given through Christ. Because of this given unity, the disunity of the visible companies of Christian people is at any time and place a challenge to the truth—even where the supreme claim of conscience seems to require separation for the truth's sake—and a rejection of the unity implicit in the saving love of the one God for our single humanity."[4]

There are those who take a different attitude. For them, the presence of many competing bodies is not only a witness to the vitality of the faith but also the way to reach more people. The free enterprise system is thought to be as beneficial for the church as for the economy. This was once put pungently by a Texas Baptist editor who described the bitter denominational rivalry on the frontier and its results in this way: "You know how it is when you hear a horrible squawking from the alley at night and expect to find it littered with dead cats in the morning? But what happens instead is more cats."[5] More sedately, but similarly, the Baptist church historian Kenneth Scott Latourette used the emergence of new religious groupings as a gauge of the degree of life within the church. One of the reasons that the eighteenth and nineteenth

[3] H. Richard Niebuhr, *The Social Sources of Denominationalism* (New York: Meridian Books, 1957), pp. 25, 264; originally published in 1929.
[4] *Consultation on Church Union 1967* (Cincinnati, Ohio: Forward Movement Publications, 1967), p. 9.
[5] Quoted from Archie Robertson, *That Old-Time Religion* (Boston: 1950), p. 80, in Ross Phares, *Bible in Pocket, Gun in Hand* (Garden City, N.Y.: Doubleday & Co., 1964), p. 129.

centuries are great eras of progress in his judgment is the fact that many newcomers arrived on the religious scene. In like fashion, the presence of new orders in Catholicism is a mark of religious vigor: "It was to the dynamic which is of the essence of Christianity that Protestantism owed its origin. It was that dynamic which chiefly accounted for the variety exhibited by Protestantism. The 'denominations,' 'confessions,' and 'communions' of Protestantism roughly corresponded to the monastic orders in the Catholic Church. Like the latter, they arose basically from a fresh surge of conviction and devotion." From this perspective the fissiparous quality of Protestantism is not an unrelieved tragedy, although it is granted that some of the schisms were the result of personal ambition rather than piety.[6]

Walter Rauschenbusch was sanguine about the march of a many-faceted faith. He praised the radicals of former years for their courage in persisting in their beliefs even though this broke through church patterns. "We were for a 'reformation without tarrying' even if we had to have the old church and break it in pieces. We were against clericalism and against all hierarchies." Although the fathers had to pay for their daring with their blood, the God of history has vindicated them. Their triumph, for Rauschenbusch, was seen in American religious life.[7] Later scholars have agreed that the free church idea has permeated American Christianity, even among the descendants of those who fought so bitterly against the early free churches at the time of the Reformation. For, "while almost all mainline American denominations have at length abandoned their sectarianism in the sense of moralistic exclusiveness and doctrinal bigotry, they are still directly or indirectly heirs or beneficiaries of the sectarian ideal of the gathered church of committed believers, living in the fellowship of mutual correction, support, and abiding hope."[8] The difference is that some are trying to shed this heritage for a more inclusive posture, whereas others maintain the free church position is preferable.

---

[6] Kenneth Scott Latourette, *A History of Christianity* (New York: Harper & Brothers, 1953), p. 970.

[7] Walter Rauschenbusch, *The Freedom of Spiritual Religion* (Philadelphia: American Baptist Publication Society, 1910), p. 13.

[8] George H. Williams, *Wilderness and Paradise in Christian Thought* (New York: Harper & Brothers, 1962), p. 214.

The Separatist Stance

The urbane Roman Catholic scholar Ronald Knox chronicled the path of separatism from the mother church in his book called *Enthusiasm*. In it he described several of the movements here denoted as Believers' Churches. For Knox there is a recurrent situation in church history which results in the spawning of new bodies: "You have a clique, an *élite*, of Christian men and . . . women, who are trying to live a less worldly life than their neighbors; to be more attentive to the guidance . . . of the Holy Spirit. More and more, by a kind of fatality, you see them draw apart from their co-religionists, a hive ready to swarm. There is provocation on both sides; on the one part, cheap jokes at the expense of over-godliness, acts of stupid repression by unsympathetic authorities; on the other, contempt of the half-Christian, ominous references to old wine and new bottles, to the kernel and the husk. Then, while you hold your breath and turn your eyes in fear, the break comes; condemnation or secession, what difference does it make? A fresh name has been added to the list of Christianities."

For Knox, the process is inevitable once the firm hold of discipline and obedience to Rome is lost. One schism breeds another. Yet, in the process of cataloging his heresies, he came to a grudging appreciation for them, so much so that he closed his book with the passage from *La Princesse lointaine*:

> Frère Trophime: Inertia is the only vice, Master Erasmus; and the only virtue is—
> Erasmus: Which?
> Frère Trophime: Enthusiasm![9]

It can hardly be denied that the radical Protestants have been among the "come-outers." George H. Williams says that the Believers' Churches have been "leavers' churches."[10] From the perspective of the establishment they have been troublers of Zion and disturbers of the peace. In seventeenth-century England the atti-

---

[9] R. A. Knox, *Enthusiasm: a Chapter in the History of Religion* (Oxford: Clarendon Press, 1950), pp. 1, 591.

[10] George H. Williams, "'Congregationalist' Luther and the Free Churches," *Lutheran Quarterly*, XIX (1967), 292.

tude of ecclesiastical authority toward them was expressed by one Howells who wrote of the Separatists and Baptists: "If I hate any 'tis those that trouble the sweet peace of our church. I could be content to see an Anabaptist go to hell on a Brownist's back."[11]

Given their convictions about the gathered church, voluntaryism in church membership, separation of church and state, and church discipline, it is not surprising that members of Believers' Churches either were expelled or chose to withdraw from the existing churches. They were unconcerned about apostolic succession and an unbroken line of church order. They shared the attitude of the Pilgrim pastor John Robinson in a dispute with an opponent:

> As for the gathering of a Church . . . I tell you, that in what place soever, by what means soever, whether by preaching the Gospel by a true Minister, by a false minister, by no minister, or by reading, conferences, or any other means of publishing it, two or three faithful people do arise, separating themselves fro[m] the world into the fellowship of the Gospel, and the covenant of Abraham, they are a Church truly gathered though never so weak, a house and temple of God rightly founded upon the doctrine of the Apostles and Prophets, Christ himself being the corner stone, against which the gates of hell shall not prevayl, nor your disgraceful invectives neyther.[12]

Although the Waldenses began simply as an expression of lay piety in a spirit of deep loyalty to the Church, their decision to continue their preaching and teaching despite churchly ban was a declaration of religious independence. Before long under persecution they had created a rival church organization, and consciously thought of themselves as the true church in distinction to the fallen papal church. Similarly, the Unity of Brethren began as faithful churchmen of Calixtine persuasion, but with the ordination of their own ministers, and the subsequent baptisms in 1467, they also became separatists. Some of the Swiss Brethren in the Zwingli circle had hopes of convincing the Zürich town council of the truth of their position, thereby making their belief the general possession of the populace, but the future development of the

[11] Quoted in Niebuhr, *op. cit.*, p. 44.
[12] Quoted from Franklin H. Littell, "The Concerns of the Believers' Church," (unpub. typescript, Conference on the Concept of the Believers' Church, 1967), pp. 5–6.

1520s showed this to be impossible. By defying the council's legislation against meetings and baptisms, they clearly drew a line
between themselves and the state. The Schleitheim Confession
(1527) spelled out the importance of separation from the world,
which included "all popish and anti-popish works and church
services, meetings and church attendance."[13]

In England, the Baptists and Quakers began among the separatist wing of Puritanism, that is among those who had already
discarded the idea of a national church, be it of episcopalian,
presbyterian, or congregationalist polity. The Quakers, especially,
found adherents among those who had parted from all organized
religious activity and who were waiting for a path to be shown to
them. The Brethren in Germany came primarily from Reformed
folk who wished to remain in the church. When, however, they
were given the choice between leaving their homes and churches,
and dropping their quiet conventicles of Bible study and mutual
edification, they chose to keep the latter at the cost of the former.
The Methodists were the most reluctant of separatists, and John
Wesley persevered in his attachment to Anglicanism. Nevertheless, the direction of his convictions and the necessity of caring for
his societies overseas led inexorably to the rupture he so dreaded.

The Restorationists—Disciples and Plymouth Brethren—were
known and cordially disliked for the fierceness of their criticisms
of church establishments, including other free churches. A Methodist pastor wrote on the American frontier that "the prowling
wolves of Campbellism, Drunkardism, and Devilism of every
grade, are ready to devour the sheep."[14] When the Evangelical
Alliance was organized in England in the 1840s, there was strong
support for enlisting all of the churches holding the "voluntary
system" in order to combat "Infidelity and Popery, Puseyism [Ox-
ford Movement], and Plymouth Brethrenism."[15] Much the same
feelings were evoked in Germany by the stubborn insistence of the
Confessing Church that it was the only true church in Hitler's
Third Reich. It can be prophesied that if the underground

---

[13] William L. Lumpkin, *Baptist Confessions of Faith* (Philadelphia: Judson
Press, 1959), p. 26.
[14] Phares, *op. cit.*, p. 127.
[15] Ruth Rouse and S. C. Neill, eds., *A History of the Ecumenical Movement, 1517–1948* (London: S.P.C.K., 1954), p. 319.

churches persist in their present critique of church authority, they will be looked upon the same way.

English free churchmen have argued that there is such a thing as "Protestant Catholicity" equally if not more valid than the catholicity so prized by high-church Anglicans. They based their discussion on the pronouncement of Ignatius writing to the early church at Smyrna that "wherever the episcopus [understood as the minister of an individual congregation, not of a diocese] appears, there let the congregation be, just as wherever Jesus Christ is, there is the Catholic Church." The catholicity of the church is determined by the presence of the living Christ, "recognized, adored, and obeyed." There is, therefore, neither hierarchical nor institutional test for catholicity. Rather, the test comes from a life which includes belief, worship, and moral witness. "Only that Church, or communion, or tradition, is in the full sense catholic which possesses the 'wholeness' of the Gospel, and such 'wholeness' can be derived only from our Lord Jesus Christ, His message of the Kingdom of God, His work of salvation, and His way of life for mankind." To the extent that the free churches attained these goals, they thereby attained catholicity.[16]

Ecumenical Emphases

This would indicate that for the Believers' Churches there is a resistance to being thought sectarian in the pejorative, rather than Troeltschian, sense of the term. In fact, the case can be made that there have been definite ecumenical tendencies within their life and practice. Because in recent decades the ecumenical movement has tended to be dominated by those confessions which place primary emphasis upon a morphological unity, the contribution of the Believers' Churches to the ecumenical story has not been fully recognized.

The very nomenclature of these churches indicates an open posture. They wished to be called simply "brethren," or "friends," or "Christian." It was only reluctantly that they accepted the labels by which they have come to be known, such as Mennonite or Methodist. Since they thought of themselves as brothers, they

[16] R. Newton Flew and Rupert E. Davies, eds., *The Catholicity of Protestantism* (London: Lutterworth Press, 1950), pp. 21–27.

were ready to receive others on an equal basis when they found themselves to be of like persuasion.

An earlier chapter has described the missionary passion of the Believers' Churches. It is a truism that the present ecumenical movement grows directly out of the mission program of the nineteenth century. Modern missions, in turn, are to a great part indebted to the groups under discussion. A blithe disregard for territorial limits characterized their activities. From the Waldenses to the Church of the Saviour, there is a pronounced international spirit. Among the early Anabaptists there was talk of going to the red Indians across the sea. A recent essay asserts that the Society of Friends can be defined best by "Catholic Quakerism" in this sense of the term: "The early Friends claimed that the truth that had been given them to proclaim was universal and that their faith was a catholic faith which was for all men to share."[17]

This urge was nowhere stronger than among the Restorationist Churches. A fundamental concern was the drive for Christian unity, best based in their view upon early Christianity. "The 'material principle' of this new reformation was the Union of All Christians, while the 'formal principle' was the Restoration of Primitive Christianity."[18] The paradoxical fact that these groups themselves solidified into denominations, and divided ones at that, does not detract from the sincerity of the intent. For Thomas Campbell the "church of Christ upon earth is essentially, intentionally, and constitutionally one." This drive for unity has remained strong among the Disciples, and has led to several merger discussions, most recently in their participation in the Consultation on Church Union. The dean of a Disciples seminary wrote an evangelistic "open letter to American Christians" calling them to move into the C.O.C.U. orbit. He quoted from Alexander Campbell to give corroboration to the four points of the Anglican-initiated Lambeth Quadrilateral.[19] The Plymouth Brethren began with a call for unity across denominational lines. According to Darby, the church was found wherever the two or three were gathered in Christ's name. Every true Christian believer wherever

---

[17] Lewis Benson, *Catholic Quakerism* (Gloucester, U.K.: the author, 1966), p. 8.
[18] Rouse and Neill, *op. cit.*, p. 238.
[19] Ronald E. Osborn, *A Church for These Times* (New York: Abingdon Press, 1965).

he might be found ecclesiastically was considered a part of the body of Christ.

The Waldensian Church has repeatedly announced its support of ecumenism. Its youth center at Agape, built by international work camps, was symbolically presented to the universal church via the World Council of Churches. Service work in Sicily and Germany is carried on by interdenominational teams. Its seminary in Rome provides training for several Protestant groups. Among the Unity of Brethren, also, there was early an ecumenical consciousness. In the sixteenth and seventeenth centuries the Unity participated in formal discussions and agreements such as the Consensus of Sendomir of 1570. In 1534 members asserted that they had gathered themselves into the Unity for the purpose of using in holy fellowship the good things of the old church and had discarded only that which was corrupt. Their most famous leader, Comenius, is ranked among the "early prophets of Christian ecumenicity." In his writings and in the course of his travels he worked against confessional bigotry. By 1632 he had drafted a detailed plan of union among Protestants, and at his death he left a monumental work in manuscript which included plans for church unity as well as for a world federation of nations.[20]

Following in Comenius' footsteps, and directly inspired by him, was Count Zinzendorf, whose biographer has called him an "Ecumenical Pioneer." Born and bred a Lutheran of pietist orientation, Zinzendorf received ordination as a Moravian bishop from Daniel Ernest Jablonski, a descendant of Comenius, serving at that time as a Reformed court preacher. Through the vehicle of the Renewed Moravian Church, Zinzendorf labored for wide cooperation of Christians. It was not necessary, in his thinking, for all to become members of one large body. Instead they should remain in their separate denominations or "tropuses," as he called them, because of the differences in ethnic background, temperament, and disposition. "Religions (Tropuses) are God's economy, machinery to bring Truth and the Love of His Son to men according to their capacity, and according to the temperature and atmosphere of the country. . . . The Saviour has all the Religions under His Protection and will not let them be destroyed." Each person

[20] Rouse and Neill, *op. cit.*, pp. 88–89. See also Ermanno Rostan, *The Waldensian Church of Italy and the Ecumenical Movement* (Genoa: Papini, n.d.).

must remain loyal to his own tradition, but not let that interfere with his overarching faithfulness to Christ, which should surpass everything. Moravian missionaries were sent out on this basis, directed to convert men to Christianity and not to a specific denomination. One Moravian converted seven hundred West Indians in 1736 but accepted only thirty into a Moravian society.[21]

Another aspect of the ecumenical leaning of these groups was their attitude to non-Christians. Anabaptists got themselves into trouble with the magistrates for not rallying to the crusade to drive the Turks from Central Europe. Quakers were prepared to find "that of God" in the Sultan to the same degree as in the pope. Pietists were deeply concerned to mount missions to Jews and pagans, and to this end established institutes and language centers at Halle.

Quite an interesting development came in the nineteenth century when descendants of those religious minorities who had found no toleration in Europe came back from North America to evangelize and establish congregations. Ernst Benz and Erich Beyreuther have both written about this "reverse migration," which has changed the religious map of Germany and other West European countries. Baptists, Methodists, United Brethren, and more recently the cult groups have found followers in the Old Country. Often migrants to America who had joined free churches upon arrival, felt themselves under deep compulsion to share their new faith with their relatives at home. Financial support from America has helped to extend these efforts in all parts of Europe. Europe was seen as a mission country along with Asia and Africa. This idea was hardly appreciated at the time, but has since become a commonplace of ecumenical discourse.[22]

In these ways, the Believers' Churches have felt themselves to be ecumenical, although not all have associated themselves with the organized movements culminating in the World Council of Churches. In some cases, the question of membership in the W.C.C. has been answered variously by the several national churches of these denominations. For example, Dutch and Ger-

[21] A. J. Lewis, *Zinzendorf: the Ecumenical Pioneer* (Philadelphia: Westminster Press, 1962), pp. 138–140.

[22] Ernst Benz, *Kirchengeschichte in ökumenischer Sicht* (Leiden: E. J. Brill, 1961), pp. 75–111; Erich Beyreuther, "Die Rückwirkung amerikanischer kirchengeschichtlicher Wandlungen auf das Evangelische Deutschland im 19. und 20. Jahrhundert," *Ökumenische Rundschau*, XIII (July 1964), 237–256.

man Mennonites and American Friends are members, but American Mennonites and British Friends are not. American (Northern) Baptists belong, but Southern Baptists do not. Of those remaining aloof, some give doctrinal reasons and others have based their objections on their view of the church.

Ecumenical Organizations

In 1805 William Carey called from his post in India for an international meeting of "Christians of all denominations" to be held at Capetown. The purpose was to pool information and experience on common missionary problems. Regular meetings thereafter would follow every ten years. This proposal was considered just a "pleasant dream" by officials of the mission agencies back in England and it never came off. But one hundred years later it was realized in the famous World Missionary Conference at Edinburgh, the beginning of the modern ecumenical movement.

Even before Carey's initiative there were those in the broader pietist movement who proposed and carried out interdenominational endeavors. Count Zinzendorf organized seven synods in Pennsylvania with the aim of bringing about greater unity especially among the churches of German background. He hoped to set up what he called the Congregation of God in the Spirit. His plan failed, but the experiment was tried. Zinzendorf was "the man who dared to attempt what the boldest ecumenical minds of the 19th century only ventured to pen."[23]

More successful was the Evangelical Alliance, the creation of individuals from fifty-two denominations, both free and state churches, in Europe and America. In 1846 they came together, some eight hundred strong, to form a confederation "on the basis of great evangelical principles held in common" by them. In its conference format and, to a lesser degree, in continuing structure it was to influence the later agencies which fed into the World Council of Churches. The Alliance pioneered in calling for weeks of united prayer, on which divided Christians found they could cooperate if they failed to find common ground in all other activity. Its most effective practical action was in the area of religious liberty. Protestant,

[23] Rouse and Neill, *op. cit.*, p. 230.

Roman Catholic, and Orthodox minorities were all defended by its representatives.[24]

Starting at roughly the same time as the Alliance was the Young Men's Christian Association, founded in England in 1844 by George Williams, a Congregationalist. This, the associated Young Women's Christian Association, and the Student Christian Movement which was closely related, are all foundation stones on which the modern ecumenical movement took shape. Four-fifths of the early leadership of the World Council of Churches came directly from these movements, and found there their first avenues for interchurch work. In all cases, free churches gave major support.

Dwight Moody, the most important evangelist of the nineteenth century, got his start in Y.M.C.A. work in Chicago, and then began to spend full time in revivalism. On one of his trips to England his message challenged Henry Drummond, a scientist, who was to become an important leader in international student work. On another trip Moody converted the "Cambridge Seven," a group of athletes and campus leaders. One of them while touring the United States to speak to college students influenced John R. Mott. As a Methodist layman, Mott was to become the key figure in several world organizations. He was chairman of the Edinburgh Conference and its continuation, the International Missionary Council, president of the World Alliance of YMCA's, founder of the World Student Christian Federation, and the honorary president of the World Council of Churches. Mott's first experience at guiding conferences came at Northfield, an institution in New England created by Moody. At Northfield a visiting Swedish churchman, the later Archbishop Nathan Söderblom, caught a vision of Christian unity. He prayed there: "Lord, give me the humility and wisdom to serve the great cause of the free unity of Thy Church." Söderblom was the soul of the so-called "Life and Work" movement which was one of the main strands forming the World Council of Churches.[25]

The student movements in many ways broke the ice for more formalized ecumenical bodies. They established the principle that it was possible for churchmen to come together and discuss com-

[24] Ibid., pp. 318–324.
[25] Norman Goodall, The Ecumenical Movement, second ed. (London: Oxford University Press, 1964), pp. 7–10.

mon concerns while remaining solidly loyal to individual church backgrounds. The personal relationships and experiences garnered at these student meetings provided the basis for the later ecumenical leadership.

In these movements the free-church element was very strong. The qualities of commitment, consensus, and willingness to experiment with new forms, all characteristic of the Believers' Churches, are found here. It is quite true that they were not alone responsible for progress. The entry of Anglicanism at the Edinburgh Conference of 1910 opened up a new world of possibilities as did the participation of Eastern Orthodoxy later. It is also true that without the innovating spirit of many of the free churchmen, the present ecumenical movement would not be in its present advanced position. This fact is not always sufficiently realized.

Openness to New Light

One quality of the Believers' Churches which has militated against a narrow sectarianism is the principle of openness. By this is meant the deliberate readiness to accept new light from the scriptures. This was expressed well in the farewell sermon said to have been made by John Robinson to the departing Pilgrims: "I charge you, before God and His blessed angels, that you follow me no further than you have seen me follow the Lord Jesus Christ. If God reveals anything to you by any other instrument of His, be as ready to receive it as you were to receive any truth by my ministry, for I am verily persuaded the Lord hath more truth yet to break forth out of His holy Word." Robinson continued by expressing his regret that the Lutherans and Calvinists tended to limit their faith to that which had been revealed to their founders. Though great men, they had not fully plumbed God's mysteries.[26]

The expectancy that further light would in fact come was a primary motivation for not adopting formal creeds. Confessions, yes, but creeds, no. In Benjamin Franklin's autobiography there is a section dealing with Michael Welfare (Wohlfahrt), a colorful leader of the Ephrata Community which broke away from the Brethren in Germantown, Pennsylvania, around 1730. In many ways they reflected Brethren thinking. Welfare complained to

[26] Horton Davies, *The English Free Churches* (London: Oxford University Press, 1952), p. 56. Some authorities question the authenticity of this sermon.

Franklin that his community was slandered and misunderstood by members of other faiths. Franklin recommended that the Ephrata people publish the articles of their belief and the rules of their discipline in order to put a stop to the abuse. Welfare's response was that this had been considered but upon reflection had been rejected:

> When we were first drawn together as a society, it had pleased God to enlighten our minds so far as to see that some doctrines which we once esteemed truths were errors, and that others which we had esteemed errors were real truths. From time to time He has been pleased to afford us further light, and our principles have been improving and our errors diminishing. Now we are not sure that we are arrived at the end of this progression and at the perfection of spiritual or theological knowledge; and we fear that if we should once print our confession of faith, we should feel ourselves as if bound and confined by it, and perhaps be unwilling to receive further improvement, and our successors still more so, as conceiving what their elders and founders had done to be something sacred, never to be departed from.[27]

Quakers built this principle into the heart of their practice, and refined techniques to be better able to apprehend and ascertain the quiet movings of the spirit in bringing new insights. "Centering down" to make possible "openings" of revealed truth played a vital role in their meetings for worship and business sessions alike. This was emphasized so much that many Quakers frowned on any evidence of prior preparation of messages. Rufus Jones, called a "master Quaker" by his biographer, was long under a cloud in some conservative Friends' meetings because he accepted invitations to speak in colleges at appointed times, which meant that he would need to prepare specifically for his talks ahead of time. D. Elton Trueblood contends that the core of the Quaker faith is the "continual effort to avoid the loss of the reality in its seemingly inevitable formalizations." Since vision tends to crust over, it is necessary for those in each generation to break through as did Fox in the seventeenth century. To this end, simple rules govern the

---

[27] H. W. Schneider, ed., *Benjamin Franklin: the Autobiography* (New York: Liberal Arts Press, 1949), p. 115.

participation in the "silent meeting," better called the "obedient meeting."[28] One should neither determine beforehand not to speak, nor to speak.

John Smyth of the Baptists was charged by his opponents among the separatists with inconstancy and instability for his changes in religious position. Raised an Anglican, he was successively a Separatist, then a Baptist, and ended his days seeking membership among the Mennonites. He was not perturbed by the attacks but replied that to remain with outgrown convictions when new insights had come was unworthy. His last publication was a moving plea for tolerance in religious matters, judged by Haller to be of such quality that it could only have come from a "truly fine spirit." "I am not of the number of those men, which answer unto themselves such plenarie knowledge and assurance of their wayes, and of the perfection and sufficience therof, as that they peremptorily censure all men except those of their owne understanding. . . ."[29] William Bradford in writing of the first Baptists noted that they formed a church estate or covenant based on the gospel "to walk in all His ways, made known, or to be made known unto them. . . ."[30]

The Presbyterian Robert Baillie called this willingness to change "mutability" and charged the left-wing Puritans with fickleness and inconsistency. The radical Puritans answered by saying that the Holy Spirit could not be squelched, and must be followed no matter if it seemed foolish to the world. They said that the hyper-Calvinists set up a paper pope, and did not let the inner word, the Spirit, illumine the outer word, the Bible. They could agree with the Independent Craddock who cried: "Goe on in love, and when it comes to that we shall see more light."[31]

Martin Niemöller likes to tell of the inhibitions he felt as a Lutheran pastor when first asked to conduct a communion service in the concentration camp. How could he in conscience break the

[28] D. Elton Trueblood, *The People Called Quakers* (New York: Harper & Row, 1966), p. 65.
[29] William Haller, *The Rise of Puritanism* (New York: Harper Torchbooks, 1957), p. 204; originally published in 1938.
[30] Quoted in Ernest A. Payne, *The Fellowship of Believers*, enlarged ed. (London: Carey Kingsgate Press, 1954), p. 18.
[31] Geoffrey F. Nuttall, *Visible Saints* (Oxford: Basil Blackwell, 1957), p. 117.

bread for those of other confessions, and even members of sects? He did, however, go through with it, and found that the deep unity in Christ became manifest in ways which put to shame his previous opinions and the letter of the church law. From that time on he would be a man of the whole church.

The same principle of openness has governed the internal church life of the Believers' Churches. Their mode of reaching decisions has usually been by seeking a consensus before acting, rather than by formal votes. They could speak with the early church: "It seemed good to the holy spirit and to us." Franklin H. Littell has shown in several writings how this method has found wider use in the political sphere and in business. Newer forms of ministry and congregational life have led to the discovery that the churches must practice this type of decision if their mission is to flourish. A pragmatism of church polity has developed from this attitude.

It is the witness of the Believers' Churches that attention to the Spirit can bring about growth in individuals in ways which they could not have predicted before. Admittedly weak personalities have taken on new robustness and daring. Insensitivity has given place to real listening. The spirit can make possible creative responses to seemingly impossible situations. This quality is movingly phrased in the dying testimony of the erring Quaker saint James Nayler:

> There is a spirit which I feel that delights to do no evil nor to revenge any wrong, but delights to endure all things in hope to enjoy its own in the end. Its hope is to out-live all wrath and contention and to weary out all exaltations and cruelty of whatever is of a nature contrary to itself. It sees to the end of all temptations. As it bears no evil in itself, so it conceives none in thoughts to any other. If it be betrayed, it bears it, for its ground and spring is the mercies and forgiveness of God. Its crown is meekness, its life is everlasting love unfeigned; and takes its kingdom with entreaty and not with contention, and keeps it by lowliness of mind. In God alone it can rejoice, though none else regard it, or can own its life.[32]

The record of the Believers' Churches undeniably bears many entries demonstrating failures to reach the goal of openness to the

---

[32] Quoted in Trueblood, op. cit., p. 16.

Spirit. Eras of rigid narrowness have all too often followed the expansive early adventures of dedication and vision. But in the best moments of these movements the world has seen evidences of what can happen in the lives of those who wish in earnest to be Christians.

Epilogue

SEVERAL questions may legitimately be asked by those who have had the patience to complete the reading of the preceding historical and topical sketches of the Believers' Church. Does not the weighting of the description on the side of the early life of these movements leave an unbalanced and overly positive impression? Have not some of them, in fact, become established churches not unlike those against which they originally reacted? May not this emphasis on one aspect of Christian history work against the long-sought-for ecumenical spirit now abroad? Could it not tend to stiffen intransigent denominations in their splendid isolationism? Is not the Roman Catholic Church, cast here largely in a repressive role, currently surpassing most of Protestantism in the intensity and scale of her reform? Has, in sum, this book a sectarian tendency?

Without question, a process of change has occurred over the years within the Believers' Churches which, to use the jargon of sociologists of religion, has brought about a shift from the sect type to the denominational pattern. Problems of nurture, ministry, institutionalism, and acculturation have shaped them in ways which would be astounding to their founding fathers. It is clear, for example, that Mennonites in nineteenth-century Russia or Southern Baptists in twentieth-century America became social and political establishments. Testimony to this general development is found in several recent studies.[1]

What is perhaps not so evident is the way in which "sectarian" characteristics, in Troeltsch's sense of the word, have persisted over the centuries in these groups, the predictions of the sect-cycle

[1] A good example would be Langdon Gilkey, *How the Church Can Minister to the World Without Losing Itself* (New York: Harper & Row, 1964), pp. 1–27.

theorists notwithstanding. Leaving aside such a group as the Hutterites, who have purchased an astonishing degree of perpetual self-identity by tactics of migration and cultural withdrawal since the sixteenth century,[2] one could point to the peace witness of the Quakers, Brethren, and Mennonites as one example. This unpopular stance has retained surprising vitality, for all the defections from it, in the face of continual and often massive societal pressure against it, and still waxes strong.[3] Baptists, to take another case, have both caused exasperation and won admiration for their determination to preserve their "distinctives."

There has also been demonstrated among the Believers' Churches a steady potential for recovery of those basic beliefs, if not their outward forms, which had motivated their religious forbears. Modern Mennonites offer perhaps the best illustration of the way in which a self-conscious "Recovery of the Anabaptist Vision" has proved fruitful, not only for the scholarly discovery of a heritage (no small achievement in itself) but also for a revitalization and focusing of energies in many areas of Christian life and witness.[4] Troeltsch himself envisioned the possibilities of this sort of renewal, an insight ignored by the analysts of sectarian behavior.

Whether these movements have been portrayed in too flattering a manner will need to be judged by the reader. The effort was made to "speak the truth in love" and to sketch their likenesses, warts and all. It does seem to be the consensus of ecumenical

[2] Note in the discussion in Bryan R. Wilson, "The Migrating Sects," *The British Journal of Sociology*, XVIII (September 1967), pp. 303–314.

[3] Otto Piper mentions them as examples of denominations who would be justified in continuing independent existence "because they bring out an aspect of the Christian faith which no other denomination represents, the complete absence of which would result in a serious impoverishment of Protestantism"; see his book *Protestantism in an Ecumenical Age* (Philadelphia: Fortress Press, 1965), p. 170.

[4] Guy F. Hershberger, ed., *The Recovery of the Anabaptist Vision* (Scottdale, Pa.: Herald Press, 1957); "Harold S. Bender Memorial Number," *Mennonite Quarterly Review*, XXXVIII (April 1964), pp. 82-228. J. H. Nichols commented: "The Mennonites have exhibited in this generation a vigor in historical studies unequaled, in proportion to their size, by any other Christian tradition in America. . . . It seems to have arisen in part from the international crisis of identity of the Mennonites and their need to identify a viable tradition"—"The History of Christianity," in Paul Ramsey, ed., *Religion* (Englewood Cliffs, N.J.: Prentice Hall, Inc., 1965), p. 188.

discussants that progress comes not by invidious dwelling upon the plentiful failures and errors, of which the histories of all churches contain many examples, but rather by directing attention to the highest aspirations and clearest witness to be found in the separate traditions. One aim of this book has been to try to describe some of the qualities and beliefs of this strand of Christianity which merit attention by those of other traditions.

It is increasingly realized that the ecumenical movement, if it is to be true to its best insights, must be broadly comprehensive. By and large, the Believers' Churches have not played a role in the movement proportionate to their numbers and abilities. This is partly owing to their own inertia and hesitancy. The oekumene needs the presence of these groups, just as they need to be in closer relationship with their Christian brethren. Paradoxically, it could be shown with little difficulty that the theological thrust of much of the current ecumenical discussion and study (at least within the orbit of the World Council of Churches) parallels in a remarkable way the concerns of the Believers' Churches. Ecumenists have hailed as exciting new ideas, postures and practices— e.g., the ministry of the laity, house churches, even the agape meal—which, as has been seen, have been part of the Believers' Church tradition for decades. The contribution of this experience could help to enrich the contemporary dialogue.

One problem which has inhibited greater interchange between the Believers' Churches and other Christian bodies has been the difference in the locus of chief interest. Whereas many within the ecumenical movement have been primarily concerned with the unity of church order and polity (such as the Anglicans with their attention upon the mutual acknowledgment of ordination and intercommunion) or with the unity of doctrine (such as the Lutherans and many Reformed), the Believers' Churches have directed their attention more to the unity of service (diakonia). Since the New Delhi Assembly of the W.C.C. (1961) recognized this aspect of the Christian life as a constitutive element, rather than as a temporary exigency, there now exists greater common ground. At the same time, there is evidence on the part of the Believers' Churches of a greater realization of the importance of theological clarity. This might be symbolized by the formation in 1957 of a theological discussion group among the Quakers, who have not been noted for their emphasis upon systematic theology in the past.[5]

With reference to the relationship with Roman Catholicism, it would be true to say that by and large the Believers' Churches have historically felt themselves to be distant from the style of Christianity practiced by those faithful to the Bishop of Rome. However, this gap is no longer so wide. One factor contributing to closer relations was the common effort in areas of social welfare and international relief and rehabilitation during and after World War II. Also, some Roman Catholic scholars are now discovering some elements in the other tradition which seem not only challenging but even appealing, in the wake of Vatican II.[6] It could be hoped that a volume of this type might be of help in introducing some Catholics to a variety of Protestantism with which they may not have in the past been very familiar.

Is this book sectarian? Decidedly not, if by this is meant that the groups depicted in it should think themselves self-sufficient and able to disregard their fellow Christians. Decidedly so, if by this is meant the conviction that the Believers' Churches are valid, if incomplete, representations of the Body of Christ. The household of God is indeed a many-roomed mansion. One wing, at least, is reserved for the Believers' Churches.

[5] The journal of the group is *Quaker Religious Thought*, begun in 1959.

[6] See Michael Novak, "The Free Churches and the Roman Church," *Journal of Ecumenical Studies*, II (Fall 1965), pp. 426–447; Rosemary Reuther, *The Church Against Itself* (London: Herder and Herder, 1967); John B. Sheerin, C.S.P., "Have the Quakers a Message?" *The Catholic World*, CCVI (October 1967), pp. 2–3.

Index

Index

(Names of places and footnote references are not included in this index.)

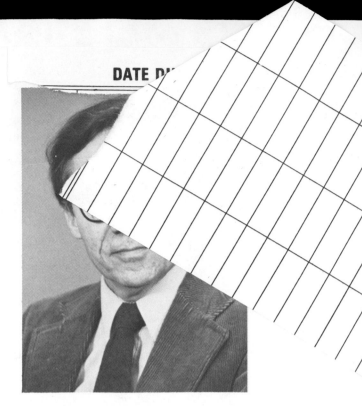

DEMCO 38-297

Donald F. Durnbaugh has taught church history at Bethany Theological Seminary, Oak Brook, Illinois, since 1962. Before that (1958-62) he was an assistant professor of history at Juniata College, Huntingdon, Pennsylvania. He did refugee resettlement work with the Brethren Service Commission in Austria and Germany (1949-51) and was Director of Program in Austria (1953-56). He directed the Brethren Colleges Abroad Program in France and Germany in 1964-65.

His academic degrees are from Manchester College, Indiana (B.A., 1949); University of Michigan (M.A., 1953); and University of Pennsylvania (Ph.D., 1960). He has written or edited ten books and has published over seventy articles in scholarly journals and denominational periodicals. He served as editor-in-chief of *The Brethren Encyclopedia,* issued in three volumes in 1983-84.

A native of Detroit, Michigan, Durnbaugh lives with his wife, Hedda (Raschka), in Lombard, Illinois. They have three children, Paul, Christopher, and Renate.